PUBLIC SUCCESS, PRIVATE SORROW

Royal Asiatic Society Hong Kong Studies Series

Royal Asiatic Society Hong Kong Studies Series is designed to make widely available important contributions on the local history, culture and society of Hong Kong and the surrounding region. Generous support from the Sir Lindsay and Lady May Ride Memorial Fund makes it possible to publish a series of high-quality works that will be of lasting appeal and value to all, both scholars and informed general readers, who share a deeper interest in and enthusiasm for the area.

Other titles in RAS Hong Kong Studies Series:

PUBLIC SUCCESS, PRIVATE SORROW

The Life and Times of Charles Henry Brewitt-Taylor (1857–1938),
China Customs Commissioner and Pioneer Translator

Isidore Cyril Cannon

香港大學出版社
HONG KONG UNIVERSITY PRESS

Hong Kong University Press
14/F Hing Wai Centre
7 Tin Wan Praya Road
Aberdeen
Hong Kong

© Isidore Cyril Cannon 2009

ISBN 978-962-209-961-6

Secure On-line Ordering
http://www.hkupress.org

British Library Cataloguing-in-Publication Data
A catalogue record for this book is available from the British Library.

Printed and bound by Liang Yu Printing Factyory Co. Ltd., in Hong Kong, China

To my dear wife Charmian, and children David, Lesley, Jonathan and Esther and grandchildren, with much love for providing deep warmth, great pleasure, constant interest and all you have taught me — sometimes against my better judgement!

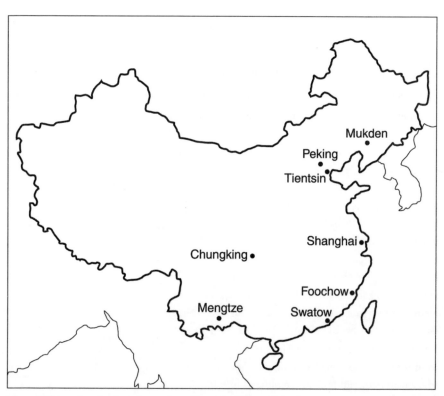

Map of China showing locations where Brewitt-Taylor worked.

Contents

Foreword for the Series

Thanks to the tremendous efforts of a great number of people, the Royal Asiatic Society Hong Kong Studies Series continues to gain momentum. With this volume, the seventh in our series, we can present to the reading public a unique collection of pieces of individual research and writing. It was not long ago that the concept of Hong Kong Studies was looked down upon as being an empty shell, with little chance of ever being otherwise. Today, however, an increasing number of schools are including the history of our city and its wider surroundings in their curricula. Furthermore, the 'Local Interest' sections of Hong Kong's many bookstores attract ever more people, both serious students of history and those who prefer a more casual dip into the subject.

The Chinese Imperial Maritime Customs service was an enormous and vitally important arm of the Chinese government from the mid-nineteenth to the early twentieth centuries. Despite Hong Kong's status as a British colony, the Chinese Customs maintained a station in Kowloon, headed by British expatriate staff. Although much is known about the service itself and the people who ran it, very little has been written about the everyday life of the many hundreds of officers who made the system work, scattered about the country often in very remote postings. In this account of the life and times of Charles Brewitt-Taylor, Cyril Cannon provides much that will be of interest to all types of reader. Historians who know about the structure of the service will be keen to read about the personal side of the life of one of its officers. And in these days when any one of us can travel freely to virtually any part of the People's Republic, those with a yen for adventure will be equally interested in the accounts of just how difficult it was to go into the interior, simply to take up one's allotted duties. The research has taken many years, and overcome many apparently blind alleys, but the result is an eminently readable account of one man and what he achieved.

The publications in the Studies Series have been made possible initially by the very generous donation of seeding capital by the Trustees of the Clague Trust Fund, representing the estate of the late Sir Douglas Clague. This donation enabled us to establish a trust fund in the name of Sir Lindsay and Lady Ride, in memory of our first Vice President and his wife. The Society itself added to this fund, as have a number of other generous donors.

The result is that we now have funding to bring to students of Hong Kong's history, culture and society a number of books that might otherwise not have seen the light of day. Furthermore, we continue to be delighted with the agreement established with Hong Kong University Press, which sets out the basis on which the Press will partner our efforts.

Robert Nield
President
Royal Asiatic Society, Hong Kong Branch
December 2008

Foreword

Charles Henry Brewitt-Taylor made a very significant contribution to Western knowledge of Chinese culture, for his *Romance of the Three Kingdoms* was the first of the great Chinese novels to be translated into English. The novel in its Chinese original also played a significant role in the development of British sinology: it was the first of the major Chinese novels to arrive in England in the early seventeenth century. Several fascicles published in 1592 were sold in Amsterdam in about 1604 and survive in Germany, Cambridge, Oxford and the British Library, having been acquired by Sir Hans Sloane (1660–1753) some time before his death. In the seventeenth and eighteenth centuries, there were no sinologists, particularly in England, who understood the structure of a Chinese book, let alone had read one, so the volumes languished unseen. Brewitt-Taylor himself later added to the collections of Chinese works in England by presenting to the British Museum volumes of the great Ming manuscript encyclopaedia, the *Yongle dadian,* which he had daringly rescued from the burning Hanlin Academy during the Boxer Siege of the Peking Legations in 1900.

Brewitt-Taylor was an outstanding example of an officer in the Imperial Chinese Maritime Customs. Robert Hart, Inspector-General of Customs from 1863 to 1911, laid stress on the importance of learning Chinese, though not many took it up with the seriousness of Brewitt-Taylor. Diplomats may have had similar encouragement but felt too grand to exercise their skills. It is striking, by contrast, to note the many publications in literary and cultural fields of members of the Customs, such as Brewitt-Taylor's translation and E. T. C. Werner's several volumes on folklore and beliefs. The language skills and openness to Chinese culture found among Customs officers is also evident in Somerset Maugham's *On a Chinese Screen* (1924), where he writes harshly of snobbish diplomats and self-satisfied merchants and missionaries in China but reserves some sympathy for a Customs officer he encountered. And in his only novel set in China, *The Painted Veil,* virtually the only sympathetic character is a Customs official. There are episodes worthy of Maugham in the story that Cyril Cannon has unveiled. His was not an easy task. Brewitt-Taylor's first draft of his translation was destroyed in the anti-foreign Boxer Uprising (he fought in the besieged Legation), along with much else. Letters have been ruined or lost and trails have run cold, but scholarly persistence over many years has resulted in a fascinating life story, quietly celebrating a modest man's achievements amid a life beset by family tragedy.

It is significant that Brewitt-Taylor worked for the Imperial Chinese Maritime Customs. Founded in 1854, though foreign-run, it was an agency of the Chinese government. Apart from assessing tariffs, the Customs gradually assumed responsibility for much more, introducing a system of modern lighthouses and buoys to protect fishermen and sailors, establishing an efficient postal service, conducting practical research into all aspects of the Chinese economy and teaching languages and modern skills to a new generation of Chinese. And while British diplomats and merchants might look only to serve British interests, the Customs officials were of necessity more involved with the daily commerce of China itself, hence their need for language skills. Often sent with their families to lonely outposts at a turbulent time in Chinese history, the experiences of the Customs officers are very little known: this makes the story of C. H. Brewitt-Taylor, his rise from very humble origins to service in far-flung corners of China, both hot and cold, dull and dangerous, all the more welcome.

Frances Wood
Curator of Chinese Collections at the British Library

Preface

Foreigners were a dominant force in nineteenth- and early-twentieth-century China; economic gain and strategic advantage their primary motivations. Most of the foreigners avoided a wider interest in their host society beyond that necessary for material or political self-interest, and much recent historiography has been in terms of this econo-imperialist agenda. Yet, though this characterization is broadly valid, there existed within the foreign community a small minority who responded sympathetically to their exotic cultural context. They became sinologists and sinologues absorbed by Chinese history and culture and were important conduits for bringing knowledge and understanding of China to the West. These individuals and their contributions have rarely been highlighted, and accounts of their lives are few.

The subject of this study is one example of a Westerner who spent most of his working life in China, mainly with the powerful Chinese Customs, a Chinese governmental organization run for almost a century by Westerners. While primarily responding to the economic and social opportunity China afforded, Charles Henry Brewitt-Taylor also achieved a considerable reputation as a scholar. His translation of the *Romance of the Three Kingdoms* (the first draft was destroyed during the Boxer Uprising) was the first full English translation of any of the major Chinese traditional novels; he thus became one of the pioneers who introduced this genre to the English-speaking world.

One framework for understanding this period in history is the interplay between three prominent features of the time: foreign domination, internal political dissent and the belated recognition that China's Manchu dynasty would need to modernize in order to contain the first two. In this broad canvas the role of the Chinese Customs is highlighted.

Acknowledgements

I have been constantly impressed by the interest shown and trouble taken to assist my enquiries. Acknowledgements are not easy — recording all the ways that people have helped would be difficult — though the attempt would make an interesting essay on one's research; simply citing a name or an institution does not always do justice to the quality of the contribution. Having said that, among those I wish to publicly acknowledge are the following.

First, I wish to express my warm thanks to Frances Wood, Curator of Chinese Collections at the British Library, for her help, encouragement, comments and enthusiasm throughout my research; meetings with her were always a delight. Graham Hutt of the same department assiduously discovered valuable materials donated by Brewitt-Taylor to the British Museum, and John Hopson, the British Library's archivist, dug out some interesting correspondence about them. It was always a joy to use that excellent institution. Rosemary Seton and her staff in the SOAS Archives were very helpful. Perry Anderson, whose father was a Customs commissioner, introduced me to Sun Xiufu of the Second Republican Historical Archive of China, who facilitated my research while I was visiting the archive and since, and also Zhang Ziqing of the Institute of Foreign Literature, Nanjing University; both helped to make my stay in Nanking a pleasurable experience, as did Wu Xinglong and especially his student, Xiao Tang, also at the university. Robert Bickers of Bristol University has done excellent work in opening up the Second Historical Archives of China, the SHAC, and has always been available to provide information from the archive; he also introduced me to a doctoral student working on Postal matters who was able to ferret out interesting material. Elizabeth Sinn of the University of Hong Kong enabled me to use the Hart correspondence held in that university's archives and kindly invited me to talk about Brewitt-Taylor's life to the Hong Kong Branch of the Royal Asiatic Society, and to contribute an article to their journal.* As a former member of the branch, these activities were particularly

---

* Cannon, 'Charles Henry Brewitt-Taylor, 1857–1938'.

pleasing, especially as Brewitt-Taylor's earliest writings were found in the journals of the China Branch of the RAS.

I must also thank others for their assistance, interest and comments: Charles Aylmer of Cambridge University Library; Adam J. Perkins, the Royal Greenwich Observatory archivist, and Hans Van der Ven, both also of Cambridge University; Deirdre Wildy of the Humanities and Special Collections, Queens University, Belfast; David Helliwell at Oxford University; Bernhard Fuehrer at SOAS; Alison Gardiner of the Lothian Health Service Archive at Edinburgh University Library; Alaister Gloag formerly of the Royal Hospital School; Edwin Green, former Group Archivist for the Hongkong and Shanghai Bank; Lane J. Harrris, Susanna Hoe, Robin Hutcheon with much appreciation for undertaking the onerous burden of the index, Hin-cheung Lovell, David Mahoney, Luke Kwong, and John Minford; and Mrs. Staggs for her knowledge of coastguards. Staff in the Worthing area of the West Sussex County Council produced enlightening material on Brewitt-Taylor's family origins; Margaret Smith of Elie Library, Fifeshire, went beyond the call of duty in locating local information, as did colleagues at the Cupar Library, Fifeshire. David Thomson, secretary/chairman of the Elie and Earlsferry History Society, Fife, for his help and invitation to address the society on Alexander Michie and Brewitt-Taylor; and David Garland, a local undertaker in Elie. Long-standing friends Professors Michael Young and Peter Newmark gave support and encouraged me to publish.

Countless staff of a variety of institutions have been helpful in addition to those already mentioned. Staff members in the various rooms at the British Library including the Newspaper Branch at Colindale, the Bodleian, the Camden Archives at Holborn Library, the former Family Record Centre, the Houghton Library of Harvard University, the National Archives of Scotland, the National Library of Scotland, the National Maritime Museum, the Needham Institute, the Probate Service, the UK National Archives (formerly the Public Record Office), Queens University, the Royal Asiatic Society, the Royal Astronomical Society, the State Library of New South Wales, the University of London Library, the Wellcome Trust and its Library for the History and Understanding of Medicine and the archives of several hospitals in England and Scotland. I also wish to thank the Universities' China Committee in London for their generous support for my visit to Nanking. My apologies are due to any who may have been inadvertently omitted.

Family members also made their contribution, providing letters, photographs, memories and other information: Edward Gordon Brewitt-Taylor (Brewitt-Taylor's grandson Teddy) and his children Colin and Frances, Joan Leaf (Brewitt-Taylor's granddaughter) and Margaret Woods. My son, Jonathan, enthusiastically shared curious discoveries, made most helpful suggestions and undertook a long journey to Mengtze, returning with photographs; his wife, Liu Hong, helped with occasional translations from the Chinese. Joe, my grandson, was impressively patient in giving invaluable computer advice to a novice.

I am greatly indebted to two unknowns, my publisher's anonymous readers, for their most useful detailed comments and recommendations for further reading. They have increased my knowledge of the period which I trust has filtered into the writing, though perhaps not as fully as they would have desired. To Colin Day of Hong Kong University Press, my very warm thanks for his initial interest, constant sensitive support and patient reassurance; he has been an excellent publisher to work with; my thanks are also due to Dennis Cheung and other staff members including the copy-editor.

Finally, I must thank my wife for her patience, her comments, her archive of letters and her bemusement at my preoccupation with a remote family connection.

I am indebted to many; any errors are, of course, entirely my own responsibility.

Photo Credits

The following providers of photographs are acknowledged with thanks:

Swatow Customs House: Queen's University Library, Belfast

Customs staff and their ladies at the Yellow Temple, near Peking: University of Washington Libraries, Special Collections, CHA 002

Customs volunteers at the end of Siege: G.E. Morrison Collection, State Library of New South Wales

Alexander Michie, Snr.: British Newspaper Library

Photographs of Brewitt-Taylor and other family members: Teddy Brewitt-Taylor, Joan Leaf, Charmian Cannon

Note on Citations

Generally, the bibliography only contains works referred to in the notes, but it also includes a few works consulted but not used.

In Fairbank, Bruner and Matheson, *The I.G in Peking,* the letter number not the page number is given unless the reference is not that of a letter.

Where the *Cambridge History of China* is used, normally just the page reference is given in addition to the volume, unless appropriate to name the author of the chapter and its title because of the chapter's special pertinence.

Sources recorded directly at the Second Republican Historical Archive are abbreviated as SHAC – Second Historical Archives of China, the number of the volume for the semi-official reports in that location is given at the first citing only, followed by the date of the report, otherwise simply SHAC followed by the date, the location will be clear from where B-T was then working. Reports deriving from the University of Bristol's material are recorded differently.

Brief explanation of the 'budges' of Margaret Ellis, known as Peg, is made in the Introduction; a further note is to be found in the chapter on B-T's Sons and the Ellises. Where a budge is cited it is simply shown as Peg followed by the date of the budge. Letters from Peg are referred to as such and the recipient is usually named.

Regarding the use of the subject's name, in general I have referred to him as 'Charles Henry' in his early years, and as 'B-T' in his later years, particularly after he established the use of the hyphen.

Note on Romanization

Names in China, particularly of towns, have changed in two main ways. First, they were altered for a variety of historical reasons, such as migration or conquest. Second, the systems adopted in attempts to romanize Chinese characters have evolved; the most recent form, known as pinyin, was introduced by China in 1958. I have used the name and the form of romanization as first encountered in the documents. Where there is a different modern place name, this is usually shown in parenthesis after its first use.

1

Introduction

This book is the result of a long and unexpected journey. I knew that the surname of my wife's aunt had become 'Brewitt-Taylor' on marriage, and I had also been aware that her father-in-law had spent time in China. I recall Aunt Evelyn pointing out to me the two volumes standing in her bookcase of his translation of some kind of Chinese work, and I had seen the three beautiful gowns that he had brought back for her and her two sisters. But it was only after I became more acquainted with the country, initially through working in Hong Kong and later by having family connections in China, that my curiosity about Charles Henry Brewitt-Taylor began to be kindled.

It was in Hong Kong that I learnt that his name was familiar to specialists in Chinese as the translator of the then only complete English version of one of the most famous Chinese novels: the *San Kuo Chih Yen-i* (in pinyin, *Sanguozhi yanyi*). His *Romance of the Three Kingdoms,* published in 1925, was the first full English translation of the work, believed to have been written by Lo Kuan-chung (Luo Guanzhong) in the fourteenth century; until the 1990s it was the only complete version in English.

Later I became conscious of the work's significance for literary history. Before the twentieth century, traditional Chinese literati did not recognize novels as literature, for they were popular stories, appealing to the less well-educated.[1] They were also written not in the literary or classical language, the medium for everything seriously regarded as literature in pre-modern China, but in the vernacular; they were, therefore, considered 'unworthy of serious consideration by traditional scholars'.[2] Poetry was more highly regarded. Many educated Chinese would, however, have been familiar with the major novels. Serious foreign study of traditional Chinese literature began to be undertaken by a remarkable group of Western scholars, initially beckoned to China to work as missionaries, Consular or Customs officers, who became sinologists. While knowledge of Chinese language and literature was becoming slowly known to the West even as early as the sixteenth and seventeenth centuries,[3] it was especially with the development of the Treaty Ports in the second half of the nineteenth century that a milieu was created which aided discourse, at least for an interested minority of Westerners. Particularly valuable was the publication of a variety of English-language journals in China devoted to the study of Chinese culture, and the establishment of various societies, including a branch of the Royal Asiatic Society. The very early foreign explorers in sinological scholarship largely confined themselves in their search for understanding Chinese culture and values to the more esteemed study of traditional Chinese literature, that is, the classics, history, philosophy and poetry.[4]

Brewitt-Taylor's (hereafter shown as B-T) work marked a milestone in the history of English translations of Chinese novels. Apart from the *Three Kingdoms,* three other novels are widely highly esteemed: *Dream of the Red Chamber, Journey to the West,* and *The Water Margin;* two others, *The Scholars* and *The Golden Lotus,* may be added as strong runners-up. These have been regarded as the six historically important landmarks of Chinese non-classical literature, each breaking new ground.[5] While there had been many excerpts translated from these over the years, none appears to have received a full English translation before that of B-T in 1925.[6] Thus, by his work, B-T pioneered the introduction of full versions of the most famous popular Chinese novels to the English-speaking world. Indeed, as we shall see later, his first complete draft had been entirely destroyed during the Boxer troubles a quarter of a century previously, otherwise the publication date would almost certainly have been considerably earlier.

I read the novel initially culturally cold, without any knowledge of the important position held by the work in Chinese culture. Later, I learnt that what B-T called the *Romance of the Three Kingdoms* (*San Kuo* or *Sanguo — Three Kingdoms —* as it is popularly known in China) has been a powerfully influential novel in China. Derived from the historical period known as the Three Kingdoms in the second and third centuries, its incidents and characters have been an important source for storytelling, drama and opera over many generations; this tradition continues to this day. On learning a little of the complexities of the Chinese language, I began to appreciate the level of application that must have been required to acquire sufficient knowledge and literary sensitivity to undertake the task of translating the novel. The work was written very early in the history of the Chinese novel; the attributed author, Lo Kuan-chung, likely lived in the fourteenth century,[7] that is, around the time of Chaucer (1345–1400). The Chinese text B-T used for his translation was probably that compiled by Mao in the 1660s.[8] Though the level of linguistic change that had taken place by the time of B-T's translation was not large, there had been some development; a good translation would not have been straightforward, requiring extra-careful attention.[9]

Translating the *San Kuo* into two massive volumes was a formidable enterprise. B-T must surely have devoted a substantial amount of time, energy and persistence preparing for and undertaking the work. What kind of person was he, what had brought him to China, how long was he there and what kind of work did he do? Why did he choose the *San Kuo* for translation? Had he published anything else? I began to wonder about the man.

Knowledge of his life is slender. Yet, it seemed that someone who had achieved a certain distinction as the translator of the *San Kuo* deserved some kind of memoir, if only a brief outline of his life. After I retired and returned to Britain from Hong Kong in 1994, this is what I initially intended to write.

Obtaining material on B-T proved obstinately difficult. This should have been a warning, presaging the elusiveness of the man himself. Even the Family Records Centre of the Office of National Statistics initially failed to come up with a record of his birth![10] Clues often led up cul-de-sacs, and alternative routes had to be found. It was as if the man had drawn a cloak of secrecy over himself. Part of the difficulty lay in the fact that certain family hearsay proved inaccurate, or partially so. The challenges of the investigation were somewhat compounded by the hyphen in his name, which eventually was found to have been adopted by him as an adult, initially inconsistently and only after being in China for some years; this meant having to deal with two surnames when trying to track down details of his life. In part, the difficulties encountered reflected my own ignorance about the limitations and pitfalls in genealogical research, as well as my limited knowledge of the specific problems of researching Chinese history. Further, I had to constantly remind myself of the dangers of trying to reconstruct 'reality' from documents — a well-ploughed academic area.[11] The problems encountered will be familiar to others embarking on biographical discovery, the frustrating gaps as well as the happy moments of serendipity, and especially the way in which the subject takes over and extends itself.

Conducting this research, meant having to, as Strachey put it, 'glean what stubbles remain after the winds of time have taken those who might have thrown more light'. B-T died in 1938. Sadly, one person who would have known more about him, his daughter-in-law, Aunt Evelyn, had already died by the time I embarked on the study. Few members of the family remaining alive had any knowledge of him, mainly a grandson, now ninety, and a granddaughter of over seventy; both were young when he was alive, and their memories of him were scanty.

B-T was a man who revealed little of himself. His grandson, Edward Gordon Brewitt-Taylor, the only grandchild carrying on the surname, and known as Teddy when young, recalls his mother, Evelyn, saying that whenever she asked him questions about his early life, he would give vague, non-committal responses. Early in my research, the impression I gained was of someone who wanted to hide something about his life, something about which he was perhaps embarrassed or felt uncomfortable.

Teddy helpfully provided what material he had, making trips to his attic to try to ferret out answers to my enquiries: a few letters to his mother from her father-in-law (Teddy's grandfather), letters from her husband (Teddy's father), awards to his grandfather for service in China, some old war medals from a great-grandfather and a few photographs. However, Teddy's actual knowledge of the man and his background were rather thin. Teddy was about twenty-one years old when his grandfather died in 1938, not an age when one is likely to ask questions, even if one were so inclined. He thought that B-T had been born in Kingston, near Brighton in Sussex, and that he had gone to China to teach mathematics in some kind of navigation school in Foochow (Fuzhou); his grandfather had also been connected with the Customs, but Teddy had understood that all records of him in China had been destroyed during the Boxer Rebellion. Sussex proved to be annoyingly liberal with its Kingstons. There is a Kingston near Lewes, Brighton, but its local records revealed nothing, similarly with a Kingston near Shoreham, but one at East Preston, near Littlehampton, proved to be the birthplace, and the local Worthing District registry office of the West Sussex County Council was most helpful. Not only did the staff locate B-T's birth certificate, but also those of his siblings, as well as an account in the local paper of B-T's father's dramatic death. This all began to reveal something of his family of origin. Any impression gained of his social origins by the double-barrelled name and a view that was held that his father may have had a commission in the Services was dispelled.

Another grandchild, Joan, was also still alive, living in the United States, and an enthusiastic correspondence ensued between us. She was only fourteen years old when B-T died; she had some impressions of him, but little knowledge. However, she did have a few interesting letters from him to her and her mother (his other daughter-in-law) and some photographs.

An unexpected quarry was much closer to hand. My wife's grandmother, Margaret Ellis (known as Peg in her family), had a tradition of exchanging monthly letters with her brothers and sisters, known as a 'budge',[12] detailing activities over the previous month; these were returned to the original writer, and they were left to my wife by her mother. They have proved an invaluable historical source, extending from 1900 to the Second World War, and they have been well-mined by my wife for other purposes.[13] While only limited information about his career and publications were discovered, the budges uncovered more about B-T's family relationships, certain of his activities and aspects of his personality.

Past advice to students (as well as to myself) on the value of reading footnotes was amply justified when a useful outline of some of the main positions B-T had held in China was found in a footnote in a book on the Chinese Customs.[14] This formed a useful structure for filling out details of his career. Enjoyable discussions with Dr. Frances Wood of the British Library provided further useful sources on the Customs and expatriate life in China generally, from her extraordinary range of knowledge. But I was not aware at that stage of the volume of academic work on the Customs that was being undertaken.

Fortuitously, around this time two interesting articles in the *London Review of Books* appeared, written by an academic whose father had also been a commissioner in the Chinese Customs.[15] This drew my attention to the existence of a highly important archive in China and the possibility of records relating to B-T being housed there.

From the time that B-T achieved the position of commissioner of Customs, details of his life became fuller. Robert Hart, Inspector General of the Imperial Chinese Maritime Customs, had introduced the practice of requiring regular semi-official reports of the local situation from those occupying the position of commissioner at the Customs posts. These reports, written in English at approximately fortnightly intervals, are a fascinating record of what was happening in all the places in China which had a Customs presence. The Second Republican Historical Archive in Nanking (Nanjing) keep most of the materials on the Customs that have been found in China, including pre-Republican documents. Reputedly, twenty-seven kilometres of Customs materials are held there.

I had announced to the director of the archive my intention to go to Nanking in the autumn of November 1999 with the hope of finding material on B-T. I had already been warned not to expect a reply. Upon my arrival, I found the splendid building in traditional Chinese architectural style most impressive, as well as numerous volumes of reports including ones written by B-T selected for me to use. These included only certain postings: Mengtze (Mengzi), Mukden (now Shenyang) and Chungking (Chongqing). Commissioners working at the headquarters in Peking (Beijing), as B-T did for some years, did not appear to write such reports; some correspondence relating to other postings became available later. Few people were using the archive when I arrived, and the spacious room where one was allowed to peruse material was fairly empty. The archive's opening hours were limited and it was subject to unexpected closure, making time-planning difficult; the occasional user I spoke to complained of the high cost of using the facilities, even for Chinese. Officials also insisted, rather inconveniently, that notes had to be made on paper provided by them and not in the user's own notebook. Hopefully much of this is changing, aided by a project that has been underway drawing on the experience of British sinologists to help local staff modernize the archive.

It was, however, an extraordinary experience to open the volumes, many probably unregarded for a hundred years, and read the reports written or typed in English by the commissioners. And there were B-T's signed reports, with comments written in the margins by Inspector General Robert Hart or Francis Aglen, who became inspector general after Hart's death. A detailed picture of the kinds of activities in which B-T engaged could be derived from these regular semi-official reports.

Other chance events led to more information. For example, meeting a researcher in the London Public Record Office who had constructed a coastguard database from which I was able to derive information about B-T's parents; happily, I was eventually able to reciprocate with information for her card index. Other clues were found in the archives of the Royal Astronomical Society, of which B-T was a member. As have others who have used archives, contemporary newspapers and official records, they have proved to be endlessly fascinating; fortunately, while it is difficult to restrain one's desire to go on reading them, the exercise is often justified, if only by the unexpected find.

Over the years, other potential sources came to light as I trawled the books, letters and diaries of people who worked in China around the time when B-T was there. Just as I thought that the flow of information was drying up, another source sprang and had to be traced, without knowing whether it would reveal more than a trickle. One exciting example is the stream which flowed from a chance comment in the diary of a friend visiting B-T mentioning a place his wife was; this led to revelations of the nature and extent of her mental illness and rendered important insights into their marital relationship. Thus, the research extended for much longer than had been expected.

Gradually, I was being drawn into a search I had not intended, and into unexpected byways of history, as I began to try to understand the world B-T inhabited. My concern moved from producing a short memoir, essentially a synopsis of his career, to seeing how his private journey was played out in the context of the wider world. In particular, as I discovered more about his life in China it became essential to try seeing his career in relation to what was happening in that historically complex country, for the changes occurring there provided opportunities and challenges for the individuals caught up in them.

Soon I became interested in the relationship between the broad historical events — evidenced in China's relationship with the West, its internal turmoils such as the Taiping and Boxer movements and its attempts at modernization — and the personal impact of these on an individual. I am aware that distilling a complex history into the confines of a few chapters is fraught with the dangers of selection, omission, and distortion, yet it seemed important to try to set out certain major developments crucial for understanding some of the context in which the individual operated. In doing this, I have made more explicit than I have found elsewhere the importance of the interplay between a triangle of forces in China which most impinged on the lives of individual expatriates, providing as they did those twin characteristics of opportunity and danger. These three major forces were foreign domination and trade, internal dissent and modernization. Each of these forces covers huge areas which cannot be done justice in a book of this kind, though one institution, the Chinese Customs, a fascinating and significant product of the interaction of all three forces, is given special prominence here because of its role in B-T's life.

Some readers may find the attempt to understand China's history through the interplay of these dimensions overly simplistic, and the marriage of the broad analysis to the individual too crude. All I can argue is that this analysis has helped my understanding of the times. But frameworks tend to be fragile, and others who are more knowledgeable may wish to demolish or, more usefully, further refine the framework. Some comfort is drawn from another observation of Strachey, which is that the first requisite of the historian is ignorance — though I would not recommend taking that too far!

Economic or strategic self-interest is the paramount explanation for foreign participation in China, and certainly the activities of those involved generally provided opportunities for financial benefit and social advancement. Often the rewards were considerably higher than those likely to be available to individuals in their home country. For the majority of foreigners who operated in China, this was the major motivation. Further, the predominant view of both Chinese and Western writers over the past half century or so has been that the Western players in the China game were agents, consciously or not, of an imperialist agenda. While not quarrelling with the general validity of this perspective, my contention is that it is by no means the whole story. The private correspondence of some of those involved reveals a contrary picture, a real desire to help China develop. Of course, it could be argued that this was a rationalization, an example of Man needing a comfortable motivation to cloud self-interest, but benevolence, albeit well-paid, should not be dismissed. Among those who went to China's shores out of self-advancement, there were a minority who became attracted, indeed engrossed, by its culture. In the study of China's history, social institutions, customs, philosophy, visual arts, literature and language, there were foreigners who became significant scholars, trying to understand a world alien to them. They communicated with one another largely through learned societies, Western language journals, newspapers and books. Some would argue that even this activity was carrying out an imperialist agenda, albeit unconsciously.[16] But this position underemphasizes the positive contributions of those so engaged, who while following their own interests, also acted as a conduit for bringing knowledge and understanding of China to the West, as well as contributing to China's development. Crudely caricatured, it could be said of some that during their working hours they intruded the West into China, but in their leisure they were the means of introducing Chinese thought and achievements to the West. Their disinterestedness should not be overstated, but neither should it go unrecognized. The motivation was sometimes dual: the strands of self-interest and altruism often interweave, sometimes too finely to tease out fully. If personal ambition led some to become, for example, expert sinologues, they did so out of self-interest, not as imperialist agents.

Most of these foreigners did not withdraw from their own culture, remaining embedded in their various European cultures and lifetstyles, though their perceptions of these may well have been modified by bestriding two cultures. B-T is centre-stage here, but his life was peopled by expatriates with deep interest in China, including Robert Hart and other Customs colleagues, H. A. Giles, Alexander Michie, Sr., G. E. Morrison and Evangeline Dora Edwards, among others.

This, then, is the product of various avenues of enquiry. Specialists in China's diverse and complex history of the late Ch'ing (Qing) period should find some interest in the slivers of detail and knowledge about certain people prominent on the China scene; they are less likely to find much of the broader canvas that is especially new. Those less familiar with China's history will be introduced to certain significant events, such as the Taiping, the Self-Strengthening movement, the Boxers, and especially the significance of the Chinese Customs, a Chinese organization that was Western led. These all had an impact on China and on China's relationship with the West. They are essentially windows into aspects of China's development, brief sketches to help illumine the context of the life of a foreigner abroad. I have tried to discover more about all of B-T's writings, but though the opinion of sinologues has been sought, there is no serious attempt here to evaluate B-T as a translator.

My central concern in relation to the subject has been the reconstruction of a life and how China provided opportunity for an individual. Historical interpretation is bounded by context, and much interpretation of modern China's history has emphasized the role of China as 'Europe's victim'.[17] Many Chinese and Western historians have stressed this interpretation, but there were actors on the scene who would have argued otherwise. The Customs Service, where B-T spent most of his career, richly exemplifies both viewpoints, being seen by some as a tool for imperialists, by others as a major force in China's modernization. By pointing up the activities of B-T and some of his circle, this study hopefully makes a modest contribution to the history of Britain in China. It also demonstrates that not all foreigners in China only focused on maximizing reward; there were also those who became interested in Chinese culture and helped to extend knowledge of China in the West.

Currently we are witnessing a rediscovery of China. The strong Western presence in China from around the Opium Wars in the 1840s to the early twentieth century enabled many outside China to gain some insight into China's culture: 'things Chinese' entered the popular imagination,[18] albeit frequently with distortion. Following the Second World War and the establishment of the People's Republic of China, the country became for a time rather impenetrable again. Now, with the opening up of China and its position as a world power, knowledge of and interest in

China is deepening. Much of the recent interest and writing has focused on the period following 1949, and especially the role of Mao Tse-tung and the Gang of Four, and the effects of policies such as the Great Leap Forward and the Cultural Revolution. Along with the current economic resurgence, interest is broadening more positively to include China's cultural achievements (witness the major exhibitions being held, films shown and literature published) and pre-1949 history, including the lives of Westerners in China.

A life of achievement is almost its own celebration, but few lives are untouched by sadness. As will become apparent, B-T, despite his modest career success and the wide recognition of his scholarship, was shadowed by a great deal of personal grief. He appeared to shoulder this with stoicism, perhaps as a defence. His was a life which, especially given his unobtrusive and somewhat secretive personality, could easily fade into obscurity. Perhaps he would not have given thanks to anyone for rescuing him from such a fate, by revealing aspects of his life which he might have preferred to have remained hidden. Whether or not one should embark on such an undertaking is a moral problem which frequently besets the biographer. The writer tends to follow where his or her inclination leads and weave his or her own rationale for decisions on what to include. B-T's achievement in the face of difficult circumstances seems to justify some kind of record.

For me, there has been a triple bonus: first, the research became a focus for becoming much more familiar with China's turbulent, extraordinarily complex and endlessly fascinating history; second, it introduced me to unfamiliar sources and the delights of using rich though little-used archives; third, and by no means least, this research has brought me in touch with a wide range of people, many well-versed in various aspects of China, providing new friendships and acquaintances.

2

Family Origins

When I started my research, knowledge of Brewitt-Taylor's social origins was scarce, his hyphenated name suggested a higher status than proved to be the case and it was rumoured his father had possibly held a commission in the forces. His marriage certificate, unseen by his family, gave his surname as Taylor. It also records his father's occupation as 'Seaman, Royal Navy'; this was only partially accurate. His father had, in fact, for most of his career until his retirement been an ordinary 'boatman' in the Coastguard Service. While it was the case that coastguards were frequently recruited from the navy, and were liable to be called back to serve in times of need, the father's occupation at the time of his son's birth and at retirement was that of coastguard.

Charles Taylor, Charles Henry's father, was born on 25 October 1820 in Lewes, Sussex, the son of a coachmaker of the same name. Shoemaking had been the trade of the son until he was nearly eighteen, when he decided to join the Royal Navy. His first vessel was the *Magnificent;* he began serving on her in September 1838. He then transferred to a sloop, the *Frolic,* on 11 November 1842, at the age of twenty-two. He was stationed in Portsmouth from 26 October 1843, and he stayed with the *Frolic* until he was appointed to the Coastguard Service in Haven Hole, Essex, on 7 July 1847. This finding was significant: it demonstrated that, contrary to what one would have expected about B-T's family background, reinforced by the deceptive hyphenated name, his social origins were humble. I felt that a major factor in his need for achievement had been uncovered.

The Coastguard Service had been created in 1822 in order to break the widespread and serious smuggling trade.[1] For centuries there had been numerous attempts to deal with the problem, and by the end of the seventeenth century, the Customs and Excise department had a small fleet of boats together with a few men on land to try to prevent evasion of the payment of customs. But the early attempts to suppress the trade, which was particularly rampant along England's south-eastern coastline, were ineffective. Smuggling was very well organized, and the men engaged to deal with the problem were frequently exposed to corruption.

Many apparently respectable pillars of the community were involved in the trade (as depicted in such novels as Daphne du Maurier's *Jamaica Inn* and Thorndike's Dr. Syn series); it was difficult to secure convictions. But commerce was becoming more significant in the economy, and evasion of duties meant a considerable loss of revenue. There are echoes here of what our subject was to find in China. Further, Napoleon had paid tribute (doubtless in both senses) to the way smugglers had aided his forces by providing useful information, even delivering French prisoners-of-war out of England. This spurred the government to action.

A committee was appointed in 1820 to look into 'every department of the customs', and a Coastguard Service was set up in January 1822. The Admiralty, which was responsible for the Service, decided in 1831 that the coastguards should be a reserve for the Royal Navy. Regulations promulgated in that year stated that vacant situations for coastguard boatmen should be filled by seamen, and that ships' captains should select men best entitled to serve and transmit their names to the Admiralty. The captains had to certify that the candidate has been sober, attentive, and obedient to command, and is a healthy, active and good seaman, not more than 30 years of age, nor under 5' 5" high. The person selected should be 'best entitled to that reward for good services of any . . . who are fit for the coastguards and desirous to enter'.

By and large the Service was attractive as it offered a relatively settled way of life, with good accommodation and the opportunity to live with one's family — not that Charles Taylor was married when he joined. The salary was five pounds a month for a boatman; he also received a small share of any reward for goods seized from smugglers, an incentive for the coastguards both to be more effective in the job and to counter corruption. Such a selective procedure would be expected to have raised the standards and the status of coastguards, yet as we have seen, the young Charles Henry preferred to refer to his father as being in the Royal Navy. Had he been aware that his future role as Customs commissioner included responsibility for coastguards, this might have been a source of satisfaction, encouraging him to be less reticent in recording his father's actual occupation.

A medal awarded to Charles Taylor for service in the Crimean War (1854–56) is held in the family by Teddy, his great-grandson. Why it had been awarded had been a source of some curiosity and had led to uncertainty as to whether Charles Taylor had been in the army; indeed, he is recorded as 'soldier' in one family tree. The explanation lay in the requirement that coastguards had to be part of the reserve and be able to serve on ships of the Royal Navy in time of need. This regulation had been activated by the start of the Crimean War, when every available coastguard was drafted. In all, during this war three thousand coastguards served in the Royal Navy, their places being taken mainly by retirees.

Gradually, the Service became less concerned with smuggling, not only because of its own increased efficiency, but also because the advent of freer trade in Europe in the 1860s would have made smuggling less lucrative. While anti-smuggling was still an important function, the Service became increasingly focused on safety at sea, with coastguards acting as lookouts, warning ships of hazards and being involved in rescues.[2]

It was while Charles Taylor was in his first coastguard post that he must have met his future wife, Ellen Brewitt. According to the 1861 Census, she had been born in 1827 in South Benfleet, Essex, and was still living there, just a few miles from Taylor's base in Haven Hole, when they married on 26 October 1848. Curiously, a later census, in 1881, states she was born in Islington.

Charles and Ellen married in the local parish church in Essex, with her father, Henry, a shoemaker, as one of the witnesses. Shoemakers were particularly associated with independent, radical thinking. Sir Robert Peel asked shoemakers who were pressing the demands of their trade society:

> How is it you people are foremost in every movement? . . . If there is a conspiracy or political movement, I always find one of you in it.[3]

Whether Henry Brewitt held radical views is not known, nor whether any such political ideals affected his daughter, Ellen.

The imminence of Charles Taylor's next posting may well have brought forward the decision on when they should marry, for nine days after the marriage, on 4 November 1848, he was posted to Brixham in Devon. During the following four years in Brixham, the Taylors produced two daughters: Ellen in 1850 and Rebecca in 1852. A posting followed to Kingston, East Preston, close to Littlehampton in Sussex, in February 1853. It was from there that Charles left for the Crimea, and shortly after his return from the war, his wife became pregnant again. On 11 December 1857 Charles Henry Brewitt Taylor was born; his mother's surname being added as a forename. He was the only one of the children to be given his mother's maiden name; it would seem that Ellen especially wished her eldest son to share an identity with her. Charles Henry's birth certificate gives his father's occupation unreservedly as 'coastguard'. So, with his father a coastguard, paternal grandfather a coachmaker and maternal grandfather a shoemaker, Charles Henry Brewitt's forebears, on both sides, were clearly working class, of the kind Booth was to label 'respectable', despite Charles Henry's later-adopted hyphen and somewhat patrician air.

Two more children were born to the Taylors in Kingston: Elizabeth Edith in December 1862 and Herbert William in October 1864. Thus, Charles Henry was the middle of five children, with two elder sisters and a younger sister and brother. The 1861 Census shows the family all living at the coastguard station at East Preston, with the mother contributing to the family income by working as a dressmaker.

What this meant is unknown — whether she actually made dresses or just did the sewing as a seamstress would have affected her income and status; Hood's 'Song of the Shirt' paints a graphic picture of the dismal conditions of the latter in the days before the widespread use of the sewing machine.

On 31 March 1867, Charles Taylor, still a boatman at Kingston, was discharged from the Service early, at the age of 46 years. At that time coastguards did retire fairly young, the normal age being 50. Fortunately for him, small pensions had just been introduced by the Service in 1866; before that date many coastguards had no pension at all, as was the case for many occupations in that period.[4]

Why Charles Taylor retired so early is not known, but a dramatic event in the following year provides some insight into a possible cause. On 19 October 1868, about eighteen months after he retired, Taylor, described as a pensioner of the Coastguard Service, committed suicide. In the graphic words of his death certificate, he 'cut his own throat not being of sound mind'.

The local paper, copies of which are now aging and are very difficult to read even with the aid of a magnifying glass, records the inquest under the heading 'Sad Suicide':

> The people in the neighbourhood of High-street [Littlehampton], were on Monday morning in consternation at hearing that Charles Taylor, a superannuated coastguardman, had destroyed himself by cutting his throat, under the following circumstances, as given in evidence before R. Hughes, Esq., coroner, on the next day. — Ellen Taylor [eighteen years old at the time] said: I am the daughter of the deceased. Our family consisted of my father, mother, and four other children. My father, who was a seaman in the Royal Navy, and afterwards in the coastguard service, was 48 years of age, and has been afflicted with asthma. He has been a pensioner since April last year. On Monday morning I took him a cup of tea while in bed; this was about eight o'clock. Shortly after I sent my brother and sister, of the ages respectively four and six, for the cup and saucer, and on reaching the room door they screamed. My mother had gone out to work. I went upstairs and found my father lying on the room floor with his throat cut and I observed that he did not breathe. He had been drinking excessively for several days previously, and was strange in his manner, and in a very nervous state. He came home intoxicated on Friday last, after having been at Lewes since the previous Saturday, on which day he went to Ford to receive his pension of £5 8s. for the last quarter. He sent home to my mother £3, and then left by train. After returning home on Friday he did not again leave the house, and seldom answered to anything said to him. I never heard him threaten to take away his life, or had any unpleasantness occurred between him and my mother or his family. It had been his habit to give my mother £5 of his pension money. When away he spent the money he took with him, and had also disposed of his gold shirt studs . . .

Thomas Evans a surgeon said: I was called in to see the deceased on Monday morning. I found him with his throat cut. A razor with blood on it was lying near. It must have been twice used, and death must have quickly ensued. The jury returned a verdict of 'suicide, while of unsound mind'. On the suggestion of the foreman, the jury as a mark of sympathy, sent their fee of one shilling each to the family of the deceased.[5]

At that time, a shilling was one-twentieth of a pound, and while the cost of living then is very difficult to compare to what it is now, some idea of the value of the annual pension of £21 12 shillings received by the family before the father's death can be assessed by estimates of other wages around that time. This level of income, 8 shillings and 6 pence weekly, would have been at the lower end of what agricultural workers would have been paid in the late 1850s, at about 8 to 10 shillings a week, and this would have been supplemented by their being able to produce much of their own food cheaply; common labourers would have received nearly twice as much, at 15 to 17 shillings.[6] In the middle of the 1860s, an economist concluded that about 19 shillings was the average weekly earnings of adult male workers, and that of adult women was 11 shillings.[7] During Charles's retirement, and even more so after his suicide, the Taylor family would have been dependant on the mother's income to relieve their poverty.

One can only guess why Charles Taylor had gone to Lewes, where, it will be recalled, he had been born. Perhaps he had been visiting family or old friends, winding up affairs, or aiding someone in need; given the references to money, maybe he was under pressure to settle old debts.

Charles's suicide no doubt would have had a considerable effect on the ten-year-old Charles Henry, who was likely to have been attending one of the many small private schools located in the area.[8] If 'the boy was father to the man', he was probably an intelligent and sensitive child, though how traumatic the loss of his father was to the young boy cannot be known. However, he would have been conscious of the sense of family shame associated with the manner of his father's death. His family's humble circumstances together with his father's suicide might well help to explain his later desire to distance himself from most of his family, his reticence over discussing them, as well as his determination to do well in life.

3

Early Years and Marriage

Trying to discover more about the life of Charles Henry Brewitt-Taylor before he went to China has been one of the many time-consuming aspects of this study. Not being aware of his social circumstances, but knowing that he might have taught mathematics in China, his family held the idea that he might have studied the subject at the University of London, at University College or Imperial College. Records at the university's Senate House do in fact show that he took his matriculation for the University of London as a mature student in June 1879. His matriculation suggests that he did at one stage have the intention to go to university. He was then aged twenty-one, and the records show that he had prepared for matriculation through private study; they also include a certificate of eligibility to enter the entrance examination registered in Littlehampton. So, the family had retained some connection in the area. At the time he obtained his matriculation, though registered in Littlehampton, he was in fact living in London, at 6 Haddington Terrace, Greenwich. What was he doing there? And where was his family?

The 1871 Census record indicates that the family had moved from the address where they had lived in Littlehampton at the time of the suicide. But they were not living in Haddington Terrace, neither then nor in 1881, when the next census was taken, by which time Charles Henry had left the country. In 1881 the little terraced house had three people living there including a male lodger, described as a shipping secretary; it was likely that the house tended to be used by lodgers with a maritime connection, given its location in Greenwich with its long tradition of naval-related activities. The registration for matriculation in Littlehampton suggests B-T's family still lived in that area in the late 1870s, and their home was probably the young man's only stable address at the time.

When B-T went to China, only a year after his matriculation, he took up a position to teach mathematics and navigation. According to his grandson, Teddy, Charles Henry turned down 'something' at Greenwich when he went to China. Might he have been a student at the naval college there? A complete blank was drawn from the scanty records on the school's students held by the National Maritime Museum at

Greenwich and also from the somewhat fuller student records at the Public Records Office in Kew. The likely school for orphans of employees with naval connections was the Royal Hospital School at Greenwich, but their records in Suffolk where they are now located also revealed nothing.

A search was then made for the Royal Hospital School in the 1871 Census, and this revealed that Charles Henry was, indeed, a boarder at that school. He was then thirteen years old, but the school's archives only started with the 1870 intake, which is why they had no record for him, for he was likely to have started earlier, in 1868 or 1869, shortly after his father's death. Boys would normally have left the school at the age of fourteen or fifteen. Further enquiry with the school, while producing nothing on Charles Henry, did show that his younger brother, Herbert William, followed him there, joining the school in December 1874 at the age of ten; he left in December 1879 aged fifteen.[1]

The Royal Hospital School was financed by the Greenwich Hospital Foundation, a charity set up by the royal charter of William and Mary in 1694. It was part of Queen Mary's concern to help veterans and the families of those who were killed or disabled in the wars of the time, and when she died in 1694, Sir Christopher Wren was appointed as architect together with his assistant Nicholas Hawksmoor. Teaching started around 1712 in the splendid buildings that were erected and still survive at Greenwich, and the school gained a reputation as a place to study mathematics and navigation. A visiting inspector in 1851 reported that the school was 'far beyond any other known to me in scientific attainment'.[2] The fine setting of the school would have contrasted hugely with Charles Henry's simple family home when he joined probably at the age of ten; if the youngster felt any lingering homesickness, this was likely to have been swiftly removed as he eagerly anticipated a new stage in his life.

But what did Charles Henry do from around 1873, when an average pupil would have left school, until the time he went to China in 1880? Could the school have provided sufficient education for him to be able to teach at the level necessary for specialist naval cadets?

He must, therefore, have further engaged in some way with navigation and/or astronomy, at the time very closely allied subjects, probably in the Greenwich area. There was another pointer to a continued Greenwich connection, for the post that he took up in China was at the Naval Yard School in Foochow. As will be seen later, the Foochow school had recently developed a relationship with the Royal Naval College, Greenwich, and it is not impossible that by being in the Greenwich area he learned about the China opportunity. To have achieved what he did in life suggests, notwithstanding his general reticent air, a confidence that facilitated a form of 'networking'; it could well be that he established the China connection in this way. Especially intriguing is the possibility, as will be considered later, that he could have known Yen Fu, a former student at the Foochow Naval Yard School, who attended the Royal Naval College, which was in the same complex of Greenwich buildings as the Royal Hospital School, at about this time. Yen Fu was to become famous as a translator of seminal Western works.

Other clues to his familiarity with astronomy emerged. Charles Henry later used the letters 'F.R.A.S.' after his name. Because of his activities and his writings for the journal of the North China Branch of the Royal Asiatic Society, I had assumed that the 'R.A.S.' derived from his membership of the main body in Britain, and that when he retired he remained involved with the R.A.S. in Britain. But there was nothing about him in the R.A.S.'s records. The only other body with the same initials was the Royal Astronomical Society, the records of which I then tried without any expectations. I thereupon discovered that he had indeed applied for and been accepted as a fellow of that body in 1885 while in China. As we shall see later, the Astronomical Society proved to be the only source of an obituary notice for him. The fellowship demonstrated that he must have had considerable knowledge of astronomy, for he was sufficiently well thought of to have been supported in his election by three existing fellows who were professional astronomers. His three sponsors were all at the Royal Observatory in Greenwich: Sir William Henry Mahoney Christie, the Astronomer Royal; Edward Walter Maunder, who worked with Christie and was very well-known in the world of astronomy; and Lewis, who, though less illustrious, was later to have the splendid title of Superintendent of Time at the Royal Observatory. Lewis had also attended the Royal Hospital School, having lost his father at an early age, a merchant sea captain who was killed in a disaster at sea. Lewis, incidentally, was to become an active freemason, an organization to which it is later hinted that B-T may have belonged.

According to the obituary, astronomy also featured in a book B-T wrote, *Problems and Theorems in Navigation and Nautical Astronomy.* No copy of the book has yet been located, and no date of publication or publisher is known. It may have been published in China during the 1880s when navigation and astronomy were included in the subjects he taught.

His familiarity with astronomy together with the Greenwich connection raised the possibility of a closer link with the Royal Observatory there. Adam Perkins, archivist of their records, which are housed in the University of Cambridge, informed me that there was some correspondence concerning a 'Taylor' around that time. A trip to Cambridge uncovered interesting material. "Charles Henry Blewitt [sic] Taylor" had in fact applied for the post of junior assistant at the Royal Observatory, Greenwich, but had been turned down on health grounds: 'Myopic in both eyes . . . Heart condition irregular, and lungs delicate, especially the upper part of the right'. Arie, then Astronomer Royal, initially refused to accept the decision and invited B-T to undertake a test of skills and 'powers of observation', after which

Arie engaged in a lengthy correspondence with members of the Civil Service to try to persuade them to change their minds about the conditions of appointment. He was particularly concerned as the post was a difficult one to fill, and B-T had been the only candidate. To support the case he pointed out that two other staff members were no less shortsighted than the candidate, and that he, Arie, was 'more shortsighted than any of them'!

Charles Henry also made an appeal (writing from Haddington Terrace where he still lived) on 25 May 1880; he was then aged twenty-two years, and this is his earliest letter to be discovered. His plea demonstrates that he was keen to secure the post, and at that stage he wished to remain in Britain:

> With reference to my late examination for the post of Junior Assistant, Greenwich Observatory, and a communication received 20/5/80 stating that I had failed to satisfy the Commissioners; I beg to state that I have been most carefully examined at the Royal Observatory as to my capability to use the instruments, and perform the duties of junior assistant, and the Astronomer Royal has promised to inform the Commissioners that I am not unfitted by my natural shortness of sight, to perform the duties required.
>
> I am sir, your obedient servant CHB Taylor.

The Lords Commissioners of the Admiralty considered the request by Arie but turned it down:

> it appears that Mr. Taylor, who is a delicate man, is very shortsighted, and . . . . the strain upon his eyes for the nature of the work . . . would most probably still further impair his vision, and render him eventually unfit for his post.

The Lords Commissioners thus demonstrated their own longsightedness, and despite further remonstrations by the eminent Arie, they were not to be persuaded, fearing to create a precedent. A curt letter from the commissioners on 3 July ended the matter.[3]

The post was eventually filled by a schoolmate of Charles Henry, Lewis, who was then occupying the post of temporary assistant master at the Dockyard School in Portsmouth, having completed a specialist teacher training programme which had been established in Greenwich in the 1870s. This was the same Lewis who was later to be one of B-T's sponsors for the F.R.A.S.; the only astronomical background that Lewis had referred to in his letter of application for the Royal Observatory post was the special training received under the headmaster of the Royal Hospital School, Greenwich. So, it is conceivable that this was the same level of education in astronomy Charles Henry had attained. But it is also possible that B-T had worked as a temporary supernumerary assistant in the observatory, which would have given him more experience and may not have required a formal application. Having worked there could also explain the eminence of his referees, but had he done so surely some reference to this would have been in the appeals, so this is unlikely. Perhaps he, like Lewis, had undertaken the training course for intending mariner teachers. Was there a precursor institution to the present Goldsmiths' College, in New Cross, close to Greenwich, which was later to engage in teacher training, and might records still exist? Maritime-related teaching in the Royal Naval School for the sons of naval officers did take place in the same building as Goldsmiths', but no institutional connection between the two colleges has been established.[4]

It looked as though B-T's years between completing school and leaving for China would remain unknown, until further research at the Public Record Office partly filled the gap. The Royal Hospital School had a 'Senior Training Course' at Greenwich which provided more formal training that enabled students to become teachers. A few of the school's students who were being used as pupil-teachers were examined when they turned nineteen for entry to the course. Among those examined in 1875 were Thomas Lewis, 'C. Taylor', and another boy. Lewis and Taylor were both under age, but despite that the former did sufficiently well in the examination to be recommended for the course; this was in all likelihood where Lewis had undergone the teacher training referred to earlier. While Taylor did not do well enough for immediate entry, it was recommended that he 'should not be passed over — may be given a silver medal' and allowed to come up again for examination at Christmas 1876, when he would be nineteen.[5] I could not establish whether Taylor did take the examinations again. Pupil-teachers often went directly into teaching, which Charles Henry might have done.

Most likely he stayed at the Royal Hospital School at least until he was nineteen and may have continued teaching there or elsewhere in the area for the following four years. His matriculation to university in 1879 at the age of twenty-one suggests an intention to take a degree which would have greatly enhanced his career in either teaching or astronomy. His application for the observatory post also suggests a strong intention to stay in Britain, and he must have been disappointed to be turned down, especially knowing that the Astronomer Royal himself was batting for him.

But there was a beguiling though somewhat more challenging compensation. Alongside his application to the Observatory he must have also applied for the teaching post in China, for which he obviously felt sufficiently qualified. As a prudent man, he must have felt he had sufficiently good prospects to be able to marry, though given later evidence of his devotion to the young lady, passion might have outweighed prudence. For immediately following the Observatory disappointment, and having secured the position in China, on 30 July 1880, Charles, still at the somewhat young age of twenty-two, married. His wife was a nineteen-year-old local girl named Alice Mary Vale. No current occupation is given for him — his status in the marriage certificate is the one anticipated in Foochow — nor is there an occupation recorded for her. They left the country some months before the next census took place in 1881, unaware that 120 years later someone would be trying to establish more about them.

At the time of their marriage in 1880, they were both living in Beresford Street, Walworth, London, he at number 249, a house which took in lodgers, she a short distance away in number 165 with her family. Both houses have since been demolished. One wonders how they met — perhaps romantically on the street, though given that he was living in Haddington Terrace in May, he must have recently moved, probably in order to be closer to her. This possible move on his part is understandable from a photograph of her showing a lively, handsome woman. She must have been attracted by the sensitive and serious young man who knew about the stars and who clearly had aspirations for a life different from the one with which they were both familiar.

Alice's father, George Vale, aged approximately forty-three, was a candlemaker, a trade well in demand before gas and electricity lighting became popular. Alice's mother, aged forty-two, had no occupation. The Vales had themselves seemingly married quite young as well, and they had a son (twenty-three years of age in the 1881 Census) also named George and also a candlemaker, as well as a daughter, given the same name as her mother, Emma; the family in common with contemporary practice obviously believed in continuity. The sister Emma was about a year older than the newly-wed wife, and she was an embroideress, so it would be interesting to know why there was no occupation recorded for Alice in the marriage certificate — perhaps she was anticipating her future status as a nonemployed housewife. Family lore has it that the Vales were opposed to the marriage because Alice was then regarded as under age. But the evidence does not point in that direction: not only were the ages of the newly-weds apparently similar to those of the parents when they married, but both the parents were witnesses to the marriage (though the George Vale recorded as witness might have been the brother of Alice). Had the Vales been firmly opposed, they could have withheld consent as Alice was under the age of twenty-one and consent would have been required. The parents may well have been understandably apprehensive, however, about their young daughter going off to the other side of the world.

Charles's mother, however, was not a witness, and we do not know whether she attended the wedding, the only witness from his side being his seventeen-year-old sister Edith Elizabeth. He must have been in contact with his family still despite living on his own in London. His mother may have felt that after her struggle to bring up a family of five children on her own on meagre resources, she was being abandoned by her eldest son, both by his marriage and by his impending departure to China. So perhaps it was she, not Alice's parents, who opposed the marriage. According to B-T's grandson, B-T would never answer questions about his mother, which suggests an estrangement.[6]

The marriage certificate describes Charles Henry as 'Professor of Mathematics'. This might seem somewhat pretentious if it describes a teaching post he then held (though the term 'professor' was far less restrictively used then), but it is more likely that he gave the title of the job he had been appointed to and was about to take up in China. Like his parents before him, he may have married quickly in anticipation of a move to a new job, in this case a more dramatic move.

From the tone of B-T's letters to the Royal Observatory, one can imagine he probably would have taken up the post there if he had passed the health test. Ironically, the strain on his eyesight from reading and writing Chinese must have been considerable, probably greater than that likely to have been endured by the work at the Royal Observatory for which he was turned down. Such is the way the world turns, and sinology was to be the gainer.

These findings present a picture of an intelligent young man, one with academic inclinations, keen to get on in life and break away from the constraints of his social origins. Frustrated in attempts to become an astronomer, B-T doubtless saw China as a means of realizing his ambition for social advancement in an intriguing context.

The newly-weds must have left England very shortly after their marriage at the end of July, for Charles Henry took up his post on 1 October 1880,[7] having had a six-week sea journey (this being well before the Trans-Siberian Railway was built in the 1890s). Both their families must have been sad about their departure, for it was likely to be some years before they would see them again. But for the couple, the long and exotic journey was likely to have added enchantment to their romance.

4

The China Background

The China that Charles Henry entered with his young bride was at a fascinating stage in its history. This chapter sketches some of the background of this world; it is intended to acquaint those readers less familiar with nineteenth-century China with its circumstances and also serves to remind others of events relevant to the foreigners' situation. To widen interest, I have used less well-known sources in addition to more familiar scholarly discourse. A framework of analysis is also proferred which may be helpful in providing a partial understanding of the period.

The Ch'ing dynasty underwent a series of shocks during the nineteenth century from both external belligerence and internal discord. China's reaction led to a slow crystallization of the view held by a small number of progressive senior mandarins that in order to strengthen China, change was necessary in a number of areas, including defence, industry, commerce and administration, and would involve infrastructural innovation in communications and education. They believed that China could learn from the West. Though pleas for change met with considerable resistance from traditionalists in positions of power, who felt threatened by change and believed in the superiority of their values, events were encouraging the voice of a small but powerful band of progressives.

Since the First Opium War (1840–42), China had felt humiliated by being forced to grant concessions to Western powers. These demands were mainly for the purposes of trade, but also for strategic reasons, exacerbated by the rivalries which existed among the foreign powers active in the area. Part of China's need to modernize was motivated by the desire to become sufficiently powerful to defend itself against foreign intrusion. Modernization was also seen as a means of dealing with internal dissent which threatened the dynasty. Interaction among these three forces — foreign domination, internal dissent and modernization — was to characterize much of China's history in the second half of the nineteenth century.

Foreign Domination

Domination may be too strong a word to describe the foreign presence in China in the nineteenth century, for though certain neighbours, particularly Japan and Russia, sought to encroach geographically, the major aim was opening up trade. For nearly a century before the First Opium War started in 1840, trade with the foreigner was confined by Chinese regulations to Canton (Guangzhou). Initially, this trade tended to be one way: foreigners purchased tea, silk and other items, such as rhubarb, paying in gold and silver. But by the second quarter of the nineteenth century, the balance of payments moved against China; this was the result of a considerable increase in the importation of opium. Concern about the wider use of opium had led to a series of government edicts during the eighteenth century prohibiting the use of opium except for medicinal purposes, but despite increasing penalties and the later provisions for dealing with addiction, the increase in consumption was not stemmed, and the trade continued.[1] The British, then masters of an extensive empire, replaced the Portuguese as the most important players in this trade in the late eighteenth century when the East India Company succeeded in establishing a monopoly on opium cultivation in India. After the abolition of the company's monopoly of the China trade in 1834, opium imports increased substantially as more British companies and traders from other countries entered the market. China lacked the apparatus to control this trade effectively.

While China grew a good deal of opium on its own soil,[2] the international opium trade became a serious economic problem; with China's exports being insufficient to compensate for the increased value of imports, the country was being drained of gold and silver. Peking was alarmed and eventually, in 1838, the Emperor appointed Lin Tse-hsu as the imperial commissioner charged with the suppression of the opium trade in Canton.[3] It was in response to Lin's attempts to carry out his mission that the Opium Wars began. After a series of truces, the power of Britain eventually prevailed when it threatened to attack Nanking, and a formal peace treaty was signed in 1842.

China and Britain had different perceptions of the conflict. For the former, it was at least ostensibly about opium; the latter saw the hostilities as an opportunity to secure wider trading arrangements and diplomatic recognition, both of which the Chinese had resisted.[4] Among the most significant provisions of the Treaty of Nanking were the ceding of Hong Kong, which secured for the British a reliable long-term base for trade; the opening up to Britain of five ports — Amoy (Xiamen), Canton, Foochow, Ningpo (Ningbo) and Shanghai; the payment by China of an indemnity of $21 million; and the beginnings of diplomatic recognition — though implementation of this was strongly resisted. Other countries, especially America and France, soon demanded and secured treaties for themselves. Thus, gunboat diplomacy had not only succeeded in opening up trade but also brought into being foreign settlements in important, strategically placed ports.[5]

British views of the war were by no means unanimous. As *The Times* put it:

> To those who have all along blushed for the cause of quarrel which has entangled us in a war with China, who feel that neither necessity, nor justice, nor honour can be pleaded for what must seem to all nations but ourselves a crusade against the wholesome and reasonable revenue laws of a distant, peaceable and independent State — to such fresh account from China must afford but fresh matter for humiliation. It must be confessed that such warfare . . . is of a shocking, and barbarous, as well as futile and ineffectual, character.[6]

One popular paper, however, held a contrary view: despite the general distaste surrounding the use of opium, its sale by the British was justified if it were the means by which China could acquire the beneficial influence of the West. The perception of China that was displayed, the pious rationalization about the activity and the period's characteristic combination of the Bible and the Flag are revealing:

> That the Tartar dynasty is tottering to its fall appears far from improbable . . . The Chinese are far too wise not to see the advantages of our just laws, giving protection to life and property, when contrasted with the arbitrary rule of their Tartar conquerors . . . Out of evil sometimes cometh good, and the opium trade, which is little understood in this country, may have been the means intended by Providence for introducing the Gospel, and altering the condition of that benighted country, for that such an event is sooner or later to take place no Christian can doubt. Speaking of the opium trade . . . the opprobrium that has been heaped upon it as having been the cause of the war is totally unfounded; the real cause may be easily traced in the many years' submission to insult during the period of the East India Company's charter . . . An immense field for British commerce is about to be opened, and the advantages offered must not be lost by a mistaken policy.[7]

Not all wielders of the Bible and the Flag were as supportive of the war as the *Illustrated London News*. The Rev. Henry Solly, an eminent Unitarian minister and a radical on many social issues, met a sergeant in a train who had just returned from serving in the war. The sergeant was far from enthusiastic:

> I didn't like it . . . A deal too much like just driving a lot of sheep before you and butchering them, I didn't like it at all.

Solly commented: 'a vile and cruel business from beginning to end'.[8]

The Treaty of 1842 was highly significant. It fundamentally altered the structure of Ch'ing relations with foreign powers, and the dynasty could no longer effectively control all the foreigners on its soil.[9] While the Treaty Ports varied considerably in their importance and the way they operated, in general they ensured a more reliable setting for trade, for commerce and for living in China. Although some foreign merchants preferred their own known methods of operating, using their bargaining strength, personal contacts and outright bribery, many wanted reliability and a base for accessing a country they saw as ripe for profit-making; in short, they wanted a context more familiar to the West.

The foreign settlements thus established gradually brought about a vastly improved municipal administration in many ports. Here, the foreigners tried to maintain lifestyles familiar to them in their own countries. The nationality of inhabitants could be recognized by the architectural style of the houses they built. Imported furnishings, culinary habits, leisure pursuits, churches and chapels, clubs and learned societies, newspapers and other publications all resulted in living styles which would not have been unfamiliar to the resident of Manchester or Berlin. Indeed, given the relative cheapness of servants, travel and living costs generally in China, many foreigners would have experienced a standard of living well beyond their reach in their home country.

The Shanghai International Settlement was a prime example of foreigners running their own affairs. The principle of 'extraterritorality' contained in a supplementary treaty to that of 1842 exempted foreigners from local Chinese laws, and foreign nationals set up their own courts and police force and were subject to their own laws.[10] As will be seen later, unexpected problems arose, for example when prosperous Chinese became attracted, because of status, safety or the fact that the area was better run, to move into areas covered by the settlement. Chinese magistrates often refused to issue summonses to Chinese offenders of superior status to themselves.[11] Problems also arose when the Chinese authorities tried to extricate Chinese political seditionists who sought refuge in the area.[12] Later, new regulations were drawn up, which included provision for the election of a Municipal Council to jointly administer the three settlements. The French eventually withdrew from the arrangement, preferring to run their own concession; but the US and British areas amalgamated in 1863 and became the basis for the famous Shanghai International Settlement, which was to last until 1943.[13] Much of the flavour of life in the Treaty Ports has been well elaborated elsewhere.[14]

As already noted, not all the terms of the 1842 treaty were readily complied with; and following a Second Opium War an Anglo-Chinese Treaty was signed in 1858, partly to enforce the Treaty of 1842 and partly to include further provisions, such as the opening of additional Treaty Ports, freedom of travel, facilitating missionary activity and the imposition of extra indemnities. When ratification became problematic, an Anglo-French force was despatched to Peking and the Summer Palace was set on fire. The resultant Convention of Peking in 1860 extended the provisions of the 1858 treaty. Further north, the Russians were also widening their area of influence. In the view of one eminent historian, 1860 ended a period of conflict, and China entered an era of submission.[15]

Exhausted by the Taiping and other rebellions (discussed later), and shaken by impotence in resisting the foreigner, China felt humiliated. Relations with the key foreign powers continued uneasily for the remainder of the century, with a process of adaptation as China came to terms with the West's norms for conducting international relations. Further Treaty Ports were also opened, and foreign powers extended their areas of interest. For some years, the demands of the foreigner centred on enforcement of the treaties, but gradually neighbouring nations' ambitions were asserted. China had been buttressed on its borders by a number of vassal states, including Siam, Annam, Burma, Mongolia, Tibet and Korea. Gradually, the country lost control of most of them. When France sought to increase its influence in Annam (roughly Vietnam), China's attempt to prevent this extension of influence to its south-west resulted in the Sino-Franco War (1884–85).

Even more humbling was China's defeat by another Asian country in the Sino-Japanese War in the mid-1890s. Japan had taken to reform and development much more energetically than China; the Ch'ing were found wanting militarily and suffered serious naval and other defeats. China not only had to give up its interest in Korea but also lost Formosa (Taiwan) to the Japanese.

Now the country was seen to be a spent force. In the scramble for concessions, known as 'slicing the melon', other foreign powers seized the opportunity to extend their spheres of influence: Britain, the dominant foreign power during the period, in the economically critical Yangtze (Yangzi) region, as well as adding the New Territories lease to the adjacent Kowloon Peninsula and Hong Kong Island; Russia in politically sensitive Manchuria; Germany in Shantung (Shandong); and France in China's south-west.[16] This subjection of China to foreigners' demands even led some observers to envisage China's break-up.[17]

There was a strong realization among some Chinese statesmen, with the recent reforms of the Emperor Meiji in Japan in mind, that more drastic reforms were needed to modernize China and that the level of reform required was unlikely to be achieved by most of the present high ministers. Emperor Kuang-hsu was persuaded that to rely on these ministers for reform would be 'like climbing a tree to seek for a fish'. He decided to embark on relatively radical changes, and from June to September 1898 some forty to fifty decrees were issued overhauling government, education, industry and international exchange. Though technically in retirement, the Empress dowager Tz'u-hsi was still very powerful, and she saw the Emperor's edicts as undermining her authority. She was likely to have agreed with the grand secretary, who observed, 'Reform benefits the Chinese but hurts the Manchus'.[18] A power struggle ensued, which the Empress Dowager, largely backed by conservative ministers, won, and most of the reforms were soon reversed.[19]

The failure of reform created more uncertainty, frustrated the progressives and confirmed revolutionaries in their view that the dynasty had to be overthrown. At the same time, anti-foreigner and anti-missionary activity also increased, culminating in the 1900 Boxer Uprising. Further attempts at reform were to follow the allied crushing of the uprising, but the reforms could not stem unrest, and the deaths on consecutive days of the Emperor and the Empress Dowager in 1908 further encouraged the existing republican movement. Revolution broke out in October 1911, the dynasty speedily collapsed and the Republic of China was established on 1 January 1912.

The immediate goals of the revolution were anti-monarchy and pro-democracy rather than anti-foreigner, and the foreign presence in China was to remain important well into the 1920s and beyond, through a period of political turmoil in which warlords extended their influence and there was conflict between the nationalist government and opposition communists. Foreign governments were aware that the presence and status of their nationals could not be sustained; with the war in Asia from the late 1930s , the role of the foreigner in China greatly diminished. The majority of foreigners finally departed with the establishment of the People's Republic of China, following the 1949 communist triumph known as 'Liberation'.[20]

Internal Dissent

As far back as early in the seventeenth century, the Manchu Ch'ing dynasty had gradually established supremacy over the native Chinese Ming dynasty, 1368–1643. However, the new regime was not regarded as having been established until October (a recurring significant month in Chinese history) 1644, when the Ch'ing dynasty court moved from Mukden (Shenyang) to Peking.

There were frequent expressions of popular discontent during the Ch'ing era. These partly derived from residual feelings about the Manchu as foreigners from Manchuria; sometimes discontent was associated with triad, secret society affiliation with their variety of motivations; often it stemmed from religious sectarianism, ethnic association or simply a reaction to oppressive taxation. One dramatic example of a group opposed to the Ch'ing was the Small Sword Society, which, as will be seen later (Chapter 6), occupied Shanghai for about eighteen months in the middle of the 1850s. The Small Swords paralleled a more famous movement, the Taiping (Great Peace), which secured extraordinary military success. The rebellion has been said to be the most destructive civil war in history with the alleged slaughter of twenty million lives.[21] Though the Taiping were finally put down, they were the greatest internal threat to the Ch'ing, a dramatic example of the dynasty's vulnerability; the experience of the rebellion was to prove significant for China.

The Taiping combined a platform of social reform with a kind of Christian belief. This mixture was not in itself an unfamiliar one in the West; indeed, the movement could be seen as a form of Christian Socialism, the nineteenth century movement in Britain. Ideologically, it was egalitarian, with men and women theoretically regarded as equal and having a share in land distribution; favoured the abolition of private ownership of land and property; and adopted various social welfare measures supporting the weak and deprived. The Taiping prohibited 'opium smoking, footbinding, slavery, and prostitution'.[22] Not surprisingly, they attracted the marginalized. More oddly, the Cantonese leader, Hung Hsiu-ch'uan, believed himself to be the younger son of God and the brother of Jesus and claimed he was founding the Kingdom of Heaven. The fascinating though poorly displayed material in Nanking's Taiping Museum, now sadly run down in what could be a fine building, hails the Taiping as the radical precursors of the founders of the Republic of 1912 and the later Communist 'Liberation' of 1949; there is not a hint of their Christian dimension.

Having declared a revolt against the Manchu in Kwangsi (Guangxi) Province in January 1851, Hung was proclaimed 'Heavenly King' of a 'Heavenly Kingdom of Great Peace'. Over subsequent years, the Taiping gained numerous impressive victories and occupied vast tracts of land, controlling important areas of China. In 1853, they took Wuhan and then Nanking, which had been a capital in previous dynasties, and which they renamed the 'Heavenly Capital'. Other conquests included Soochow (Suzhou) and Hangchow (Hangzhou). So successful were they that initially the foreign powers were uncertain whether to back them or the Ch'ing. Individual foreigners did indeed support the Taiping, attracted by their programme of social reform, and some missionaries saw them as a step towards the fulfilment of biblical prophecy.[23]

Foreigners were to become sceptical of the Taiping. Alexander Michie, a businessman who much later was to become closely related to B-T, visited the Taiping in Nanking in 1861 to find out more about them. He contrasted their intentions in theory with their actual practice:

> I have no hope of any good ever coming out of the rebel movement . . .
> They do nothing but burn, murder, and destroy . . . They have held Nanking
> eight years, and there is not a symptom of rebuilding it. Trade and industry
> are prohibited. Their land-taxes are three times heavier than those of the
> Imperialists; they adopt no measures to soothe and conciliate the people.[24]

Eventually, partly through this kind of disillusion with the Taiping and partly as a result of new treaties with the Ch'ing, aid was provided to the imperial forces by the foreign powers.[25] Soochow was retaken in December 1863, Hangchow in March 1864 and Nanking itself in July of the same year. After the slaughter of millions, and Hung having committed suicide, the Taiping rebellion was over.

While the Taiping rebellion was the most dramatic, it was not the only one. The period from the early 1850s to the mid-1870s witnessed a number of others. Of these rebellions, the Nien in Shantung and Honan (Henan) was seen as one of the most effective despite having no clear political ideology, religious affiliation or even effective leadership. They waged war over the North China Plain, coming close to Peking. Also important during the period was a series of Muslim revolts in the North-West centring on Sinkiang (Xinjiang), as well as in the South-West in Yunnan.[26]

These revolts further demonstrated the dynasty's vulnerability and dependence on the West, especially Britain and France, who were able to exploit the situation by securing more advantages. Foreigners had demonstrated, both by their assistance and their 1860 campaign 'lesson', their technical and military superiority. To some commentators, this combination of domestic uprising and foreign invasion bore the characteristics of a possible dynastic collapse.[27]

Modernization

Foreign aggrandizement and the internal vulnerability of the Ch'ing were major triggers for China to attempt to change in order to survive. The problem was how to learn from the West while retaining China's perceived superior culture — a familiar recurring theme in China's history of modernization: 'Socialism with Chinese Characteristics' and 'Capitalism with a Chinese Face'.

Chinese attitudes towards foreigners varied considerably. There was strong resentment at having to accept Western influence and to see China's sovereignty undermined. Many scorned foreigners, who were perceived as having an inferior culture, and extreme hostility toward and rejection of certain Western values were frequently expressed. But there were also those who appreciated the West's achievements; later, there are many examples of true affection and loyal devotion from local Chinese who became friends or, more frequently, loyal servants to Westerners.

One early view of 'the foreigner' and of the vulnerability of the dynasty stemming from internal dissent was expressed in 1860 by Prince Kung in a dispatch to the Emperor:

> If we think the barbarians are sincere we shall be greatly deceived. They [the Russians] talk of helping us to put down the rebels, but say we must not let the British and French know. In my opinion all the barbarians have the nature of brute beasts. The British are the most unruly, but the Russians are the most cunning. The rebels menace our heart, the Russians our trunk, while the British are merely a threat to our limbs. First of all we must extirpate the rebels: then we must settle accounts with Russia. Britain's turn comes last.[28]

But a more realistic and pragmatic view than this of what was necessary for China to overcome external and internal threats began to emerge.

The Taiping rebellion had brought to prominence a number of important Chinese who were to become the torch bearers for China's attempts at modernization. Five were particularly significant. The first was Prince Kung himself, chief minister of the Imperial Household, who moderated his view of the foreigner and became head of the Tsungli Yamen, the office dealing with foreigners. The second was Wen-hsiang, a Grand Councillor and major supporter of both diplomatic and economic modernization. And there were three others who illustrate the rise of Han Chinese within the Manchu-dominated hierarchy: Tseng Kuo-fen, who later was in charge of four rich provinces (Kiangsu (Jiangsu), Kiangsi (Jiangxi), Anhwei [Anhui] and Chekiang [Zhejiang]); Li Hung-chang, who was to become one of the most important and powerful mandarins and a 'virtual prime minister';[29] and Tso Tsung-t'ang, who became governor general of Chekiang, Fukien (Fujian) and then Shensi (Shaanxi) and Kansu (Gansu). In the operations against the Taiping, they had witnessed what the foreign powers could achieve, especially with their superior weaponry and naval capability. These administrators and others like them realized that only by modernization could China establish itself as an equal.[30]

In 1864, Li Hung-chang addressed the following memorial to Prince Kung:

> In China, our civilian officials are plunged in the elucidation of classical texts and in the refinement of calligraphy, while our military men are for the most part ignorant dullards. Our education seems quite divorced from utility . . . It is my submission that to turn China into a strong country we must acquire the use of modern weapons, and for this must install machinery for making these weapons. By learning the foreigners' methods for ourselves, we shall no longer depend on their services.[31]

Li's view of the foreigner was more favourable than that of Kung (whose view did change later): responding to a departmental circular in 1867, Li stressed that from 'several years' experience in conducting business . . . he has found that . . . they act honourably without deceit or falsehood.'[32] In his argument for modernization, Li cites the way Japan learnt from the foreigner in order to become a great power. Doubly ironically, however, it was not until China's humiliating defeat by Japan in 1895 and Li's perceived failure over the war that change was seen to be essential. Li also expressed the hope that military arsenals could be of value to the wider economy more generally, producing machinery for use in, for example, agriculture, weaving, printing and the pottery industry.[33]

The need to change, however grudgingly acknowledged from the time of the Taiping, marked the beginning of what has become known as the period of 'Self-Strengthening'.[34] This period has been divided into a number of stages: the first, from 1861 to 1872, emphasized the development of military, including naval, industries and also changes in education. The second, from 1872 to 1884, recognized the need for wealth creation if China was to develop an adequate infrastructure; major commercial, industrial and communication enterprises were established during this period. The third stage also lasted for about ten years, from 1885, and in addition to further developing the military, extended changes into light industry, especially textiles.[35]

Despite political turmoil, the Chinese economy had improved considerably beginning especially in the early 1880s. In the development of commerce and the banking system, the exploitation of natural resources such as coal and iron mining, improved communications through railways, roads, the telegraph, telephones and the postal services, foreigners were highly active, often in concert with Chinese traders and entrepreneurs. As will be seen later, the development of a much improved Western-led Customs Service was to play a significant role. Though China remained desperately poor, overall living standards did improve with economic development, and during the Republican period China was to increase its participation in world trade.[36]

Modernization also required, whatever the merits of the classical system of education, a differently educated population. While there was an awareness of the need to change, many Chinese saw their educational system, along with other institutions and customs, as in many respects superior to those of foreigners; higher education institutions in China tended to regard Western knowledge merely as a supplement to traditional teaching. There was still much distrust of 'the foreigner', and many Chinese who got on well and worked closely with foreigners were themselves distrusted. Western knowledge was regarded with ambivalence — partly respected, but also resisted; for as with all change, it undermined the position of those, such as the Confucian-trained elite, who had achieved success through being educated in a very different tradition. Prejudice was reinforced by their understanding of the qualities necessary to function in public life. Having spent years poring over classical books in order to enter government service, mandarin traditionalists would not be enthusiastic if others were given the opportunity for officialdom without enduring the same ordeal.

Nevertheless, attitudes more receptive to the need for educational reform emerged with the slow realization that this was the key to sustaining modernization. The 1860s saw the beginning of an awakening and a growing awareness that entirely new institutions needed to be created. Between 1861 and 1870, four modern schools were built, at Peking, Shanghai, Canton and Foochow, where modern mathematics and science were to be taught. The practice of sending students abroad was also justified by the need to learn the superior techniques of the 'barbarians' in order to control them.

By the end of the century, new universities were being established, often funded by foreign religious bodies with a strong missionary presence, such as the Non-Conformists and Roman Catholics; they also employed Western staff. These institutions, though in the main less a direct result of Self-Strengthening, were to make a significant contribution to the process of modernization and would themselves eventually begin to influence established institutions.

This, then, was the climate, created out of both foreign domination and internal dissent, which gave rise to groping yet more conscious steps towards modernization. Though a catalogue of the achievements of Self-Strengthening might seem limited compared with what was needed in China, it did have some effect in bringing about significant changes, not only in developing new institutions but also in adopting modes of operating and administrative procedures from the West. Further, the longer-term significance of the period should be seen to include the encouragement, whether intentional or otherwise, of new cultural and political attitudes, which questioned the values and practices that underlay much of traditional Chinese society.

A brief introduction of this kind cannot do justice to the complexity of the currents and eddies of this period of China's history. Different forces within China interacted with foreign powers who were also competing with one another. The interplay of all these, especially given their changing position and relationships, is too intricate to fully dissect. I argue here that the three themes of foreign domination, internal dissent and modernization were played out in China's discordant society, counterpointing one another. While these strands were not the only ones that can be discerned during the period, it can be argued that they were significant for the foreign presence in China.

Opportunities for Foreigners

Foreign domination, trade and modernization provided rich sources of opportunity for expatriates in China. Many derived employment in foreign trade and industry, others in the diplomatic and consular services and the foreign military; church missionary societies provided another source. The Treaty Port settlements were important recruiters, not only for their administrators and law enforcers, such as the police, but also for the supply of various services demanded in the foreigner's world, such as banking and the importation of familiar goods; the shopkeepers, lawyers, accountants, architects, schoolteachers, barbers, printers, workers on newspapers and journals, and operators of bars and clubs; these and others could be regarded as among the 'servants of empire'.[37] By providing opportunities in China for individuals from abroad, such as B-T, the settlements both reaffirmed the foreign presence and contributed to change.

It will become clear how some of the events outlined here had an impact on B-T. One of the major achievements of Self-Strengthening, the Foochow Naval Dockyard and its school, provided B-T with his first employment in China. The occupation of Shanghai by the Small Sword rebels provided the opportunity for the setting up of a better regulated Customs Service, which provided B-T his second job and his major career.

Another skein in the historical tapestry should not be ignored; it is the difficulty of distinguishing self-interest from altruism. Just as individual Chinese saw value in modernization, not only to counter Western domination or reduce vulnerability to internal dissent but for the betterment it could bring to China, so were there individual Westerners who could stand apart from their own situation. These individuals were able to appreciate the value of Chinese culture, and some were also motivated to help China improve its situation. While these motives were not for most the dominant ones in responding to opportunity, there did exist individual foreigners who, usually after being attracted to the rewards of working in China, either materially or spiritually (by capturing souls), also wanted to contribute to China's well-being. For some, this goal might have been a rationalization, that is, an ideology to justify economic self-interest, but not for all. These individuals should not be overlooked when assessing the more obvious economic and political self-interests of the merchants and diplomats operating in China.

Certainly there is no evidence that our man was initially motivated by the idea of being of service to a developing society, rather than simply satisfying his own ambitions. Yet, B-T clearly developed at a very early stage a deep interest in traditional Chinese culture, and there is some indication in his writings that this was accompanied by some desire to assist the society that provided him opportunity for advancement, considerable status, an interesting lifestyle, and his later identity as a scholar-official.

5

Life in Foochow: Family, Teaching, Writing

B-T's appointment to Foochow lasted eleven years, a period which saw him establish his teaching career, family life, early mastery of Chinese and a reputation through his publications as a translator, but it also witnessed the destruction of his home and ended with the devastating loss of his wife.

The dockyard school B-T taught in was part of the Foochow Naval Dockyard established around a dozen years before he arrived. We saw in the last chapter that among those aware of the need for change in China was Tso Tsung-t'ang, the governor-general[1] of Fukien and Chekiang 1863-66. Tso urged in a memorial of 25 June 1866 the building of a modern naval yard, with a school attached, in Foochow. This was one of the early Treaty Ports which had been stipulated in the 1842 Nanking Treaty. Here, Tso advised that Europeans be recruited to train Chinese 'from all levels of society' in ship construction as engineers, technicians and ships' officers. He stressed the need to learn from foreigners and rejected the attitude that was widespread among the tradition-ridden bureaucracy that it would be humiliating for China to imitate Western ship construction; he recalled that the Chinese had found it advisable two centuries earlier to adopt Western cannon and pointed out that Japan had already sent people to England to study ship building[2] One view held that in promoting the arsenal, Tso took a great personal risk:

> According to the system followed by the government at Peking, which never takes the initiative in any new undertaking but contents itself with vetoing or sanctioning what is proposed to it, Viceroy Tso had to assume the entire responsibility of his project and a failure of the experiment would have ruined one of the most successful careers that the mandarinate could present.[3]

That the memorial was regarded as urgent can be seen from the fact that the proposal was accepted and authorized by imperial edict on 14 July 1866, within three weeks of the memorial's being despatched; the building was designed and construction was underway by the end of the year. The French especially were involved in the naval yard's establishment, and it has been alleged that many

Chinese who worked in the area spoke French, though this is questionable.[4] This dockyard, which was built in Mamoi (Mawei), just outside Foochow, was regarded as one of the outstanding achievements of China's Self-Strengthening period. Tso took up another appointment before the plans were realized; his successor, Imperial Commissioner Shen, had wondered whether the Europeans would fully give up the secrets of their science and industry. When they did, he recommended that the director of the enterprise and other Europeans be rewarded with bonuses and honours.[5]

The Foochow school was largely funded by the Imperial Chinese Maritime Customs, which B-T was later to join. Robert Hart, head of the Customs Service, supported the Foochow Naval Dockyard project, which he regarded as a major step toward the modernization of China.[6] One of the proposed foreign directors of the enterprise, Prosper Marie Giquel, was in the Service, having served as Customs Commissioner in Ningpo and in Hankow (Hankou); he had also commanded the Ever-Triumphant Army fighting the Taiping rebels and had been awarded the honorary rank of brigadier-general by the Chinese government, so he was well-regarded by the authorities.[7] The Customs Service was involved with a number of the new naval schools that were created, and these schools featured in the reports of that organization.

The Foochow Naval Yard School had two divisions with five-year courses: the French, where ship construction and design were taught, and the English, specializing in navigation and the training of deck and engine officers for the ships to be built in the naval yard. Partly because foreign instructors were used, each division also taught its own language, French or English.[8] The Naval Yard School appears to have opened around the end of 1869, and it was intended originally that foreigners would no longer be needed as teachers after five years, that is, by 1874. This plan proved to be optimistic, and in the mid-1870s the director-general of the school, Ting Jih-ch'ang, was arguing that experienced Western teachers were still needed.

It was to the English Division of this school that B-T came in the autumn of 1880, to teach mathematics and navigation, which included navigational astronomy.

Why China?

What had decided the young B-T to apply for the post at the school? One interesting feature of the Foochow naval school may well have been significant in his decision to go to China. As part of the Self-Strengthening programme, some students were sent by China to study abroad. The school sponsored several students to study in England in 1877 (and also in 1882 and 1886), for at least three years; they divided their time between first undertaking courses at the Royal Naval College, Greenwich,[9] and then serving on British warships. Those students who proved insufficiently physically fit to serve in the naval yard or on board ship were to teach astronomy, mathematics and geography in the various modern Chinese schools on their return from England.

It could well be that young Charles Henry met some of these students or their accompanying teacher in the Greenwich area. He appears to have made very rapid progress in learning Chinese when he arrived in China, so it is not difficult to imagine that the studious and assiduous young man might even have begun to learn Chinese from one of them, though this seems highly unlikely given that his apparent original priority would have involved remaining in Britain. There would have been little time for this anyway, for he must have been offered the appointment around the time he was turned down for the Royal Observatory post. Either from the students or one of their staff he may have learnt about the post that had become vacant on the death of another teacher at the Foochow Naval Yard School, James Carroll of the Navigation Department.[10] Given the school's link with the Chinese Customs Service, the appointment might have been processed through the organization's London office, but any documentation on this, if there were any, appears to have been destroyed. B-T took up the position in Foochow on 1 October 1880.

The Foochow Naval Yard came to be regarded as the leading naval ship building establishment in China. Though it has been alleged that the dockyard was in decline by 1905, its position being replaced by the Kiangnan (Jiangnan) arsenal and dockyard in Shanghai, the school even as late as 1928 was seen as one of the principal naval academies.[11] Graduates from the school contributed to the development of a modern navy and to the general modernization of China; a few of them rose to positions of influence and leadership in the early years of the twentieth century.[12]

One of the students from Foochow who was to become famous in another field, translation, has already been mentioned: Yen Fu (1853–1921).[13] The work of Yen Fu has been regarded as the first sustained Chinese attempt to understand Western thought. Yen graduated in 1871 and was selected to go to the Royal Naval College in Britain in 1877. There, he came into contact with and developed an appreciation of Western ideas and culture. He was a young man with broad concerns, and he studied the economic, legal, political, philosophical, sociological as well as the scientific thinking of the time. Later, he translated into Chinese works by Darwin, Huxley, J.S. Mill and Herbert Spencer, among others. He was concerned with the cultural and ideological underpinnings of Western power and wealth compared with those of China, and he concluded that Western culture was essentially activity-orientated whereas China's was stability-orientated. After returning to China in 1879, he became Dean of Instruction at the Naval Academy in Tientsin (Tianjin), where he stayed for about twenty years, becoming head of the academy in 1890.[14] Later, he was to become President of Peking University. Although he was originally an admirer of the West, he became a traditionalist who despised Western civilization; he even backed Yuan Shih-k'ai's bid to restore the monarchy and become emperor.[15] A near-contemporary of B-T in age, it is not inconceivable that they could have met each other in London. Given their maritime connections and common interest in translation, they may have met again in China, for their paths overlapped for some years when they both worked in Tientsin; each was clearly attracted to the other's culture.

Life in Foochow

China was an exotic and fascinating country for the young Taylors, though it also had its dangers, particularly in terms of health, which the couple was to experience. Foochow, approximately five hundred miles south of Shanghai, is situated in a beautiful region which still had panthers and tigers living close to the city in the late nineteenth century.[16] Living there must have been an exciting challenge for the expatriates. Foochow is about seventy miles from where the central depot for the great black bohea tea hills was located, and the city became the chief tea port of China. The harbour at Pagoda Anchorage was crowded with 'the finest sailing ships in the world', and the great improvement in clipper ship design dated from the races of the tea-carrying ships from Foochow back to Britain.

> The [foreign] settlement became a model business centre. The residents worked hard and incessantly during the season and enjoyed themselves during the rest of the year, and the old luxurious 'China' style of living survived longest in Foochow.[17]

But with the development of tea plantations in India, the demand for Chinese tea diminished, and economic activity surrounding the trade began to decline in China. By the 1880s, the British in Pagoda Island, where B-T lived, were part of a very small expatriate satellite community located about ten miles downriver from Foochow. Among those living there, considerable social interaction would have taken place.[18]

The world the Taylors encountered, especially in the wider Foochow society, was not only different because it was China: the social life of the expatriate community was also likely to be unfamiliar to the young couple coming as they both did from fairly humble backgrounds with probably little of the social experience possessed by many of their expatriate contacts. While many of those expatriates tried to replicate the world they had left behind, the lifestyle they would have introduced to China would have generally been that of a social status higher than that familiar to the young Taylors. This is not to suggest that expatriates of a lower social origin were unknown: there were many such examples.[19] But the particular group the Taylors were mixing with were likely to be professionals, consuls, teachers and others from a different class background from themselves; many would have received their education in private schools, and some would have attended university. These expatriates would be endeavouring to continue a familiar lifstyle, the Taylors would be discovering a new one.

Thus, in terms of cultural adaptation, they would be learning on two levels — becoming familiar with Chinese manners, mores and customs, as well as those of another social class (though this blending into a higher class was possibly aided by engaging with different foreign nationalities, making class somewhat less homogenous). One wonders how much and for how long they would have felt aware of social difference and whether they had some feeling of marginality. For Charles, who probably had begun this orientation through the kind of world he had already started to move in before leaving England, his involvement in work, learning Chinese and writing would be all-absorbing. A sense of marginality may have affected his desire to establish himself through his literary interests, and it may even have been a factor in his sympathy for a different culture in that he did not share quite the same 'social baggage' as many of the expatriates with whom he mixed. The social milieu he encountered, and indeed aspired to, also contributed to the distance he appears to have felt in relation to his family of origin. Awareness of social difference was likely to have been felt even more sharply by Alice, who was likely to be in everyday social contact with other wives in the small expatriate community.

'Most arrivals in China would be male, young, single.'[20] Being married may have facilitated the social acceptance of the Taylors within the expatriate community. For foreign men, ports of any size would have 'the club' for the elite among the consuls, Customs commissioners and merchants, together with their respective juniors, and another group, 'the customs club', for the lower-ranking tide waiters (customs men who waited for the tide to change to facilitate boarding ships), consular constables and the like.[21] Life for expatriate wives could be demanding whatever one's status. For Alice there would have been much to learn on her social visits about domestic issues, such as the organization of the household, how best to manage servants, dealing with food (including instructing the cook in British cuisine), raising children in China and health concerns.

Relations with Chinese tended to be more formal; differences in taste, upbringing, education and domestic habits being 'too dissimilar for common ground to be readily found', though there were rare exceptions.[22] Also, some expatriate children made very close attachments to amahs and other domestic helpers.[23]

Embarking on a family as quickly as the Taylors did would probably have facilitated their integration into expatriate society. There was much to consider:

health conditions were poor, especially for those encountering childbirth, and infant mortality as well as maternal mortality rates were high. The dangers for both child and mother are described in portrayals of Treaty Port life.[24] Sharing the experience of family life with others in the community was likely to have been psychologically reassuring. According to a recently discovered family tree, Alice may have had altogether six babies who died at birth or in infancy; this number seems particularly high, and Consular records for only four babies born alive to Alice have been found.[25] The Taylors' first baby, Charles Burney Taylor, was born in August 1881, having been conceived soon after their arrival in China, but he died aged just ten months in 1882. However, another son, born in June 1884, survived, he was named Leonard.

Shortly after Leonard's birth, the Taylors suffered a distressing experience when Foochow was the scene of a major battle. At the time, the French were successfully extending their influence in Annam and were in conflict with China over the shared border in its south-west. China received suzerain tribute from Annam and was most concerned about the increasing influence of France. There were battles at land and sea, and while attempts were made to try to resolve problems, in mid-July of 1885 the French sent their warships to Foochow.[26] The following month, the tranquillity of the port, busy with commercial activity and the grace of naval movement, was shattered by the blaze and roar of French guns attacking the naval arsenal, where B-T's school was located:

> In less than one hour every Chinese ship in the anchorage had been sunk or set afire and the dock had been blown up.[27]

Certainly, much of the local Chinese fleet was destroyed, and estimates of the number of Chinese killed ranged from one to three thousand; total French losses were six men.[28] The initial task accomplished, the French turned their guns on the dockyard, leisurely putting it to ruins.[29] The French organizers and teachers of ship building in the Naval Yard school must have felt a heavy-hearted ambivalence about the destruction of their workplace by their co-nationals. Certainly, the loyalties of the French dockyard director, Giquel, were severely tested by the war; he was bitterly upset by the enormity of the damage, and he did what he could to put China's position to France.[30]

Although the dockyard was not entirely destroyed,[31] according to B-T's obituary notice, 'his house was wrecked in the bombardment by the French fleet'.[32] The attack must have been a hair-raising induction into life in China.

War and infant mortality were not the only threats. Disastrous fires were to sweep Foochow whilst B-T was there. In January 1890, a great fire in the foreign settlement caused 'immense destruction of property, native and foreign', and in April of the same year, another major fire was reported: 'disastrous fire at Foochow;

hundreds of houses destroyed'.[33] War, fires, and children dying in infancy were the kinds of hazards that were not infrequent in China, but to have suffered all three would have been exceedingly distressing.

Alice and her baby did not directly experience the French bombardment, as they appear to have left Foochow beforehand. A letter dated June 1885 from B-T written in Foochow is in the archives of the Royal Astronomical Society. This letter indicates that his wife must have already gone home, anticipating that B-T would join her on leave. Alice was staying at an address which a census revealed to be that of B-T's married sister, Rebecca, in Southsea, Hampshire, along with her gas-fitter husband, Albert H. Barber, and their two babies, Bertha Florence and Charles H., the latter presumably named after his uncle, Charles Henry. This is a rare reference to continued contact with any of B-T's sisters, though there is another example much later of contact with the same sister. Perhaps Alice felt comfortable in this working-class family, sharing the experience of having young babies with her sister-in-law. B-T joined his wife and son there when he went on leave.

After the Taylors returned to China the following year, another son, Raymond, was born in September 1887. B-T appears to have thrown himself into his work, for though he was a reserved man, he was also ambitious. On Raymond's birth certificate, he is described as Acting Foreign Secretary, Mamoi Arsenal. This presumably refers to an administrative post he held at the school, alongside being 'Professor of Navigation and Mathematics, Imperial Arsenal', as he is also described on the certificate; he was probably undertaking a temporary role for someone who was away, for this was the last reference to the acting foreign secretary position.

B-T performed his work well enough to be awarded the Double Dragon, Second Class, Third Division after five years in his post; this was conferred by imperial decree on 21 September 1885 at the instance of Special Commissioner P'ei, who commanded the naval arsenal at Foochow.[34] The citation states that the award was granted to C. H. B-T, who was 'then Professor of Navigation in the naval school of Foochow after five years of markedly meritorious service'. Honours in China were hierarchically ranked according to status, and this level of award was for vice-consuls or people of equivalent rank. B-T's grandson, Teddy, still has the medal and the associated document which shows that B-T had by then been given a Chinese name, Deng Luo, a transliteration of 'Taylor'.

It was at about this time, quite early into B-T's Foochow period, that he began to adopt the hyphenated surname. 'Brewitt' was the maiden name of his mother and was the last of his forenames; he was the only child of the family to be given the name, and so the only one who could suitably hyphenate it. When he married in 1880, just before leaving for China at the age of twenty-two, he didn't use the hyphen. Apparently, according to his grandson, B-T had explained the hyphen by the wish to differentiate himself from all the other Taylors in the organization; this would have been, perhaps, also more acceptable to his family of origin. However, given the fact that the hyphen was adopted in the smaller work community of Foochow, before he joined the larger Customs organization, this seems rather unlikely; other explanations are that he may have wished to make himself more distinctive as a writer or distance himself from his family. At least equally plausible is that in his situation in China, largely mixing with people whose background was socially superior to his own, the hyphen would have suggested a higher status in his origins than he actually had.

At first, B-T did not use the hyphen consistently; he seems to have experimented with its use, sometimes using C. H. Brewitt Taylor without the hyphen. His son Leonard was not given the hyphen at birth in 1884, simply having 'Brewitt' as a forename. When B-T first joined the North China Branch of the Royal Asiatic Society in 1885, his surname is given in the membership list as 'Taylor'. But in the same year, a short translated story in the society's journal is signed 'C. H. Brewitt-Taylor', the first known reference to this usage by B-T, then aged just twenty-seven years. Raymond, his second son, was given the hyphen when he was born in 1887. The early inconsistency is understandable, for one does not generally lightly change the way one is known.

Early Writings

B-T began his translation activities at a very early stage in his career. How did he learn Chinese so quickly? He almost certainly would have employed a Chinese tutor, the norm at the time for anyone seriously wanting to study the language. A young student interpreter in the Consular Service described his learning regime undertaken under the supervision of Thomas Wade, the diplomat and sinologist. For about eighteen months, the student had a language teacher who didn't speak a word of English:

> My sien-shang[35] is a little dried up old fellow, but one of the most perfect gentleman I ever saw. He comes to me for two hours and a half before breakfast . . . and as long afterwards as I choose to keep him, I generally put on the tea-pot and give him a good cup . . . I am doing about six hours a day with the teacher, and occasionally an hour or two more by myself.[36]

Another account of learning Chinese, by a young army officer, uses another term for the teacher: the officer records that when he was sent to Peking by the War Office to learn the language, he began by engaging a *munshi* for five hours a day.[37] *Munshi* is a word of Arabic and Hindi origins meaning 'to educate', and it was used by Europeans to describe native teachers of languages. The term was imported more widely into Europe and the East, along with other words of similar origin, by those engaged in the military, trade and administration.[38]

It is highly likely that B-T was encouraged very early into writing and publishing by H. A. Giles, the well-known sinologist. In a review of B-T's translation of the *San Kuo,* he claims as much:

> Much impressed by his literary as well as by his scientific gifts, I urged him to take up the Chinese language and fit himself for a permanent position in China.[39]

Giles spent twenty-five years in the Consular Service in China, starting in 1867. One view of him was that he was

> too much of an individual to settle easily into a Civil Service mould, his career as a consular officer was not outstanding. But he was fascinated by Chinese people, their language, and their civilization, a fascination that in later years became an obsession . . . [Giles] set out to transform current European ideas about China . . . to the view that China was a country with an unsurpassed record of civilization and culture, where scholarship was revered.[40]

Giles is another example of someone who by his position would stereotypically be seen as part of the 'imperialist agenda' yet whose concerns extended well beyond this. Giles's name is frequently used in conjunction with that of Wade, who devised a system of transliteration of Chinese to English for his *Peking Syllabary* of 1859 that was later modified by Giles for his Chinese-English Dictionary. This became known as the Wade-Giles system and was in general use by students of Chinese until replaced by pinyin in 1958.[41] Given the familiar connection between the two authors of the system, it is worth noting the scorn that Giles expressed for Wade:

> He was a bogus scholar, who has left not a scratch of any importance behind him, and was a diplomatic failure into the bargain.[42]

After Wade's retirement in 1895, Giles was to succeed him as professor of Chinese at Cambridge from 1897 to 1932; denigrating one's predecessors is not an unfamiliar form of self-enhancement.

Giles and B-T met very early in the latter's career. Giles had become Vice-Consul at Pagoda Island, Foochow, in February 1880, and he got to know B-T when the latter arrived later in the same year. Proximity and shared interests would have encouraged considerable interaction in the small expatriate community. Giles actually signed the death certificate for B-T's firstborn son. Giles left China in 1893, but his opinion of B-T must have lingered; when Giles received the Gold Medal of the Royal Asiatic Society in London in 1922 (the first time the medal was awarded for Chinese studies), he named B-T in his words of thanks as one of a 'tidal wave rolling up' of British sinologues helping to establish the study of Chinese.[43] As B-T was by then sixty-five years of age, the term 'rolling up' was hardly appropriate!

Freemasonry was one of Giles's interests. He had been initiated into the society in 1870 and soon reached senior positions, being appointed Worshipful Master of the Ionic Lodge of Amoy. In 1881, he became the first Worshipful Master of the Foochow Lodge.[44] As a zealous member of 'the craft', he may have encouraged B-T to join the fraternity. Freemasonry seems to have flourished in the British expatriate community; it also resonated with the *kuan-hsi* (*guanxi* in pinyin, meaning 'personal connections or networking') mores of Chinese society where 'secret societies' flourished. As one observer commented, Freemasonry performed similar functions to other clubs, imposing its own 'discipline on social interaction and personal behaviour' encouraging 'participation in communal life, and playing by communal rules'.[45] Membership could well have facilitated social connections for a man making his way in the world: for example, 'A.H. Rasmussen's climb from customs outdoorman to business manager was accompanied by enthusiastic Masonry.'[46] Membership of bodies such as Masonic Lodges would also have helped to initiate 'griffens' (new arrivals) into expatriate life. Given B-T's close contact with active Freemasons such as Giles and at least one of his FRAS sponsors, together with the fact that Masonry was fairly widespread amongst expatriates and in the Chinese Customs, it would not have been surprising if B-T had become a member, but no record of this could be found.[47]

Giles lost his wife at Pagoda Anchorage in 1882; she was worn out by repeated pregnancies, the strain of looking after her children (she bore eight with two dying in infancy) lacking many of the things considered essential to child welfare. All her children were under nine when she died.[48] Perhaps this loss brought Giles and the B-Ts closer. Having been in Foochow for three years, in June 1883 Giles was transferred to Shanghai. A member of the China Branch of the Royal Asiatic Society, Giles became more involved with the society in Shanghai. In his memoirs,[49] reference is made to his 'scanty leisure' time being taken up with meetings of the society, and he was elected President in March 1885. He also organized a number of symposia, which 'were most successful in giving new life' to the society and 'attracting new members in considerable numbers'. B-T was one of those recruited that year, probably with the encouragement of Giles, and he became a life member of the society. The society attracted many eminent China scholars, including Chinese Customs staff such as Morse, the historian, and Hirth, the translator and writer on Chinese culture.[50]

B-T's first foray into publication is to be found in a translation in the Royal Asiatic Society's journal for 1885.[51] This was less than five years after he arrived in China. It is worth emphasizing the high level of knowledge of Chinese he must have acquired by this time: the ability to read and write thousands of characters, as well as the mastery of Chinese usage. Attaining this level would have been very demanding, especially bearing in mind that B-T was adjusting to a new life, holding down a new job, and establishing a family. In addition to a good Chinese tutor, he clearly possessed the qualities of application, persistence and scholarship. He also must have had considerable confidence to feel able to publish at such an early stage, for his first piece would have been written no more than about four years after he arrived in China. Concern for scholarship is not always totally untinged by self-interest, and his devotion to study was likely fostered by an awareness that proficiency in Chinese could only aid his career prospects.

Among expatriates, Westerners who were fluent in Chinese were rare, and they were frequently treated with disdain by compatriots. Somerset Maugham, the famous novelist who travelled in China, criticized the insularity of many Westerners in a description of a Treaty Port dinner party:

> Perhaps the conversation was less varied than the courses, for guests and hosts had seen one another nearly every day for an intolerable number of years . . . they talked of racing and golf and shooting. They would have thought it bad form to touch upon the abstract and there were no politics for them to discuss. China bored them all, they did not want to speak of that; they only knew just so much about it as was necessary to their business, and they looked with distrust upon any young man who studied the Chinese language . . . It was well known that all those fellows who went in for Chinese grew queer in the head.[52]

A light-hearted warning advised the new arrival not to become a sinologue, for you'll 'cease to be an Englishman'.[53] A more restrained though similar view was held even by a competent scholar of Chinese, J O. P. Bland, who worked for the Customs Service and later the Shanghai International Settlement's Municipal Council:

> I observed that the mentality of Europeans who became absorbed in the intensive study of Chinese gradually assumes an oriental complexion and, in the end, becomes estranged from the European outlook on life, habits of thought and standards of conduct.[54]

The attitudes described here would have been familiar to B-T. Fortunately, he was not deterred.

His first piece of published writing, in 1885, was a translation of a chapter: 'How Snow Inspired Verse and a Rash Order Made the Flowers Bloom'. This was not from the *San Kuo*, for which he was to become well-known as translator, but the *Ching-hua yüan* (*Jinghuayuan*), a popular Chinese novel by Li Ju-chen (Li Ruzhen), who lived from 1763 to 1830. This novel was not fully translated into English, as *Flowers in the Mirror*, until 1965.[55] The *Ching-hua yüan* is a satirical allegorical fairy tale with a background in popular Daoism. The story is about the T'ang (Tang) dynasty Empress Wu who reigned from 684 to 705; she felt herself to be all-powerful as the 'first female emperor'. One day, elated by the sight of falling snow, which signifies an upcoming year of plenty, she decides to celebrate by listening to poetry and drinking a glass of wine for every verse. She is soon in a very happy condition and commands all the flowers on earth to bloom by the following morning. They all do, apart from the camellia, which was thereupon banished to Honan (Henan) where it grows in abundance. Given when this tale was written, it is worth mentioning that the novel discusses social problems such as 'the double moral standard between the sexes, the evils of footbinding, the neglect of women's education, and concubinage'. The book has thus been regarded as 'worthy of a permanent place in the world history of the emancipation of women'.[56] Perhaps B-T initially intended to translate the *Ching-hua yüan* but was persuaded to shift focus to the more renowned and influential *San Kuo Chih Yen-i*.

Another translation published the same year was in the genre of filial piety, where there are numerous widely known macabre stories showing the length that children, especially sons, would go for the sake of parents. These stories often have a cannibalistic element. The piece B-T translated, entitled 'A Dutiful and Unselfish Heart', is a sad account of a poor family in which the grandmother has a strong desire to eat meat. Her filial son wants to satisfy her need and raises the money to do so from a pawnbroker, but a thug steals the money while the son is making his way home. The son nearly attempts suicide but is restrained by his wife. His own little son sees his father's grief and commits suicide. When the father discovers his son's body, he sees this as a way of providing meat for his mother; the old lady sends for the grandson to share the treat, and the situation is revealed. She charges her son with impiety; in the court, just when the magistrate cannot decide the case, the little boy's spirit appears, explains what happened and leaves money for the father, who is acquitted. The thug is struck by lightning.[57] Given what had happened to B-T's own father, one wonders whether the reference to suicide was a morbid factor in attracting B-T to the piece.

Other brief notes by B-T appear in the 'Notes and Queries' section of the same Journal, where B-T signed himself simply as 'CBT'. Two samples obviously responding to queries from readers show the character of the notes; one reads:

> The Empress Wu of the T'ang dynasty used to wear a false beard when in Council on a matter of great importance.

The second note reveals the prevailing strength of superstition even in officialdom at the time B-T was working:

> Once each day for three successive days, some three hundred soldiers marched round the buildings of the Imperial Arsenal Foochow firing blank

cartridges. This was to scare away the evil spirits which have lately brought much sickness. Three years ago towards the end of an outbreak a similar ceremony was gone through.[58]

In 1886, a number of members of the Royal Asiatic Society were invited to express their views on the 'Advisability or the Reverse of Endeavouring to convey Western Knowledge through the Medium of their own Language'. B-T is one of fourteen who contributed papers to a meeting of the society on 26 May 1886. His paper, probably invited by Giles, rather magisterially and seemingly sensibly observes that 'as an abstract question it is advisable, but with reference to particular circumstances, not advisable, and I pronounce against it.' He states his reason — the lack of scientific language in Chinese — and explains that a terminology in that language 'needs to be developed, otherwise the knowledge will be seen as an ornamental extra and not useful'. He didn't actually attend the meeting, as attendance would have entailed a five-hundred-mile sea journey, and his name therefore is not among the discussants; his contribution was sent in and read out.[59] One wonders whether he was relieved or disappointed in not being exposed to the challenge: a young novice delivering his thoughts to an audience of old China hands.

Over the following few years more of B-T's writings appeared in a number of journals, especially the *China Review*. Mostly, they are translated extracts that were simply presented without being given an introductory context, which apparently was customary at the time, or very brief notes on a variety of subjects.[60]

There is a rather charming and more personal little piece which uncharacteristically reveals something about B-T himself, entitled 'A Handful of Cash'. This is an account of B-T's going through a random handful of cash which he happens to have with him; the cash rather extraordinarily includes currency dating from 1017 and 1022 (during the Sung [Song] dynasty) and still in use. He makes a sympathetic comment on Chinese custom, somewhat critical of the meddling expatriate:

> Surely a people who use everyday, coins of such an age have something to be proud of, and is it to be wondered at that they do not throw aside their time-worn customs on the advice of any smart diplomatic fledgling.[61] [See Appendix III, (ii)]

This statement is indicative of an independence of thought in B-T as well as a sympathetic attitude to cultural diversity; his sensitive observation may not have endeared him in certain more conventional circles — if they were aware of the comment.

It was about this time that more of B-T's writings become concerned with translations from the *San Kuo*. One extract, published in 1889 or 1890, is an account of the death of Sun Tse (Sunzi), one of the characters from the *San Kuo*.[62] Another piece, on 'Conjuring', published in 1891, is also taken from the work.[63] A book review by B-T of a critique and overview of the *San Kuo* also appeared around the same time. In this review, he writes that 'the masterly critique of Chiu Sheng-Tan leaves little more to be said'; he concludes,

> With all humility I venture to say that in my opinion the book is very interesting and the interest grows as the story developed. It well repays the toil of reading.

So, even B-T found the *San Kuo* a toil! This review is particularly interesting in its discussion of the problem of describing the work.[64] [See Appendix III, (i)]

Another extract from the *San Kuo* 'A Deep-Laid Plot and a Love Scene',[65] was published in 1892–93. It was the last of B-T's writings to be found in a contemporary journal. As we shall see, this is the period when he experiences major domestic changes and starts a new life.

It has been suggested that the idea of a full translation of the *San Kuo* might have come from Giles,[66] who recognized B-T as having both the ability and the tenacity to undertake the task. More evidence of a continued strong connection with Giles arises around this time; B-T wrote 'an exhaustive review' of Giles's dictionary which was turned down by the editor of the *North-China Daily News* 'on the ground of want of space!' as Giles comments with a sarcastic exclamation mark. There follows a characteristically caustic note by Giles that the editor of the paper, R. W. Little, had omitted to notice his dictionary 'because he thought I ought to have sent a free copy to his wealthy firm'.[67]

As B-T's interest in the *San Kuo* grew so also did his determination to focus his literary work. Having by now begun to establish his reputation as a scholar of Chinese, he became more confident about completing a full translation. As was noted in the introduction, this major classic, attributed to Lo Kuan-chung, who bestrode the thirteenth and fourteenth centuries, had been, and is still today, highly significant in Chinese culture. Though set long ago, in the third century, the period of the Minor Han dynasty (AD 221–263), its legends have been long told in oral stories, dramatized in plays and performed in opera; popular still, many present-day films and television programmes derive their plots from the work.

A Devastating Loss

Another baby for the Brewitt-Taylors, Stanley, born in October 1889, survived for about nine months, to July 1890. But less than four weeks before this baby's death there occurred what was certainly one of the most traumatic events in B-T's life. His wife, Alice, never fully recovered from the birth, and she died on 21 June 1890.

Nothing else is known for certain about the kind of life Charles and Alice led, but they had lived through a good deal in the ten years they had together: adjustment to China, the loss of several babies, and the destruction of their home. B-T was devastated.

One of the few memories recounted to me about B-T is that he was said to be very much in love with his first wife, and throughout the rest of his life, despite his second marriage, he kept a photograph of her in a bamboo Chinese frame on his study table. Now he was left desolate, only thirty-two years old and with two young sons, Leonard aged six and Raymond less than three years old, to bring up on his own, apart from the servants he undoubtedly would have had. The loss of Alice was a watershed in B-T's life.

6

Change of Career: The Chinese Customs

The death of B-T's wife may have triggered him to make the change that he was probably already contemplating. In the following year, B-T decided to leave teaching and embark on a new career, one which offered potentially far better prospects. On 1 November 1891, he joined the Imperial Chinese Maritime Customs. B-T was to spend the next thirty of his forty years in China working for the Service, the same body which had helped finance his Foochow appointment. This chapter outlines this unique Chinese institution run by Westerners — its origins and the scope of its work — and portrays the powerful, attractive, controversial personality who ran it for nearly half a century.

The ICMC was one of the most fascinating organizations to be established in late imperial China. It was set up by the Chinese government with the active help of foreigners, indeed, at their instigation. Much has been written about the Service in various histories, many of which are referred to in the following text. But there is still no history which does full justice to the contribution made by the Customs Service to China (complex and controversial though such a history is bound to be), and how through that organization China interacted with foreigners, especially with their governments, Consular Services and merchants. There are abundant materials in China's archives, in Foreign Office and Consular records in Britain and elsewhere and in the archives of some of the larger firms which operated in China, as well as in the correspondence, diaries and reminiscences of people who worked in or with the Customs. Much of this material still awaits further investigation to throw more light on how these organizations interacted and their different perspectives on significant events.

There had been some kind of customs collection in China for centuries before the ICMC was established. In the Sung and Ming dynasties, there existed an office known as Maritime Customs (Shibosi). A Customs house in Shanghai existed from around 1658, and there was a Customs house in Canton in 1685, which became most significant for trade when all other ports were closed to foreigners in 1757.[1] But the collection of dues was erratic, inconsistent and subject to personal influence and bargaining. This suited some of the foreign traders: a little 'squeeze' here and there was a small price to pay to secure profits in a potentially lucrative market. Senior Chinese officials were aware that local Customs officials were not always honest, and saw receipts as a source of self-enrichment. According to Prince Kung, 'embezzlement and smuggling and a hundred malpractices flourished, and were a great hindrance in the collection of customs revenues'.[2]

The origins of a more modern Customs Service came about as a by-product of the activities of a political organization that has already been mentioned, the Small Sword Society which was associated with the Taiping. From the autumn of 1853 to February 1855, this anti-Manchu secret society established itself in Shanghai, taking control of the city. The situation was to lead to the birth of a highly influential and multifaceted Chinese organization led by foreigners. It provides another example of the effect of the interplay between internal dissent, the power and influence of foreigners and modernization.

Foreign powers operating in the area had for some time been aware of the need for better arrangements for trade. Despite the establishment of the Treaty Ports, smuggling was still rife and bargaining between merchants and Customs officials over Customs duties 'flourished like the green bay tree'.[3] For the Chinese, imperial revenues were denuded; for the West, foreign traders were uncertain of their profits.

Some merchants saw the seizure of the city as an opportunity for freeing trade from all levies; other traders, however, preferred a greater degree of consistency in Customs practices. Further, representatives of certain foreign powers were conscious of their responsibilities for their nationals under treaty obligations. Faced with a delicate political situation brought about by the occupation, in a city which had only recently been opened as a Treaty Port under the Treaty of Nanking, there was an awareness that trading activities could easily be impeded. The consuls of Britain and the United States quickly informed their merchants that the capture of a seaport by rebels did not abrogate their obligation to pay Customs dues. Acting together with France, the consuls of the three countries which then had settlements in Shanghai saw the opportunity to involve themselves in a better regulative system. The British consul in Shanghai, Rutherford Alcock, was the prime mover. He acknowledged his treaty responsibility to ensure that British merchants paid their dues (otherwise, Britain would have been liable) and allowed a Customs house to be set up in the British settlement on condition that the Chinese authorities engaged reliable foreigners to supervise the Customs operations under a foreign inspector.[4] At a meeting on 29 June 1854, the three consuls and the Chinese representative, after some initial reluctance, decided the basis for reorganizing the Customs House in order to aid the equitable collection of Customs dues. This marked the beginning of a modern Chinese Customs Service.[5]

Initially, a triumvirate of foreign inspectors was appointed to run the Customs Service, consisting of Thomas Wade of Britain, Lewis Carr of the United States and Arthur Smith of France. Being familiar both with the Chinese language and with Customs procedure, Wade undertook the bulk of the work, but he resigned the following year, 1855, in order to devote more time to his sinological studies.[6] Horatio N. Lay, an able if rather arrogant twenty-three-year-old British acting vice-consul in Shanghai, secured Wade's position and established a more efficient Service. The Shanghai-style foreign inspectorate could not have been confined there or trade would have simply shifted to other ports. The Shanghai system therefore became the model adopted for all the Treaty Ports; it oversaw the assessment of Customs dues and attempted to ensure the payment of dues by foreign merchants. Each local inspector, later called 'commissioner', took orders from the inspector general in Shanghai. Prince Kung, the prince regent and front man for the Empress Dowager who was also head of the Tsungli Yamen,[7] appointed Lay Inspector General on 7 April 1861. He was given the specific duty of

> exercising a general surveillance over all things pertaining to the revenue, of ordering the Chinese superintendants to collect the revenue at the various ports, of preventing frauds upon the revenue, and of standing sponsor for the good conduct of the foreigners engaged in the customs service.

Lay, following his appointment, took a trip back to England, designating G. H. Fitzroy and the young Robert Hart, then Deputy Commissioner of Customs in Canton, to act as joint inspector generals until he returned. Of the two, the Chinese found the tactful and patient Hart both congenial and the more able, and he was sent to Peking to take his orders from Prince Kung. While Lay was away, he undertook the purchase of a steam fleet on behalf of the Chinese government, but he overstepped his authority by making agreements without securing prior approval. In 1863, he was replaced by Hart.[8]

Under Hart's leadership, the ICMC became a unique and powerful body, responsible not only for the determination of Customs dues but also engaging in a diverse range of related infrastructural activities. Included in these were surveying and charting coastal areas and rivers (this was before a national hydrographic survey was founded); dredging channels; establishing lightships and lighthouses; developing a coastguard service (concerned both with safety and the prevention of smuggling); installing beacons and buoys; and developing wharves and harbour facilities. The Customs Service also supervised measures for the prevention of the spreading of diseases from seaborne infection, until a National Quarantine Bureau was established. The statistics the Service published were to become most useful for determining policy on trade. Cruisers of the ICMC stood in for warships during times of crisis, and it became customary for at least one Customs cruiser to be in attendance at fleet reviews.[9] Such was the confidence in Hart and the Service that it was later given the task of modernizing and administering the postal service; this lasted for about fifteen years, until the creation of a new Ministry of Posts and Communications in 1911.[10] Customs staff were sometimes asked for diplomatic advice and were involved in delicate negotiations following conflicts between China and foreign powers.[11] For example, Customs was involved in the negotiations with Portugal over Macao in 1866 and also in the Chinese war with France in 1884 and 1885.[12] Ten years later, the prominent government mandarin Li Hung-chang tried to use a Customs commissioner, Gustav Detring, in peace negotiations with Japan, but the Japanese insisted that a senior Chinese person, such as Li himself, attend.[13] Even as early as 1861, Hart had recognized the need for a diplomatic service in China and later supported a college which enabled the training of diplomats.This college, the T'ung Wen Kwan, was one of the pioneers of modern education in China.[14]

The ICMC was also deemed competent and trustworthy enough to handle complex financial matters, including loans, and to be the channel for the payment of indemnities which were intermittently imposed on China by the foreign powers.[15] However, until the 1894–95 Sino-Japanese War, and the particularly onerous indemnities imposed by the powers concerned after the Boxer Rebellion in 1900, the burden of indemnities for the Customs may not have been as great as was once believed.[16]

The Service played a significant role in China's modernization, and the revenues it brought in contributed to this. To give some indication of the importance of the revenues produced, by the end of the nineteenth century, the Service accounted for a quarter of all the revenue available to the government.[17] One view holds that without the Customs revenue, the Ch'ing dynasty may well not have survived as long as it did.[18]

Hart, early in his career, laid down the principles by which the Service was to be conducted: he made clear to his staff their primary allegiance and 'repeatedly emphasized to his foreign staff that they and he were employees of the Chinese government'.[19] His view of the Chinese and of the behaviour expected of Western staff was consistent throughout his long term of office. The year following his appointment, he distributed a keynote circular which read as follows:

> It is to be distinctly and constantly kept in mind that the Inspectorate of Customs is a Chinese and not a Foreign Service, and that, as such, it is the duty of each of its members to conduct himself towards the Chinese, people as well as officials, in such a way as to avoid all cause of offence and ill-feeling … It is to be expected from those who take the pay, and who are the servants of the Chinese Government, that they, at least, will so act as to neither offend susceptibilities, nor excite jealousies, suspicion, and dislike.[20]

Hart goes on to remind his foreign staff that they are the 'brother officers' of Chinese officials, and, 'in a sense, the countrymen' of the Chinese people. He exhorted them to learn Chinese, act with patience and without superiority, to convince rather than to dictate. But he also recognized the dilemma of commissioners trying to consider what was in the best interests of China, yet still having their own personal values and sympathies: commissioners shouldn't forget, he states ambiguously, that they are also representatives of 'a civilization of a progressive kind, which differs in almost every respect from this country'.[21]

While Hart would have been aware that the tone of the circular might help endear him to Prince Kung and the Tsungli Yamen, this would not have been his sole or even primary motivation for producing it.[22] Even after Hart's experiences in the Boxer uprising, and near the end of his career, he expressed similar sentiments. In a personal letter written in March 1910, to Francis Aglen, who had then replaced Robert Bredon as Acting I-G, Hart proffers this advice: 'serve Chinese . . . interests first . . . see the questions from the Chinese point of view'.[23] Later, in what was to be his final letter to Aglen, Hart wrote: 'The Chinese are very good-hearted and large-minded and can easily be worked with.'[24]

In stressing to foreign staff that they were working for a Chinese organization, Hart would have had another concern. Social relationships among expatriates were close. Members of the Customs, Consulate staff and those with commercial, business or other interests dined, shared leisure pursuits or met at the clubs or at the variety of functions that took place in the expatriate community. Further, as Coates's major history of the British consuls in China shows, a number of Consulate staff moved to the Customs Service, especially during its early years. Later, many saw career opportunities in the Customs for family members as well as sons of friends; so, not infrequently, Consulate and Customs staff were related to one another, directly or through marriage.[25] This level of social interaction could well have created some ambivalence among senior Customs staff over where their loyalty lay: to China, to their expatriate community or even to friends or family. Hart needed to constantly remind his staff that their primary duty was to those who paid them their salaries; otherwise, the objectivity of the Service would be undermined.

Hart's insistence that he was a servant of China was by no means overmodest. Recent work has demonstrated how the Tsungli Yamen played a significant part in shaping the Service. In particular, it is worth stressing that while the Service assessed the amount of duty to be paid, during Hart's time the actual money was paid into Chinese Customs banks. Thus, the government had a controlling role over how these revenues, which were unexpectedly high, were to be spent.[26] However, there is little doubt that Hart became one of the most famous and influential foreigners ever to operate in China.

Given Hart's significance in China and in the life of B-T, it is worth detailing something of his career. Hart was born in 1835 in Ulster, and in 1854, at the age of nineteen, he went to Hong Kong; he had been in the Consular Service before taking up his Customs post in Canton. Of the fifty-four years he was in China, forty-nine of them were spent in the Customs Service, and he worked there until very near the end of his life. Hart left China in the spring of 1908, going on leave, but with the likelihood of not returning (for he was then seventy-three years old and very weary), though he never publicly, nor even privately in his correspondence, gave up the possibility of return. He was on extended leave until he died in Marlow, England, in September 1911,[27] just prior to the overthrow of the Ch'ing dynasty and the establishment of the Republic. Hart was regarded by many as a sinophile; he 'admired the Chinese whom he considered to be intelligent and cultivated',[28] and he believed in the fundamental reasonableness of Chinese people.[29] He also saw himself engaged in an enterprise to help build up China. In one of his letters to Campbell, his London secretary, representative and confidante, with whom he had a very frank correspondence, he wrote, 'I want to make China strong and I want her to make England her best friend.'[30] In China and elsewhere, there has been a different interpretation of this man, seeing him as pro-imperialist.[31] Both aspects of Hart are discernible, and they are not mutually exclusive.

Hart was an extremely hard-working administrator and a powerful and respected influence not only on his staff, but also on the Chinese, though he always insisted that his wider role was advisory; he also at times influenced the British and other foreign authorities. Doubtless also he was wily and had the ability to 'play both sides against the middle'. He was offered, accepted and then declined the position of British Minister to China in 1885.[32] The reputation he speedily achieved for producing an efficient and incorruptible Customs Service was deserved. Impartiality did not always go down well with certain merchants who often tried to avoid or reduce duties, though they were happy to invoke the Service if Chinese bureaucrats proved inefficient or overbearing.[33] The Service's reputation for propriety made it an example for other organizations: it was said by Chinese that the Customs was a model which could help 'uphold righteousness amongst other local organs'.[34]

Such a man as Hart was bound to invite criticism. A humorous but pointed account of life in the Service with a comment on Hart appeared in a satirical journal, *The Rattle*, which was published in Hankow in 1896. This account took the form of an open letter to a fourth assistant B grade, the lowliest position in the administrative 'Indoor Staff' in the Service. Hart's appreciation of pretty women was well-known as was his predilection for Northern Ireland compatriots; he enjoyed music (he played the violin, probably owning a Stradivarius[35]), and held regular socials at which both a Western and a Chinese band played. An invitation to one of these events was regarded as highly desirable, a sign of social acceptance, and for younger staff it was an indication of being considered as having the potential for promotion. The novice was advised to

> learn an instrument, have a connection with N. Ireland, and develop a relationship with lovely women . . . Be ready to take up any office: inspector of ports, naval commander, postmaster-general, drill serjeant, or secret agent.[36]

Hart was seemingly not averse to a little nepotism of his own, recruiting not only the family of his friends, but also his own family, including a son, a brother, three nephews and a cousin, as well as a brother-in-law who was appointed directly into a commissioner post which not unsurprisingly scandalized the Service at the time.[37] The Ulster preference was well acknowledged in a Service clearly seen as highly desirable. Customs provided better opportunities than the Consular Service, which was staffed with people of similar social background. As early as the late 1860s, a young entrant into the Consular Service in China from Ulster urged his mother to encourage two of his brothers to apply for a Customs post, noting that the Customs was a better Service, with higher pay and allowances and good promotion prospects. He also noted that Robert Hart would make a direct appointment for a Queen's University graduate, bypassing the entrance examination. However, the letter contains a warning even then that there was a chance that China might get rid of its foreign servants.[38]

The company of pretty women was especially appreciated by Hart, and he often made comments about them in his letters. He allegedly struggled between his religious conscience and his sexual yearnings, and in his early years in China he had a Chinese concubine.[39] Ayaou was a boat girl whom he met and lived with in Ningpo; she is said to have died around 1865, apparently soon after childbirth. While she may not have been able to improve Hart's Mandarin Chinese, given that she was probably illiterate and would have spoken the local dialect, she could have extended his knowledge of Chinese traditions. One consular officer who later faced criticism for having a Chinese mistress claimed that she deepened his knowledge of 'language, customs, and mentality' and therefore improved his work as interpreter.[40] Ayoau's social origins were typical of a concubine:

> Mistresses were certainly low class, for rarely would a respectable Chinese family have consented to a daughter becoming the wife, let alone the concubine, of a foreign devil.[41]

Hart had three children with her: Anna, born in 1858 or 1859, Herbert in 1862 and Arthur in 1865.[42] When he decided it was time to settle down 'properly' and marry, he didn't abandon them, as frequently would have happened in those circumstances, but arranged for them to be brought up in England in 1866 (the youngest still a baby), initially with the wife of a bookkeeper in one of the firms with which he had dealings.[43] Though Hart supported them financially quite well, he did not appear to have kept up a warm relationship with them and distanced himself with the designation 'ward' rather than 'father'.[44] Arthur was later to turn up in the ICMC-maintained London office, trying to get money from Hart's representative there.[45]

Hart's leave in 1866 (the first of only two home leaves he was to take in fifty-four years) had two purposes domestically:[46] one was to place his children into care, the other was to find a suitable wife. Rather breathtakingly, he met Hestor Bredon on 31 May, proposed after seeing her four times, married her on 22 August and left with her for China in September! She was eighteen, he thirty-one years of age. They, too, had three children: Evelyn Amy born in 1869, Edgar Bruce in 1873 and Mabel Milbourne in 1879.[47] However, his wife wasn't happy in China, and she returned home after sixteen years in 1882 with the children. They were not to see each other again for almost a quarter of a century,[48] but they kept up a frequent and affectionate correspondence. These can be read with difficulty as Hart's writing was almost indecipherable — rather ironically, he laid great store by his senior staff having 'a good hand'.

A clue to Hart's wife's interests and part of her possible motivation in leaving China is to be found in one of the letters he wrote to her when he began to anticipate retirement. He expresses concern to his wife about how they will find life together after such a long separation:

> If I ever get home I wonder what I shall do about going anywhere as my health does not allow me to be long out. As far as I am concerned, I can do without either outings, society, or public amusement . . . Your fate has carried you in just the opposite direction — you must have all three.[49]

Hart's letters, especially those to Francis Aglen, the son of a friend and something of a protégé, are especially frank. In them he reveals much of his approach to running the Service and his thinking about other Western countries and the Chinese: 'Be careful about the French wharfage dues question: on one side don't give away any of China's rights — on the other don't get into a row with these touchy Frenchmen'; 'Keep up acquaintance with [China's] Viceroy. See him once a fortnight, but don't bore him . . . Do not relax vigilance, but put plenty of "velvet" on the iron hand.'[50] One can understand how Hart survived for so long through a turbulent period in China, balancing different interest groups.

For some years, Hart had indicated to his confidante, Campbell, who ran the Customs Service's London office, a desire to retire. But there was protracted uncertainty about his future even when he went on retirement leave. There was quite a tussle over who would succeed him. As early as 1898, the Tsungli Yamen had reached an understanding with Sir Claude M. MacDonald, the British minister, that while British trade predominated, a Briton would be the inspector general.[51] Britain also wished to influence the decision on who that person would be and protested when a decree announced the appointment of Sir Robert Bredon, Hart's brother-in-law, as acting inspector general for the time Hart was on leave. Bredon had been appointed Deputy Inspector-General in 1898, and so he remained until he resigned in 1910; the post was abolished in 1911. It is noteworthy that Hart's view of Bredon was not without criticism, complaining to someone less senior than Bredon (and who was to replace him over six years later) that Bredon did not relieve him of much work.[52]

Britain made strong representation against Bredon becoming permanent. China responded with a memorandum in February 1908 giving assurance that there was no intention to appoint Bredon to the substantive post and that if Hart did not return in a year a suitable person other than Bredon would be appointed.[53] Bredon, having returned to the Service on the understanding that he would eventually succeed Hart,[54] was deeply disappointed when Francis Aglen was appointed Acting Inspector General, in April 1910. Bredon resigned from the Service but continued to live in China; he died in Peking a few years later.[55] After Aglen's appointment, Hart gives him the advice of a calculating survivor:

> During your Acting period, follow old lines rather than introduce new methods. If you are confirmed, you can then take your own course.[56]

In Hart's letters to Aglen, he reveals that almost up to his death he never quite gave up the possibility of returning to his post: 'I think you are doing very well . . . I see nothing to revise should I reappear.'[57] This comment might have been made just to tweak Aglen, as Hart enjoyed demonstrating his power to affect the careers of others, but it also probably reflects the difficulty of resigning himself to giving up a position in the Service with which he was utterly identified. Paul King, a Customs commissioner at the time, states that Hart's return was widely expected. Recording a visit to Hart in London in February 1911, King confirms that at that time 'and for months afterwards, [it was] generally supposed that he was on the eve of resuming duty at Peking'.[58] Certainly as late as April 1911, the Foreign Office was concerned that Hart might return to China; this prompted a secret telegram to its Peking office:

> Sir Robert Hart — apparently under Bredon's advice — proposes to return to China. This is greatly to be deprecated. If he seriously contemplates returning hint should be given him that we shall be under painful necessity of asking Chinese Government to consider wisdom of man of his age etc being entrusted with such important interests.[59]

Not until Hart's letter to Aglen in September 1911, just six days before his death on 20 September, does Hart openly admit to not being able to return:

> My health has been bad and I daily grow feebler. So I fear China will see me no more. I am glad to leave things in your hands.[60]

There was a view that China had seen Hart's early announcement of his intention to retire as an opportunity to strengthen its hold over the ICMC.[61] Though it was by no means clear who would replace him, especially with both Britain and China probably wanting someone who could be influenced yet who would maintain widespread confidence in the office. After considerable agonizing, Aglen was deemed acceptable to both and was duly appointed.[62]

The decree formalizing the permanent appointment of Aglen was issued in October 1911, after the death of Hart, who had actually retained the title of Inspector General until then. This was a measure of the regard with which he was held, though it might also be a reflection of China's desire to keep open the possibility of his return or of uncertainty about his replacement.

Resentment within China that the country still had to be dependant on foreigners to run such a powerful body must have been strong in some quarters, but the Ch'ing had other preoccupations, given the major political changes afoot and the power struggles that followed the deaths of the Empress Dowager and the Emperor. With existing and threatened upheavals, influential Chinese modernizers would have been well aware of the need to sustain revenue, the value of the training in administrative expertise and efficiency, and other advantages of the Customs Service. The organization also acted as an important bridge between China and the West.

The ICMC, given the important role of foreigners in it and the range of nationalities employed, has been seen as 'an early essay in internationalism'.[63] This view echoes that of a young Australian doctor, George Ernest Morrison, later famous as the first full-time China correspondent of *The Times,* who traversed the country in 1894. He was eulogistic in his description of the ICMC's international flavour, writing about

> the customs service, that marvellous organization which is more impartially open to all the world than any other service in the world. As an example, I note that among the Commissioners of Customs at the ports of the River Yangtse alone, at the time of my voyage the Commissioner at Shanghai was an Austrian, at Kiukiang a Frenchman, at Hankow an Englishman, at Ichang a Scandinavian, and at Chungking a German.[64]

It is, however, a curious fact that not a single Chinese was appointed to a senior level until after the establishment of the Republic. The British were clearly the most prevalent group. In 1905, for example, there were 34 commissioners, of whom 18 were British; of 22 deputy commissioners 17 were British; and of 249 assistant commissioners 111 were British. To none of these positions, not even the lowliest of the four grades of assistant commissioner, was a Chinese appointed. By 1915, four years after the Revolution, the figures were as follows: 43 commissioners of whom 23 were British; 22 deputies with 11 of these being British; and 247 assistants with 76 British. However, by this time there were 60 Chinese assistant commissioners.[65]

Hart had cited the reluctance of officials in Peking to promote able Chinese clerks to assistant commissioner, which it is alleged he had proposed. He attributed this reluctance to the likelihood of many of the able ones coming from mission schools or from the southern provinces, against whom there was prejudice by the Manchu authorities,[66] but there are other possible explanations. Clerks were different from officials who came through the examination system; many in the Chinese government wished to ensure a Service that was clearly free from corruption, and local clerks might have been more amenable to the 'squeeze'. They were also less likely, especially during the early years of the Service, to be sufficiently fluent in English to operate at high levels. Another factor might have been that, in view of the Service's fairness and efficiency, it was likely to incur hostility from both Chinese and foreign merchants; perhaps it was seen as convenient to have non-Chinese receiving the anger of the merchants. An able man who enjoyed control, Hart might well have felt that non-Chinese senior staff would be more dependent on him and less subject to influence from Chinese authorities. Foreign governments also probably preferred non-Chinese in important positions and wanted to retain a significant presence of their own nationals in the Service. This preference might not have been just for the possibility of influencing Customs decisions, but as a potential source of strategic information. Numerous factors thus stacked up against the appointment of Chinese to important positions. Nonetheless, by 1907 pressure was coming for more senior appointments: the Chinese were 'growing restive' and 'also wanted front seats', wrote Hart to Campbell in February 1907. Soon afterwards, Chinese began to be appointed into the Indoor Staff, and a circular was issued which required commissioners to make greater use of Chinese to do assistant work as well as more senior Outdoor Staff work.[67] This was part of the background leading to the establishment of a Customs College in 1908, with which B-T was to be involved.

Personal views of Hart by contemporaries were varied. His was a complex character which demands a much more detailed study. Paul King, who felt bitter about his delayed promotion, was uncomplimentary about him. Two accounts, which seem to have been heretofore unused, by people who knew him well present contrasting views.

One view that we have already noted was by another Customs man, B-T's brother-in-law, Alexander Michie, Jr. Hart had a positive view of Michie when first appointed, 'a very capable and promising man, I should say', and Michie had become Hart's private secretary, probably briefly.[68] His promotion was even more limited than King's, yet he held a view of Hart which was much more positive. He penned an article in 1923 that contained numerous incidents illustrating aspects of Hart's character: his humour, memory and insistence on accuracy.[69] Frederick W. Maze wrote the author a word of appreciation, and Michie responded fulsomely:

> Fate had allowed me to pay this little personal tribute to the memory of a man whom I honoured, reverenced , and — I would almost say — loved and to whom anyhow, I owed a deep debt of gratitude for many kindnesses.[70]

The other example challenges the picture of Hart as a cold, sober, rational operator. Charles Addis, later to become a highly regarded banker[71] and whom we shall meet again, noted that he used to see a good deal of Hart (in the late 1880s) and was 'struck by the curious strain of mysticism underlying a cool and calculating exterior.' He had a reputation for omniscience, Addis wrote, so that people believed that his apparently arbitrary acts were based on reason, which they also would have understood had they known the facts. But often Hart acted as he did

> because he was a dreamer of dreams, because voices spoke to him in the night, and the results, he told me, justified the action taken on what to most men would have been childish superstition.[72]

Addis also criticizes the view of Hart as

> the man who of all men knows most about China. Of course that is all nonsense. Hart has been cooped up in Peking for a generation and knows less about China than most of his commissioners.[73]

That may be partially the case, but what he must have known to last as long as he did was how to handle his superiors in the government and at the same time avoid too much criticism from expatriate sources.

Recent studies deepen the picture of Hart.[74] One presents him as

> a political man who leavened his principled arguments for an independent Customs Service and administrative honesty with an ample concern for his own self-interest.

Another emphasizes his structural situation: 'a man in the middle' with multiple loyalties, occupying a nodal point in a complex network of transnational elites, tying together leading diplomats, merchants, bankers, journalists and academics, as well as Chinese government representatives at national, provincial and local levels, and Treaty Port institutions, such as municipal councils, all in addition to the Service itself.

Hart operated in a context. Especially in his early years, there existed a small, highly influential group of enlightened mandarins who, though influenced by traditional values and the idea of rule by moral example, saw the need for change. These men, including Wen-hsiang, Tseng Kuo-fen, Tso Tsung-t'ang, and Li Hung-chang, were led by Prince Kung; they supported Self-Strengthening and, whatever their individual views of Hart, helped to provide a climate receptive to Hart's endeavours. Wen-hsiang, for example, was the principal official under Kung and was the most influential Manchu with which Hart dealt while building up the Service. Without such men, Hart was unlikely to have achieved as much as he did.[75]

While the history of what happened to the Service after Hart's death takes us out of our time frame, it may be of interest to briefly outline the story of what occurred after Hart died. Aglen turned out to be a somewhat more prickly character than Hart, though he operated at a difficult time: for much of his tenure the Peking government had considerable difficulties in functioning. It was under these conditions following the 1911 Revolution that the Service added the function of collecting as well as assessing Customs dues; as imperial authorities at the ports were ousted, fled or went over to the revolutionaries, local Customs commissioners took control and the revolutionary leaders didn't interfere.[76] Customs commissioners also had the tricky task of dealing with local powerful personages and warlords. Aglen stayed in the post until 1927, when he was dismissed for refusing to carry out government policy to increase tariffs on foreign trade.[77] Then, after a temporary appointment left, Hart's shadow hovered again when Maze, Customs Commissioner in Shanghai and Hart's nephew, was appointed in 1929. The appointment was not the British Legation's first preference,[78] and one wonders whether Chinese predilection for family connections, or nostalgia for Hart, might have played any part in the choice. Maze was a controversial figure too, though he clearly took on Hart's mantle in striving to serve China and was highly critical of his predecessor, Aglen, for attempting to perform as if the Service could act independently of the government.[79] At one point, Maze was shunned by the foreign community for his stance in protecting China's interests, and he did accelerate the promotion of Chinese staff in the Service.[80]

When Nanking became the Nationalist capital, it was convenient to transfer the inspector general's office from faraway Peking to Shanghai. During the Second World War the headquarters moved to Chungking. Following Maze's resignation in 1942, C. H. B. Joly was put in charge of Customs offices and staff at places not occupied by the Japanese. In 1943, the tradition of the inspector general being British was broken when an American, Lester K. Little, was appointed. After the war ended, the headquarters returned to Shanghai in 1946, and in 1949 the Nationalists moved the Service to Taiwan. Little retired in 1950, ending a hundred years of non-Chinese leadership of the Service.[81]

At least until recently in China, the ICMC has been regarded more as the tool of Western imperialists than as having served China's long-term development. The use of the Service as the means for the payment of indemnities especially following the Boxer episode gave this view credence, but to label the organization in general in this way is far too simplistic. While it is true that foreign powers saw advantage in having their nationals in top positions in the hierarchy of the organization, there was frequent disagreement between the perceived self-interest of the foreign merchants and the Service's view, constantly stressed, that its prime duty was to act in the best interests of China. At an early stage, merchants tried persuading their consuls to argue that operating in Treaty Ports should give immunity from duties — obviously, if this principle had been granted, the whole of the income derived from Treaty Port duties would have been undermined.[82] There were obvious benefits too for the foreign powers in having a reliable body for more dispassionate interpretation and adjudication in dealing with trading regulations and Customs levies, as well as being a conduit for the payment of loans or indemnities imposed on China.[83] Of course, the individuals working in the organization were pursuing their own economic self-interest in holding well-paid jobs, but this was primarily for themselves rather than for their home country. For some, self-interest was accompanied by a strong interest in the culture and well-being of the host society, which after all provided their income. Reading extant personal reminiscences and private correspondence of the time, one is struck by the high level of professionalism and the dominant concern to serve China well.

That this view of foreign Customs officers was shared by Chinese staff is testified in interviews with three Chinese who became commissioners:

> The efficiency and integrity of the Chinese Maritime Customs were attributed by the former officials to its foreign style of administration . . . Instead of disparaging the foreign Inspectorate as a tool of Western imperialism, as their nationalistic compatriots have, they saw it in a more favourable light . . . As one of them put it, the foreign inspectorate 'did do good work for China'.[84]

One of these commissioners paid tribute to the role of the Customs in establishing 'a good civil service system comparable to that adopted in foreign countries'.[85] It would be too easy to dismiss such assessments merely as rationalizations of those who prospered by the Service. Other reform-minded Chinese wrote in 1901 of the Chinese people's appreciation of certain qualities of foreigners and their being 'delighted at the fair play of the Maritime Customs Service'.[86]

Both the opportunity provided and the culture of the organization probably appealed to B-T. By the time he joined the Service, it is likely that he would have viewed sympathetically the kind of attitudes Hart instilled, particularly so in his perception of the ICMC as a Chinese organization and of the importance of treating

Chinese as equals, an attitude which was by no means universal amongst expatriates in China. Certainly, B-T would have conveyed some of the characteristics of dignified and courteous behaviour expected of the 'mandarin' he was to become.

7

Tientsin: Marriage and the Michies

It is highly likely that B-T was already known in the Customs Service when he joined in 1891. Staff would have had some contact with him in Foochow where the Service had helped finance the Naval Yard school and (as was noted earlier) had provided staff for the Naval Dockyard project. In addition, there would also have been informal social contact between B-T and members of the Customs Service in the small expatriate community in the Foochow area. Further, though seemingly reserved, B-T was becoming known through his writings and participation in the North China Branch of the Royal Asiatic Society. In order to obtain more information on B-T's earlier background, I attempted to find an application for the Customs Service post, but this did not materialize; appointment procedures were not formalized at that stage, especially regarding known applicants from within China — *kuan-hsi* (*guanxi;* contacts and the connections they provide) being common in expatriate circles as well as among the Chinese. It was not unusual for expatriates to move across different areas of work in China, as happens elsewhere, especially in developing parts of the world, as people became better known or more familiar with what was available. As we have already seen, there are other instances of expatriates moving to Customs from, for example, the Consular Service.

Hart favoured staff with a good command of Chinese, and the young B-T had probably already demonstrated his tact, discretion and sense of fairness — and hopefully enough of his personality to suggest freedom from corruption. B-T, with his excellent Chinese, marine-related experience and qualities of good sense and dependability, felt confident that he would do well in the Customs Service. He would have met Hart's requirement for expected behaviour and would have seemed a very useful person to have on his staff. B-T was not to disappoint.

The Customs Service was composed of a number of departments or branches. Given B-T's background, it might have seemed appropriate for him to have joined the Marine Branch, but the Indoor Staff to which B-T was appointed was within Revenue, the executive arm of the Service, dealing with administration and accounting. The Indoor Staff would have been by far more prestigious than the

Outdoor Staff which included a variety of posts, such as tidesurveyors, examiners, and tidewaiters. As one study of the Customs puts it, those fortunate enough to be enlisted into the Indoor Staff enjoyed a privileged life. Despite the often harsh realities of an underdeveloped environment, Customs employees led comfortable lives in well-equipped, spacious homes attended by servants, and they moved in the elite social circles of the Treaty Ports.[1] A large office at one of these ports would include the commissioner, a deputy, and up to four grades of assistant, with each grade being subdivided.[2] The work provided considerable opportunity for advancement and probably suited B-T's temperament.

The normal process of appointing Indoor Staff meant that selection was generally confined to candidates from the middle or upper classes

> their social origins, education, salary levels, and lifestyle, all fitted them to mix with treaty port foreign officials and wealthy merchants on terms of equality.[3]

With B-T's acculturation over the previous ten years or so, he would probably not have felt uncomfortable in this milieu.

Nearly thirty-four years old, B-T was rather late entering the Service at assistant level. He joined as a fairly lowly Third Assistant A, three steps up from the lowest rank of Fourth Assistant B, where a raw recruit, normally aged between nineteen and twenty-three years, would have been placed. Though his age and experience were given small weight he must have felt confident that he would perform well.

B-T almost certainly would have travelled north by boat to take up his post in November 1891 in the much cooler city of Tientsin, just about to enter its winter. This large city, about ninety miles from Peking, was opened as a Treaty Port in 1860 or 1861; it was to become one of the most prosperous ports, second only to Shanghai.[4] At one time, there were nine foreign concessions in the city. Within the foreign Settlement there were regulations over the purchase of land, which the Chinese were forbidden to own directly. The settlement was organized by an elected municipal council with tax-raising powers.[5] As with other major settlements, this one had many Western-style buildings, a public garden (Victoria Park), and its own well-regarded English newspaper.

The Michies

The Tientsin English paper, the *Chinese Times,* was published and edited from 1886 until 1893 by Alexander Michie, a prominent businessman, who moved in political circles. He preferred writing to business, which he was less good at. Michie became China correspondent for *The Times* (of London), and in his retirement he was its special correspondent covering the Sino-Japanese War (1894–95). A well-known figure on the China expatriate scene, he was soon to become significant in the life of B-T, who arrived in the city as a young widower, with his two young boys, seven and four years old. For, having been in Tientsin for less than eighteen months, B-T and Michie's daughter, Ann Amy Jane, became engaged in early 1893; they married the following year.

B-T and Ann probably came to know each other through her brother, who also worked for the ICMC. He, Alexander Michie, Jnr., was at Foochow for his first posting in the Customs Service, which he joined as a Fourth Assistant B, the bottom rung of the Indoor Staff ladder, in 1890. Given the socializing that probably went on in the small expatriate community, especially with new arrivals, it is highly likely that he would have met B-T there. Hart, who incidentally liked the father (Michie, Sr.), though he was given to understand that the father did not like him,[6] also thought well of 'young Michie'.[7] Michie, Jnr., also wrote a little, generally in a light-hearted style.[8] But he did not seem to have fulfilled his promise, for he took well over twenty years to rise from the lowest to the highest rung of the assistant commissioner ranks, which he achieved in 1913. Drinking may have been at least a partial explanation for his sluggish progress, and he was to suffer from mental health problems as well.[9]

B-T and Ann might have met in Foochow when she visited her brother, or the young Michie might have provided an introduction (with perhaps a commendation for the sister) to the Michies in Tientsin. Evidence that she lived in Tientsin with her father was initially confirmed in a legal document stating that they both were living in Tientsin in 1889.[10] Various other sources show that she continued to live there until her marriage. One of these was the correspondence of Sir Charles Addis, who was to become the senior manager of the London office of the Hongkong and Shanghai Banking Corporation, one of the most respected leaders in the City of London, a Director of the Bank of England, and trusted adviser to the British government. Bankers were to become among the most influential of all British unofficial representatives in China, and of these the most outstanding was said to be Addis.[11] He came to know Michie, Snr. well, after the latter persuaded him to write for the *Chinese Times*; they became close friends and kept up a lengthy correspondence on political, social and family affairs until Michie's death. Little has been written about Michie, yet his story is worth the telling. Using a variety of sources, including the letters and diaries of Addis, I made a sketch of Michie's life that will be found in Appendix I.

On the couple's engagement in 1893, Addis makes to Michie in Tientsin one of the rare comments we have on B-T:

> Please convey my congratulations to your daughter. I never met Brewitt-
> Taylor but I have heard pleasant things about him from others and of course

> I have read his Chinese papers from time to time. A few years ago he was
> beginning to establish a reputation as a budding sinologue, which should
> stand him in good stead in the Customs.[12]

Clearly, as will be seen from the portrayal of Michie presented in Appendix I,
the family B-T was marrying into had a strong China presence and identity. Both his
wife's parents had connections there: her father held prominent positions in China;
her paternal uncles, the Thins, worked in the country as doctors; her maternal uncles,
the Robisons, probably engaged in the silk trade there; and she and her brother had
been born in Shanghai. It would be interesting to know what kind of relationship
Michie had with his son-in-law. They were such different characters, though they
shared one striking similarity: both were emotionally distressed by losing beloved
wives at around the same age, in their early thirties, and both were left with two
young children; one hopes this would have created some kind of sympathy between
them. Unlike B-T, Michie was an expansive, larger-than-life character, and though
difficult to get to know, he clearly elicited strong affections in those he befriended;
people commented in writing on Michie, rarely on B-T. Sport did not appear to be
B-T's métier, though he rode, occasionally had a round of golf and may have played
tennis a little; Michie became a fencing champion. Furthermore, Michie differed
from B-T in knowing no Chinese. Their writings reflected the men: Michie elaborate,
flowery, never recoiling from presenting his views; B-T rarely did. Reactions to their
deaths were similarly contrasting: Michie had several obituaries, full of his lively
personality, but only one could be found for B-T, an impersonal and brief resume of
his life.

B-T's Second Marriage

There is little doubt that marrying into the Michie family would have considerably
enhanced B-T's social prestige in the community. Especially with his growing
reputation as a sinologue, B-T was imbedding himself more securely into an elite
layer of the expatriate social world, mixing with many with a long-standing China
connection. Being the son-in-law of Michie would have done no harm to B-T's
prestige in the Customs Service, too, in that Robert Hart knew and liked Michie
Sr.[13]

Ann and B-T were married by the Right Reverend Bishop Burdon on 28 March
1894 in the rather imposing environment of St. John's Cathedral, in far-off Hong
Kong.[14] B-T was thirty-six years old, and his wife ten years younger. Though *The
Times* obituary states that Alexander Michie retired from China in 1895, it seems
that Michie had already left, for in a letter to Addis in that year he says that he is
staying with his daughter and that 'he came out to China I confess with reluctance,

to marry off my daughter'.[15] Perhaps Michie encouraged the marriage to take place in Hong Kong, the place where he first worked and made an impact as a young man. This is one possible explanation for what would have been a long journey from Tientsin, probably a few days by sea, for the marriage; another is that Hong Kong would have been a congenial place to honeymoon. The newly-weds probably knew people there through Michie and were able to arrange for the marriage to take place in the cathedral.

A copy of the marriage certificate might have been revealing, as it would have shown, for example, who the witnesses were and the addresses of each member of the couple, for it is not clear where Ann was living. Unfortunately, the certificate is not to be found: Hong Kong's special status meant records for that year would have been available only there and not in Britain, and the Hong Kong records were destroyed during the Japanese occupation in the Second World War. The local *Peking and Tientsin Times* announced the marriage and also their return from Hong Kong on 13 April.

Less handsome than his first wife, photos of Ann suggest a certain pert flirtatiousness. She was also talented musically, and the local paper reported several concert performances she gave in Tientsin. When still only nineteen, she sang a couple of Burns songs at a Burns Anniversary in late January 1888; this was followed by a piano performance at a charity concert in February 1889. In March 1890, she played at a concert in Tientsin given in aid of a worthy cause: the Training and Industrial School for Chinese Girls. The piano duet in which she performed was 'brilliantly executed'. A couple of months later she performed again, and this time in addition to performing piano duets, she also sang, winning fulsome praise

> her clear enunciation and altogether charming rendering of the favourite 'Caller Herrin' would have procured her in any case the encore which she merited doubly by her courage and energy.

The reference to 'her courage' was apparently due to the difficulty of singing in the exceedingly hot climate in May, when most ladies had left the city. Ann was the only one of those remaining 'to rise to the occasion and defy the heat'.[16]

Shortly after the couple's return from their wedding, Ann again displayed her skills at a gathering held by the Tientsin Literary and Debating Society. It was chaired on that occasion by her father, Alexander Michie, having returned to China for his daughter's marriage and been 'welcomed back in his old role as chairman of the Society'. B-T, doubtless among the audience, must have sat proud of his talented new wife, daughter of a famous father. It is hoped he loved her dearly, for future years with her were to prove most trying, but at this stage she demonstrated a confidence which later was to be undermined. A report of the occasion informs us that Mrs. Brewitt-Taylor sang and played the piano, including Mendelssohn's Andante and

Capriccioso, 'a difficult composition brilliantly rendered'.[17] The newly-weds were becoming involved as a couple in the social round of Tientsin.

B-T's bride had received the kind of education traditional at the time for girls of her class, for she was not only talented musically but also acquainted with foreign languages, and as we shall see she wrote with some eloquence. On 11 February 1896 in Tientsin, Ann Amy Jane gave birth to a daughter, also named Ann, but though born alive, the baby died the same day, as Ann herself nearly did; she was to experience further birth complications, and no child of hers survived.

Other than this event, little is known of B-T's life in Tientsin. Work was likely to be fairly relaxed, and the day tended to follow a pattern; one such was described by Paul King:

> Tiffin at noon in the mess-room, preceded by the inevitable and noxious cold drink in cocktail shape. Tiffin was quite a substantial meal, the feature being 'spatch-cock' chicken. We had no ice. Any meat had to be quickly cooked and eaten, and could only be got from the good-natured skippers of visiting steamers.
>
> Office hours in the Customs were ten to four. A cup of tea also served on the verandah to the consumer lying in a long cane chair helped to tone up the system for the evening exercises. Sometimes, when credit was more plentiful than reason, a 'hsiao-ping-tzu' anglice, a small bottle of champagne, from the cool depths of the Club well, was substituted for the tea and generally tossed for. The chit system was in full swing and the 'end of the month' troubled only a few.
>
> Dinner was late — eight to half-past as a rule. White linen mess jackets and duck trousers — the dandies with red sashes — were mostly worn. Sherry, claret and soda, and bottled beer were generally drunk at table, with whisky and soda afterwards — sometimes, when card-playing was in vogue, deep into the night. Dinner was necessarily 'metallic'. Tinned soup, tinned fish, tinned meat, tinned vegetables, and Christmas tinned plum pudding.[18]

B-T appears to have been frugal and temperate in his tastes, and probably did not socialize more than was necessary to maintain a presence; there would have been ample opportunity to engage in his writing. While there is no record of any publications appearing during the short period following his marriage that he remained in Tientsin, he was probably deep into his translation of the *San Kuo* at this time, as will be seen later. He was also actively involved in the local expatriate community's library, and he became honorary treasurer, the committee recording when he resigned its 'deep sense of the invaluable services of Mr. Taylor during the last four years'.[19]

An early opportunity for B-T to demonstrate his prowess in Chinese came very shortly after his arrival in Tientsin. In February 1892, seventieth birthday celebrations were held for Li Hung-chang, Viceroy of Chihli (Zhili) and Imperial Commissioner for Northern Trade. Li gave a special banquet for foreigners. B-T, who was invited, was asked to translate a eulogistic address to Li by Chang Chih-tung, another viceroy.[20] B-T might have been recommended to do the translation by Gustav Detring, Customs Commissioner in Tientsin, and one of Li's trusted advisers. Detring was one of the most powerful commissioners in the Service, having a problematic relationship with Hart and uniquely staying in his Tientsin posting for nearly three decades.[21] Placing B-T under Detring's watch may say something about how Hart wished to test his new entrant. It would have been most interesting to have known Detring's view of B-T, but his personal reports could not be found.

It is just conceivable that another possible acquaintance of B-T's in Tientsin might have been Yen Fu, the translator and, initially, modernizer, who it will be remembered might also have known B-T in London. At that time Yen Fu would have been well established in his post in the well-regarded local naval school, having become President in 1890. He and B-T shared common backgrounds in the world of naval education in London as well as Foochow, in the same Arsenal school where Yen Fu had been a student and teacher.[22] It would be surprising if they were not aware of each other, especially given B-T's developing literary reputation and his contacts now doubtless enhanced by the Michie connection. However, the intellectual and other preoccupations of the two men would have been very different. B-T's focus of interest in traditional Chinese would have contrasted sharply with that of the early Yen Fu, whose major concerns were the lessons which could be learnt from the West to maximize the energies of Chinese society, unfettered by old hierarchical bonds.[23] Also, at least one eminent historian of China has observed that at this time, expatriate sinologists often worked in isolation from Chinese people.[24] During this period, China was suffering from the problems of the 1894–95 Sino-Japanese War, and Yen Fu was most likely to have been highly concerned in this matter, especially given the sensitive location of Tientsin. About this time, too, he was translating Huxley's *Evolution and Ethics*, which was serialized in a Tientsin journal before a complete version was published in book form in 1898. Given these factors, even had they known each other, much contact between the two men was unlikely, particularly given B-T's lowly position.

The Brewitt-Taylors left for Britain in the early summer of 1896, about three months after the death of their baby. A letter from Hart to Aglen in April 1896 refers to B-T not returning to Tientsin when he returned from home leave, but going to Foochow instead.[25] There he took up a promoted position, probably on his return from leave, as Second Assistant B grade. In a letter to Addis on 2 February 1898, Michie refers to his daughter being in Foochow. But she and her husband could not have been there long, for in June 1898 they were on their way to a posting in Peking, dining with the Addis family in Shanghai on 20 June.[26]

What happened to B-T's sons after the death of his first wife? According to Joan, the daughter of the elder son, Leonard, her mother had told her that she understood that the boys had remained in China, attending some kind of monastic institution for their education; this may have been a missionary establishment of some kind, for the missionaries were active in educational provision, or even one of the boarding schools that were being set up in China.[27] That the boys remained in China is confirmed by a letter from Michie to Addis on 3 March 1895, while the B-Ts were still in Tientsin; Michie writes that he is trying to persuade his daughter to come with him to Japan, and 'she is half disposed to go with her two boys'.

So, it would appear that the boys were in China until the home leave taken in 1896. Not long after the family's return to Britain, Leonard started school in London, his father taking him there. Leonard was then twelve, and he went to University College School, Hampstead, where the junior part of the school had moved in 1891.[28] This school was an understandable choice: it had developed a good reputation and attracted the children of a number of expatriate families in China, Japan and elsewhere. Unusually for the period, it had a non-sectarian policy which would have appealed to B-T. Family members were within easy contact: the sons' paternal uncle lived in South London, and their stepmother's paternal uncle and maternal grandfather both lived close by. Raymond joined his brother at the school two years later, in 1898, at the age of eleven. They probably would have boarded outside the school as it was a day school. It is quite possible that at the end of his home-leave B-T left his younger son, Raymond, with his own family to be looked after for the year remaining before he was admitted to University College School. It was most unlikely that B-T was able to accompany Raymond back from China the following year — though children were often sent to Britain by boat on their own or under the care of a friend or family member. If Raymond did stay in Britain, this could have been with B-T's married brother, Herbert, the sibling with whom he kept the closest contact. Living with remote family members from a very different background may well have given rise to Raymond's later comment that he did not like his cousins.

Sending young children back 'home' was a regular feature of expatriate life. This frequently took place at a much younger age than Leonard and Raymond experienced, as we saw with Michie's children, who were returned as babies. Children were often shunted around various family members or paid foster parents. This could prove an affectionless experience,[29] if not worse, as will be seen in the account of Ann's childhood.[30]

So this is what seems to have happened with B-T's sons from his first marriage. The boys would have experienced little more than two to three years of mothering from Ann. They called her 'Mother', but the relationship, though dutiful, one suspects out of loyalty to their father and natural courtesy, did not appear to be close.

The University College School the brothers attended was to become particularly important for both the boys, for the friendships they made there and their later relationships. These connections turned out to be valuable sources of friendship and emotional warmth for B-T too.

8

Upheaval in Peking

Following a short spell in Foochow, B-T took up a position in Peking in July 1898 as a Second Assistant A, another promotion, at the headquarters of the Customs Inspectorate. There, he was Assistant Chinese Secretary in charge of the Chinese Department, involved in drafting Chinese official and semi-official correspondence and documents.

Around this time, he produced a little booklet in Chinese on economic policy, a guide to Chinese traders to the kinds of goods foreign traders wanted and how they valued them. Mentioned are such commodities as leopard skin, musk, sesame seeds, lanolin, beeswax, straw braid for hats and rhubarb (which rotted in transit to Europe and therefore should be tinned, advised the booklet). Chinese traders were encouraged to use the Customs to gain access to foreign merchants for a more detailed understanding of the market. The wording of the booklet suggests that it was based on the writing of another staff member:

> The Customs Commissioner has lived in China for a long time, working hard
> all the time. How could he keep silent about everything he has seen? So in
> his leisure, he frequented merchants everywhere to learn their ideas. He is
> ashamed that he knows so little . . . it is offered for your criticism.[1]

Working in headquarters where, under the eye of the I-G he would be noticed could be beneficial for a man of ability. B-T's further promotion was rapid. By early 1899, after just over seven years in the Service, he was promoted to Deputy Commissioner in Peking. Very shortly afterwards, in 1900, he was appointed to his first commissioner post, as Acting Commissioner of Swatow (Shantou). H. B. Morse, another Customs commissioner and a historian of some repute,[2] suggested that it took on average about twenty years to become a commissioner. It had taken Morse himself fifteen to get his first acting commissioner post,[3] and Paul King, whose relationship with Hart was uncertain, took twenty-four years to reach acting commissioner, though he got his full rank just two years later.[4] Another authoritative source noted that at one stage a good man could achieve that position in eight to ten years.[5] It isn't clear whether this space of time would have included 'acting' periods, the usual transitional route before appointment to the substantive post.

B-T must have been very well regarded in order to have obtained even an acting commissioner rank in approximately eight years, at the lower end of the unusual range; though, it took another seven years, which included a three-year secondment posting, to obtain the substantive position. Doubtless, his facility in Chinese helped. Early in 1897, Hart complained to Campbell about the problem of finding Chinese-speaking commissioners, and in 1901 Hart repeated his concerns: 'We are shockingly badly off for *good* senior assistants up in *Chinese*'.[6] B-T had sensibly calculated the value of Chinese proficiency for his career, but though very useful, proficiency in the language would not have been sufficient reason alone for such rapid promotion.

Senior staff tended to move around a good deal in the ICMC. There were always posts that needed filling at short notice, for example if someone died or took retirement earlier than expected. One of the sensitive factors was the nationality of the commissioner, as countries jealously tried to ensure that once one of their nationals had obtained that grade, another would replace him if he left. While performance in the job should not have been affected by nationality, especially as the ICMC was responsible to the Chinese government, foreign governments obviously saw advantage in holding onto commissioner positions. For posts located in politically sensitive areas, in terms of rivalries among the foreign powers operating there, appointments could be seen as useful, not so much for their Customs role, but as 'listening posts'; incumbents of posts possibly differed in the extent to which they exercised scruples about passing on strategic or other useful information especially if it were knowledge unrelated to their Customs work. The tentacles of the ICMC ran out in numerous directions, and the range of responsibilities changed over time, so there were frequent reasons for movement, especially for those in senior positions. Those being groomed for, or just entering, senior ranks could also be tested in a range of situations.

A photograph taken around this time in 1900 shows B-T displaying an uncharacteristically jaunty air, picnicking with colleagues and their wives at the Yellow Temple. He had completed a draft of his translation of the *Three Kingdoms* by this time and he must have been highly satisfied by the rapidity of his promotion to the coveted position of commissioner, albeit acting.

Having made his mark, he would have been considerably frustrated by being prevented from taking up his position at the planned time; the Brewitt-Taylors were all packed and ready to leave Peking for Swatow when the Boxer disturbances, which were already underway, intensified. The railway line to Swatow was cut off, and the couple was forced to abandon their departure.

The Boxers, Summer 1900

Numerous accounts of the Boxer Rebellion trace the momentous days of the Siege of the Legations in the summer of 1900. Whilst the siege only lasted just under eight weeks, from 21 June, the first full day of the siege,[7] until the relief on 14 August, its effects were traumatic. Some of the complexities of analyzing and interpreting the events of the time are to be found in the many accounts of the siege. More analyses, using both foreign historical as well as modern Chinese scholarship, drawing on contemporary Chinese sources from that time, may well be made. So much change has taken place since that eventful incident that even a century may not have been sufficient for all new sources to be revealed and revised appraisals to be formulated. In all likelihood, the affair will remain controversial.

Among the more immediate factors leading to the rise of the Boxers, so-called because of their style of martial art physical exercise, was the effect of China's ignominious defeat in the Sino-Japanese war of 1894–95, a defeat suffered despite the reform attempts of Self-Strengthening. As a consequence, there was a further undermining of the standing of the Ch'ing. Exacerbating this unsettlement was the scramble for concessions by the foreign powers who seized on China's weak condition to secure or strengthen their position. As one Western observer was later to put it:

> The rapacity of the West was never more shamelessly exhibited than during the years 1895–1900. Spheres of influence were a commonplace topic of conversation and publicists and politicians openly discussed attempts to extend these areas of influence, what the Chinese termed 'the dividing of the melon' … What, the Chinese asked, could be the end of all this aggression — demanding the building of railways, insisting on opening up the interior waterways, carving up slices of territories for political and commercial purposes?[8]

These actions further encouraged demonstrations of xenophobia amenable to manipulation for local or national political advantage. The Boxer movement appears to have been similarly used.

The Boxers did not form a unified movement; they contained very diverse strands and motivations. In some areas, they were likely to have been associated with secret societies or exploited by local bandits. While there has been a focus on their dominant and probably most consistent anti-Westerner, and especially anti-missionary, views,[9] the anti-Manchu factor seemed to be there at least early in their activities. On the issue of when the Boxers focused solely on the foreigner as the target, it should be noted that the word 'foreigner' could be employed ambiguously, including anti-Manchu. Even as late as early 1899, there were those in the movement who adopted the slogan 'Overthrow the Ch'ing, Destroy the Foreigner'. Certain dynastic officials would enthusiastically support the latter part of the slogan, emphasizing its anti-Westerner xenophobia to deflect popular opinion against themselves.[10] At some point it appears that the dominant slogan became 'Cherish the Dynasty and Exterminate the Foreigner', targeting Westerners more clearly. Expatriate observers in Shanghai had been predicting problems:

> The Empress Dowager intends that her favourite General Tung Fu-hsiang shall carry out his plans proposed a year ago last September of driving all foreigners into the Yellow Sea. Towards this end the Boxer contingent is thought to be a most serviceable ally . . . The coming Spring will witness a rising such as foreigners in China have never seen before.[11]

Later in May, reporting troubles in Peking and Tientsin, The *North China Herald* was suspicious that while the Empress Dowager puts out 'condemnatory proclamations to amuse the Legations, [she] has been throughout encouraging the Boxer movement'.[12] Certainly, there were divisions among the authorities, and Sir Claude MacDonald, the British resident minister, stated that some provincial governers, especially in the South, refused to recognize the Peking government's policy. Government representatives in the Yangtze provinces and further south made a compact with the allied foreign powers to oppose any spread of the Boxers in their area; in return, the allies would only use force against the Boxers or those opposing the allied rescue.[13] Even in Peking at the height of the siege, some ministers opposed the Boxers and urged the protection of the legation quarter. They paid for their dissension.[14]

This level of ambivalence among the leadership might have helped prevent a complete annihilation of the besieged in the legations, which the Chinese could probably have achieved if they were sufficiently single-minded. Some officials probably realized that this would undoubtedly have led to major reprisals by the foreign allied powers. The humiliations that China had recently experienced in the Sino-Japanese War and the further wresting of concessions by European powers had demonstrated China's weakness, encouraged the rise of a xenophobic patriotism, but also tempered its expression.

Those besieged were devastated by the experience, unable to maintain contact with the forces of the foreign powers which eventually relieved them; they woke every day wondering whether it would be their last. Hart, who was sympathetic to China, saw the Shantung Boxers as 'a patriotic association for which the world has to thank the irritation felt in that province against converts and foreigners,'[15] and initially he was not overly concerned about them. He was already feeling his age and beginning to tire from his years of dedication to the Service. It may be that his judgement about events was not as sharp as it would have been earlier. Yet if he were complacent he was by no means alone, and it should be noted that even the previous year he had voiced apprehension over the political climate. In May 1899, in a letter to Campbell, he criticized the West for their extravagant actions which had outraged the people, adding:

> Some Chinese say that revolt and disorder are fast coming on — that the rioters will wipe out every foreigner they come across.[16]

In the following month, he wrote:

> There is a curious feeling of unrest among the Chinese just now and they seem to expect something serious to occur this summer — whether a change of Emperor or a big and general demonstration against foreigners, I can't make out.[17]

By the time the siege was underway and its daily enormity realized, Hart was very disturbed. He notes his relief that a number of the spouses of his staff had arrived to stay in the British legation, including the wife of B-T, who was welcomed by Lady MacDonald, wife of the British minister, into their home.[18] B-T himself initially stayed on in the Customs headquarters to help in its defence until the staff had to withdraw from the building. According to G. E. Morrison, who was also in the siege, had Hart and his staff remained in the Customs building, 'he and every member of his staff would have been murdered'.[19]

There was continual anxiety about what would happen to those incarcerated in the legations should the Boxers overrun them, and the women were particularly concerned about their fate, with reports of some preferring to be shot by their husbands or friends if danger were imminent. If an emergency came at night, everyone was to be awakened, and occasionally this happened unnecessarily. Lady MacDonald reported one such incident, when Mrs. Brewitt-Taylor and another colleague's wife, Mrs. Brent, were woken without real cause: 'They both looked frightened nearly out of their wits, causing unnecessary pain to the already taxed nerves of the women.'[20] The comment proved to carry a prophetic note.

Over eight hundred people were crammed into the British legation, which was regarded as the best place for defence, then about seven hundred yards long and two hundred wide.[21] Conditions for those confined in the legations were initially chaotic, until the American missionaries proposed a number of committees to take charge of certain key areas: general comfort, health and sanitation, water, fuel, labour, food supply, and fortification. It is interesting to note that not a single woman served on any of the committees.[22] Though the women did strive to keep up standards, one of them when foraging for materials for the hospital commented, 'Are we semi-civilized that we do not think it improper to pack men's clothing with women's?'[23] While the siege varied in intensity, the besieged experienced attack on most days.

By the siege's end, 66 foreigners were dead, and 114 were wounded; 6 babies had died from the heat and lack of suitable food. There is no record of the actual number of casualties among the three thousand vulnerable Chinese converts, whom the missionaries had gathered separately in the East and South Cathedrals, as well as in the Fu palace, though many were killed.[24]

Horrendous though the experience was, it was not without its bizarre moments. One example is the frequently cited and controversially interpreted action of the Empress Dowager in sending two cart loads of provisions, containing watermelons, cucumbers, and aubergines, regarded as a gift of distinction in China.[25] Another was during a truce, when Japanese troops started a market in eggs brought by Chinese soldiers and also bought rifles and ammunition from them! The Tsungli Yamen, the government office responsible for the ICMC, sent messages to Hart during the siege, when each day might have been the last for the besieged who were experiencing frequent distress. The messages complained of the loss of Customs revenue due to the resultant disorganization and sought advice from Hart! Of course, little could be done about that, especially as the plea for help may have been a trap,[26] but it could well have been sincere if rather naive. In fact, arrangements were made to organize the Service from Shanghai, and the Statistical Secretary, F. E. Taylor, who was based there, agreed to take charge temporarily, on condition that the Chinese authorities formally recognize the arrangements; this was approved by the Western powers.[27]

Views differed over Hart's activities during the siege; some were complimentary, others derisory:

> Sir Robert Hart, an awful old footler told his ladies that . . . the town was filled with troops who had orders to wipe us out . . . [it] . . . scared Customs ladies, rushing about frightening our ladies, all women kin depressed re news. What an old woman Sir R. is.

The same observer also summarized the behaviour of the other foreign combatants: the Germans were hardworking and had splendid discipline but were jumpy; the French fought well but didn't understand the need for adequate defences; the Austrians and Italians were cowardly, always retreating from forward positions; the Russians were strong but stupid and brutal; and the Americans had dash but no discipline, were often drunk on duty and were unreliable, boasting. After the British, the Japanese were best, 'far superior to any other', being plucky, cheerful, obedient, persevering, and innovative.[28]

Hart, then around sixty-five years of age, but worn and world-weary from his industrious life, never really recovered from the events of that summer. He was particularly distraught by the destruction of his dearly beloved home in Peking together with much of its contents. There, in his house and large garden, he had enjoyed playing host at regular parties. He was aware of the destruction even before the end of the siege and noted wearily that he was fed up with the loss of his house and garden and was now prepared to leave China sooner than he had intended. In a letter to his wife written during the siege, he explains: 'I feel I have lost all my family and I am anxious to go to Heaven via home and not directly.'[29] A couple of days after the siege was lifted, he wrote: 'I have lost everything — and it is heartbreaking.'

Hart, despite his loss and weariness, was able to see the longer-term implications of the Boxer event, predicting with foresight:

> This episode of to-day is not meaningless — it is the prelude to a century of change and the keynote of the future history of the Far East: the China of the year 2000 will be very different from the China of 1900![30]

He also tried to restrain the impulse to adopt severe and hasty retaliatory measures by the foreign powers.[31]

Xenophobia doesn't readily distinguish between the unsympathetic and the friendly foreigner, and Hart was not the only one to lose possessions during the uprising. B-T was among those whose house was destroyed. Lancelot Giles, the son of the famous H. A. Giles, records the incident. During the night of 13 June, just a few days after the Brewitt-Taylors had sought protection in the legation, the Boxers lit huge fires, burning down the Roman Catholic mission, the London mission, and an asylum for blind converts:

> What affected us perhaps even more was the burning down of an outlying portion of the Customs . . . in the north-east of the city. The Brewitt-Taylors' house was burned to the ground, their boxes etc. were all ready packed for departure to Swatow. They were only waiting for the railway to be opened. Their losses and those of many of the Customs' junior assistants must be irreparable.[32]

Another observer amplified what happened on 13 June:

> When we rose in the morning [of 14 June] the fire at the East Cathedral was still burning. The Boy belonging to Mr. Brewitt Taylor of the Customs came in and reported that the Boxers had made no attempt on the previous night to loot his master's house, though all Mr. Taylor's things were packed up in boxes ready for a move, as he had been ordered south. The Boxers had simply set fire to the buildings and gone on. That seemed to point to a deeper hatred of the foreigner and a more sincere zeal than was to be expected. To destroy, but not to rob, is evidence of strange frenzy in the Chinese.[33]

By the time the troubles began, B-T had completed a full draft of his translation of the *San Kuo,* the work of at least a decade and a half; it was entirely destroyed.[34] Though the ever-present prospect of death during the siege would have anaesthetized the immediate feelings of loss, one could only imagine what the destruction of this work would have meant to him. Ironically, the Boxers' pantheon of heroes contained figures from traditional literature, including the *San Kuo*.[35] It was to be another quarter of a century before the final translation was completed and published. In addition to this most shattering blow, B-T also lost parts of another book he was engaged on, *Chats in Chinese*. This was a translation of a small textbook for the teaching of Chinese, the preface to which records that he was particularly upset by the loss of the whole of a Chinese-English vocabulary, setting back the date of publication.

To many in the outside world, the survival of the foreigners was not expected. Ceremonies of mourning were arranged and obituaries appeared based on assumption and erroneous rumour. *The Times* carried an obituary on Hart,[36] and another on G. E. Morrison, their resident correspondent in Peking, stating that all communcations had been cut off since 14 June:

> One shudders to think of the awful days and nights that were to follow waiting for the help that never came before the tragedy was finally consummated and the last heroic remnants of Western civilization in the doomed city were engulfed beneath the overwhelming floods of Asiatic barbarism.[37]

With reports like this, any family and friends back home who knew people still in Peking must have been distraught. One wonders how much B-T's young sons were aware of the situation. Of Michie, always concerned about his daughter's condition, it was said that

> there can be no doubt that the mental agony of the father when his daughter was in Peking, shortened his life.[38]

For his activities during the Siege of the Legations, B-T was awarded, along with about twenty other members of the Imperial Customs, the China Medal with clasp for Defence of Legations designed for Britons and others who had 'distinguished themselves' during the siege. There is no detailing of any specific action that had merited the award, except that recipients had 'performed exceptionally good service during the siege of Peking', though B-T was highlighted by Sir Claude MacDonald for special mention.[39] B-T was alleged to have received a wound in his leg during the siege, and there is a reference later to a knee problem, but his name doesn't appear in the list of those wounded. Sir Claude argued with the Foreign Office for several months before the awards were granted.[40]

Criticism was also voiced about the lack of recognition given to women despite the British Minister's commendation:

> I cannot conclude this despatch without saying a word of praise respecting the ladies of all nationalities who so ably and devotedly assisted the defence,

notwithstanding the terrible shadow which at all times hung over the legation
. . . assisting in every way the work of defence.

Other attempts to pressure the War and Foreign Offices to extend awards to
women proved fruitless, to the disappointment of expatriates in China:

> British ladies who nursed the sick and wounded and did so much to keep up
> the spirit of the defenders of the legation, whilst themselves subjected to all
> the dangers and privations of the siege have not been awarded the medal and
> clasp which would have been given them had they been Army nurses.[41]

The award would have been some consolation for the distresses undergone and
the losses that were borne.

The surprising lack of earlier looting by the Boxers was not reciprocated by
the eventually victorious allied forces. They didn't miss out on their opportunity,
customary at the time, for looting arrangements were often negotiated in advance of
action. A recent study also argues that the looting represented a desire to humiliate
the Chinese involved and to teach an imperialist lesson.[42] Some of those who had
been besieged compensated themselves by purchasing the looted goods cheaply, a
practice not always passing without criticism. Even the MacDonalds were alleged to
be engaged in the activity, though they denied this later.[43] According to one observer,
'Everyone was in the hunt: Ministers plenipotentiary, Customs staff, journalists,
even missionaries.'[44] Lancelot Giles boasted to his father: 'Every day looting parties
go out and get what they can. I have done some splendid looting already.'[45] Among
the goods which attracted looters were expensive fur coats, including sables. There
is a picture of B-T's wife, looking rather splendid in a fine fur coat; one cannot
help wondering whether this was acquired by regular purchase or from someone's
loot. Having experienced the ordeal of being in the siege would have helped to
salve consciences. Hart sent his wife two sables that year; in a letter to Francis
Aglen, he was anxious to assure him that they were not the result of looting but
were purchased from someone who wanted to clear out his goods — how the owner
acquired them is not considered.[46] Much of the loot was sold by auction for private
gain, but some of the missionaries dealt in the goods either to care for their converts
who had lost their possessions or to help rebuild their missions.[47] Perhaps it was for
this somewhat worthier cause that Mrs. Brewitt-Taylor acquired her fur.

In the British Library, there are a number of volumes, or sections (*chüan*), of
the famous Ming encyclopedia, the *Yongle dadian,* the original of which ran into
several thousand volumes. The work, completed in 1407, has been described as 'an
encyclopaedia of scope and size unprecedented in history'.[48] The original was said
to have been kept in Nanking, and one or perhaps two copies were made in 1567 and
kept in Peking. The original and possibly one of the copies perished after the fall of
the Ming. The *Encyclopaedia Sinica* records that the remaining copy

nearly complete, was kept, but not cared for, in the Han-lin College till 1900, when the Boxers fired the Library, which adjoined the British Legation, and the last copy of the work was destroyed; though a few score volumes were afterwards picked up by foreigners.[49]

Three of the valuable volumes in the British Library collection were donated by B-T.

One of the volumes he donated (dealing with aspects of architecture) is very slightly charred; this could have been the result of a fire or, more prosaically, caused by a smoker inadvertently! Be that as it may, the volumes were almost certainly picked up at this time. The Hanlin was fired by the Boxers on 23 June for strategic purposes. This was entirely unexpected — 'No one could believe that the Chinese would dare to burn it' — because it was thought to be too sacred. However, 'at this time the people acted as barbarians and set fire to the place. It was a monstrous act'.[50] Under Captain Poole, a detachment of marines and others, including five Customs volunteers, entered the Hanlin.[51] Allen suggests that some of the items were 'gathered into a place of security', but several of those entering the Hanlin kept volumes for themselves. Given his awareness of the significance of the *Yongle dadian*, B-T could well have been one of the volunteers, and perhaps even persuaded the need for action, giving rise to MacDonald's special commendation noted earlier. It may be then that he picked up the volumes, or he may have bought them later.

It took many months of wrangling both between the allies and between them and China over the size of the indemnities that would be paid by China. Eventually, on 26 May 1901, the sum agreed was announced by imperial edict: the amount was £67,500,000. Estimates suggested that it would take China thirty-nine years to pay this.[52] The Chinese Customs was to be the vehicle for payment, adding to the proportion of its revenue that was used for paying foreigners for loans and the like and encouraging the view that the organization was a tool of foreign domination. Much of the money was eventually used to good purpose, for example, for aiding educational developments in China and funding scholarships and visits overseas. Eventually, in June 1925, an act was passed in Britain which

> provided that money from the Indemnity Fund . . . be applied to such educational and other purposes as the Secretary of State for Foreign Affairs after consultation with the [British Indemnity] Advisory Committee [believed] were beneficial to the mutual interests of Great Britain and China.[53]

While the Boxers were eventually put down, the movement and its aftermath could be said to have presaged the Republican Revolution, which brought the Ch'ing dynasty to an end. Indeed, in present-day China, the Boxers are presented as precursors of the 1912 Republican Revolution and the 1949 Communist Liberation. The indemnities extracted by the foreign powers were seen as another example of imperialist extortion. In particular, they rebounded on the Customs Service: instead of being associated with China's modernization, it became a symbol of foreign imperialism, its foreign staff perceived not as modernizers but as tax collectors for foreign governments.[54]

With the ending of the seige on 14 August, those involved resumed their lives, and the Brewitt-Taylors made preparations to take up the planned posting to Swatow.

9

Career Advancement; Family Concerns

Swatow 1900–01

After the distressing events in Peking, the Brewitt-Taylors must have been relieved to travel to Swatow, despite its relative isolation from the centre of Customs activity. B-T took up his first appointment at commissioner level as Acting Commissioner. Swatow had been opened as a Treaty Port in 1861, following the 1860 Convention of Peking. In the early days, the city had been regarded as extremely dangerous, but already by the 1870s the area had a reputation as being very safe, having been pacified by the provincial authorities. Office hours in the Customs, from ten to four, were sufficiently relaxed to leave plenty of time for leisure;[1] the Customs had a good club and reputedly an excellent library.[2]

Both the consul and the Customs commissioner had leading roles in their communities; in some respects they could be in competition with each other, for the commissioner, as an important expatriate as well as a Chinese government official, would often be seen as having a nominal leadership role for the wider foreign community.[3] Promotion to commissioner, full or acting, extended the status to wives: one newly promoted commissioner wrote to Hart: 'My wife was immensely pleased to hear that she was a Mrs. Commissioner.'[4] Commissioners sometimes also assumed consular responsibility for the subjects of nations which had no treaty relations with China.[5] This would appear to have rested oddly with the fact that the commissioner was an employee of the Chinese government. The position of commissioner, with its multiple roles, could clearly be a tricky one. As one commentator put it, 'the Commissioner of Customs was by far the most important man in town'.[6]

B-T and his wife arrived in Swatow on 21 September 1900. He reports in October that though the town had been quiet, Chinese Christian converts had been attacked and chapels destroyed; there were also rumours of murders, and the German consul had called for a cruiser to be stationed there. While B-T gives no indication of being under threat from such activity, disease was another source of danger: Swatow was listed as a plague port. His view was that there was no plague at that time, but there was smallpox.[7]

At work, B-T discovered that undesirable activities had been allowed to develop, and in January 1901 he expresses concern at evidence that a practice had grown up among Outdoor Staff supervisors of obtaining bribes for appointing people, resulting in inferior recruitment. He promises to try to abolish 'the mischievous custom', but does not report whether he had been successful — he might have discovered that his position of authority was not sufficient to abolish undesirable but long-entrenched methods of supplementing income, especially in the Outdoor area. He did not expect to stay in Swatow long, with so many seniors awaiting promotion: 'Commissioners will be as common as Captains in Shanghai soon.' He was right. In April he handed over and left for home.

B-T's father-in-law, Alexander Michie, aware of Ann's vulnerability and concerned to know how his daughter was getting on following the siege ordeal, came out to visit the Brewitt-Taylors in Swatow. He clearly enjoyed his stay: 'I am having a delightful time here, weather pleasant, situation open and bright, house commodious, and society congenial.'[8] Michie was making a round of it: after Swatow he intended to go to Hong Kong, Shanghai, Tientsin, and Peking before returning home via Japan and the United States; he expected to arrive back in England in August that year.

B-T may have hoped for more time to engage in his writing with his boys away at boarding school in England, but his new responsibilities would have been demanding for the novice commissioner. In addition to work commitments, which in his new role would be different, the kind of relationships he would have within the community would also have changed, demanding much more formal social interaction. Life would take on a new dimension.

Despite many preoccupations, B-T was able to complete his *Chats in Chinese* in Swatow, writing the preface in April 1901, and sending the manuscript off to the publisher and printer in Peking. In the preface he explains the delay in its publication:

> The MS. of the text was in the printer's hands in October 1899; the first vocabulary soon after. But pressure of other work kept this behind and the outbreak of trouble in Peking found it less than half done. Worse than this, the MS. of the English-Chinese vocabulary was entirely destroyed.

He pays tribute, in the gracious and fulsome style of the time, to a colleague who recompiled the missing vocabulary, 'a labour for which I am unable to sufficiently express my gratitude'.[9] Being able to complete the book says much for B-T's single-mindedness.

His experiences over the previous year had been demanding: the traumatic excitements of Peking, becoming familiar with new responsibilities in an unfamiliar environment, his domestic concerns with his wife pregnant again, and getting a book to press. He must have looked forward to home leave and seeing his boys again.

Distressing Leave

The Brewitt-Taylors left China for a very different world. There were by this time three main routes to Britain to choose from: the newly opened Trans-Siberian Railway; across the Pacific to the United States, and then over land through Canada or the United States; or by steamer all the way via Singapore. On this occasion, B-T took the opportunity to take his wife on the US route. This he clearly enjoyed, for in a letter to one of his daughters-in-law who was about to visit California many years later, he writes:

> How nice [it would be] to be going with [you] to share the sunshine of San F!
> You can greet the city for us; remind it of two appreciative visitors of 1901.[10]

A few months after B-T's return to Britain, another shock hit the family. His wife again experienced an extremely difficult birth around December: the baby died and B-T nearly lost his second wife. Michie, her father, had clearly been most distressed, and in January 1902 wrote to Addis about the episode:

> I was plunged into serious trouble on account of my daughter. None of us I think as yet fully realises what has happened least of all perhaps the principal victim, but it is sufficient to say that her hopes of successful maternity were suddenly dashed. The experience of years ago in Tientsin has been rehearsed . . . for the third time I have received my living child from the very jaws of death.[11]

Ann's sister-in-law, Kathleen Michie, wrote to Hart (responding to a Christmas card from him and sending him a present), referring to the situation:

> We have been very worried about Mrs. Brewitt-Taylor lately, she has been seriously ill, and even now is only allowed to see my father-in-law for ten minutes at a time. It will be an awful disappointment to her, and I'm afraid she will feel it, if possible, more than her similar misfortune in 1896.[12]

Such were the difficulties Ann had that B-T's leave had to be extended. On 7 March 1902, he wrote to Hart:

> 'Tis a long time since my last letter but I can now give you better news of my wife. She has been pretty low at times but has so far proved too tough a morsel for old Death and is really mending. The present trouble is mental instead of physical. Somehow the brain lagged behind and after consulting Dr. Savage,

the mental specialist, it was decided that the best chance lay in putting her where she would be properly treated and kept from all harm. So she is an inmate of St. Andrew's Hospital at Northampton [she was received there on 10 February] and thence come satisfactory reports of her state. The opinion is that the cure is only a matter of a few months. To the outer world she has been ordered complete rest and is away in the country. To you I can tell the real truth. Such a thing was quite unnecessary in my leave, but one must put up with [it] and the two boys and I are keeping house as best we can.[13]

There is a distant feel to the letter; B-T is either stoical or emotionally detached, for he goes on to refer, inter alia, to a professorship in Chinese being established in the United States and the purchasing power of the $5,000 salary. Perhaps this was a hint to Hart that he might consider other pastures, so Hart had better speed up further promotion! Ann was in fact suicidal and suffering from melancholia as well as acute mania; she remained in hospital for some months.[14]

Ann was allowed to go home on trial in June, and she improved sufficiently for the couple to join Alexander Michie at his birthplace, Earlsferry in Scotland. Given what was to happen in the future, it is interesting to note that Michie together with his half-brother, George Thin, had owned a property in Earlsferry, near Elie, in Fifeshire on which there still stands a house called Cathay;[15] according to the title deeds to the house, they had disposed of their interest in the property in favour of Ann Amy Jane in September 1889, a few months after she became 21 years of age. She was then living with her father in Tientsin, several years before she married. Why did they do this, and why to her alone and not her brother? Could it be that they were aware that she was vulnerable in some way and might be in need of support?[16] It was in the garden of this property that Ann had a substantial house built in which B-T spent his retirement, rather resentfully it would seem from his will, and where he was to die.

Michie and the Brewitt-Taylors had gone up to Earlsferry to deal with designs for the house which she was to call 'Cathay',[17] reflecting the strong connections of the family with China, the land of Ann's birth. There, they were to experience yet another shock. Ann's father had returned to London alone, was taken ill on the train, and died unexpectedly on 7 August (two days after Ann had been officially discharged as 'recovered'); the B-Ts had to return to London. He wrote again to Hart from London:

> The shock to my wife was very severe, but we came South on the 9th and the funeral is to take place tomorrow. This leaves us both well and we hope it finds you enjoying the first coolth of Autumn.[18]

The B-T's extended leave had not proved restful. Later, he writes to Hart again, anticipating his return to China and specifically Shanghai. He first requests that he go directly to Shanghai, to save the cost of a separate passage there from Hong Kong, where he would initially be on the Canton List.[19] It is unclear why he should have been on the List or whether his request was granted, it may be he did some Customs work while in Hong Kong. B-T later writes from Cairo, where his sons joined him for Christmas, that he is returning to China with his wife, via Hong Kong.[20] Several of his communications to Hart contain references to money, perhaps a shared interest.

District Postmaster, Shanghai

One of the areas with which the ICMC had been entrusted was the Imperial Post Office; later, in May 1910, this responsibility was ordered to separate from the Customs and was actually transferred the following year, in May 1911, to the Ministry of Posts and Communications.[21] But at this point, the Post was still under the ICMC, and after returning from leave early in 1903, B-T was detached from duty with the Customs to take up a post in Shanghai as the District Postmaster.

For many years since the 1860s, there had been attempts to bring about an organization for the Post at the national level, but it was not until 1896 that a decree established an Imperial Post for the whole of China. Such was the confidence in the ICMC that Hart was given the task to run the Service, and the two organizations operated under the same umbrella, Hart being appointed Postmaster General in addition to being Inspector General; the headquarters of the Chinese Imperial Post Office, under a Postal Secretary, was located in Peking. The role of Hart and the Customs Service in establishing a modern institution has been acknowledged by historians: 'the Chinese Post Office became a model of efficiency and probity'.[22] Yet until around 1917–18, six treaty powers, including Britain, maintained their separate and independent post offices and services.[23]

The volume of postal activity was a useful barometer of the economy. Of 66 million letters and other documents dealt with by the Imperial Post, Shanghai handled 13 million, twice the volume of the next in importance, Tientsin, with 6.5 million; then came Newchwang (now Yingkou) with 5 million, Peking and Canton with 3 million each, and Foochow with 2 million.[24] These statistics, recorded in 1905, reflect the fact that Shanghai was the major economic centre of China, and a new post office was built while B-T was there. Communications in China were often problematic; notices, signed by the district postmaster, were placed in newspapers when delays were expected. B-T, with his unflappable personality, gave a good account of himself.

Generally, Customs commissioners were also ex officio the local postmasters, but Shanghai was sufficiently important for the posts to be separate, with some kind of overall responsibility by the Customs commissioner. Ambiguity between the respective roles could give rise to tensions. Further, T. Piry, the Postal Secretary under Hart, was concerned to create administrative space between the Customs and the Post. He encouraged B-T to keep independent from the Customs while remaining friendly. B-T responds:

> I have taken to heart the advice you gave me as to relations with the Commissioner and, while keeping on friendly terms with him, shall try to make the Post Office independent . . . I think I have tact enough to hold my own without breeding any ill-feeling . . . You know the Post office is not popular in the Service [it was seen as a drain on funds and a bit of empire building by Hart]. You humbly call yourself a 'learner'. I, alas, am only an apprentice in his first year; not yet beyond fetching the workman's beer! But I shall get along.

He goes on to refer to his domestic troubles:

> My wife was dreadfully ill at home but was pulled through. Now she is a veritable anomaly — an invalid, yet in better health than she has been for years and as fat and rosy as a milkmaid.[25]

A related issue to role ambiguity and independence, and one which strongly vexed B-T as the District Postmaster, was his social standing in the Shanghai community.[26] Within a couple of weeks of taking up his post, he complained to Piry, 'I should really rank with a Commissioner — perhaps as Acting Commissioner — and this should be known here.' Another letter around the same time has him stating:

> I do not wish this to be referred to Sir Robert now, but the outer world thinks I'm under a cloud to be sent here and look upon it as Irish promotion [this comment may have been intentionally ironic given Hart's origins!]. The Commissioner's doorkeeper does not think me worth rising from his chair for! But I soon corrected that!'[27]

Conscious of his social origins and having tasted prestige as commissioner in Swatow, he was not intending to lose it.

B-T's concerns became widely known in the Service. Mayer, the Customs commissioner in Canton, later commented to Piry:

> It is well-known that Brewitt-Taylor has found his position in Shanghai a great social handicap — though this may possibly be partly his own fault [no explanation given]. Still with his experience before them, other people are naturally not keen on being appointed 'Postmasters.'

He goes on, concurring with B-T's view about designation and reflecting something of the expatriate social hierarchy:

> My own opinion is that if it is considered necessary to have specially responsible people in charge of certain postal districts, they should be called 'Postal Commissioners'. In view of the somewhat common class of people in charge of the foreign post offices in China, it is not desirable that Service men who are supposed to rank with Commissioners should be called 'Postmasters'.[28]

B-T was to broaden the issue to include problems in recruiting foreigners generally in the Imperial Post Office and wrote a 'Memorandum on the Recruiting of the Foreign Staff of the Imperial Post Office':

> The number of Foreigners on the IPO staff will always be, and must be, small compared with the number of Chinese. Their part being to stiffen the ranks rather than to do the actual fighting, each one should be quite reliable, a condition difficult of attainment so long as men are engaged under the present system, under which choice is practically confined to the flotsam and jetsam of the port.[29]

Preoccupation with status, especially important in that period, tended to be intensified in societies where prestige powerfully determined the nature of social relations. B-T was not immune from the status concerns of the time, his feelings doubtless fostered by the consciousness of his own humble origins.

Status concerns were by no means confined to expatriates, and social inequalities could have odd judicial results. Influential Chinese were attracted to live in the prestigious and relatively well-run International Settlement. A letter from the British Consul General to the British Minister complained that the Mixed Court Chinese magistrate refused to issue summonses on the grounds that the parties concerned were of a higher rank than himself, and therefore he could not hear any case brought against them:

> This means, practically that there is no remedy against Chinese living in the Settlement who may be of higher rank than the magistrate.[30]

It is of course possible that this was a ploy by the magistrate to secure for himself a higher ranking! More likely, the situation reflected prevailing culture.

A flavour of the political and cultural climate B-T engaged in can be seen in other opportunities for tension between the mores of the expatriate community in the International Settlement and those of the local Chinese society. The operation of the Mixed Court, which dealt with legal cases and contained both expatriate and Chinese representation, showed this particularly starkly. Numerically, Chinese in the International Settlement always far exceeded the expatriates, and the Mixed Court dealt with police cases and disputes involving Chinese. A Chinese official represented Shanghai's magistrate and a British consular official sat with him, ensuring that the laws of the International Settlement were implemented.[31]

One example of tension was seen in a controversy which arose around the time that B-T was in Shanghai in 1903 over the handing over of dissidents charged with sedition for producing anti-dynastic literature. The city authorities had initially sentenced the two principal accused men to decapitation, but the International Settlement refused to hand over the defendants. The British Foreign Office argued that as they were arrested in the International Settlement they should be tried in the Mixed Court and not handed over to the Chinese authorities, 'having regard to the barbarous manner in which recent executions was carried out at Peking'. A special sedition trial was held, involving a Chinese representative of the City of Shanghai, the Chinese magistrate of the Mixed Court, and a British assessor. The sentence was commuted to life imprisonment, but even then the assessor would not agree, and the case had to be referred to the central government and the ministers of the foreign powers. It is interesting to note that the Foreign Office raised the hypothetical question with the Consulate whether if there were to be serious danger to the prisoners and an escape to Hong Kong was arranged for them, would such an act raise difficulties between the consuls and the municipality. The episode demonstrates the power exercised by expatriates and their willingness to impose their own values on the local Chinese society.[32] It may be argued this could have had some educative influence on human rights, but at that stage it was more likely simply to increase resentment against the foreigner.

Shanghai was a colourful place to be at the turn of the century, with much going on in its diverse foreign population of around ten thousand. It had become the most dynamic city in China and acquired the reputation of being 'the wickedest city in the World'.[33] At the time B-T was there, the foreign resident was offered opportunity to join a variety of activities. For those, such as B-T, who were less attracted by a hectic social round and the glitter of the city's nightlife, an active intellectual life was also available. Newspapers, such as the well-written *North China Herald,* which had a very wide-ranging coverage of news, and journals, libraries and bookshops of a good standard were close at hand. This is also where the North China Branch of the Royal Asiatic Society was based, with its lectures and discussion groups; it was the meeting place for those with common interests, especially in Chinese language and culture.

One would have thought that B-T would have enjoyed the greater ease of contact with other expatriates, especially those with kindred interests, by being able, for example, to attend meetings more easily in Shanghai than when he was hundreds of miles distant. But as we shall see in the next chapter, the city's dynamism and opportunities held little appeal for our quiet scholar-administrator. It says something about the man that he did not enjoy his life in Shanghai; aside from his concerns over status, he found the city too expensive, busy and noisy. His wife would probably have enjoyed Shanghai, as she was fond of society though she admits her husband was not. The Brewitt-Taylors stayed there for nearly three years, leaving around early December 1905, with B-T taking up position in January 1906 as Acting Commissioner and ex-officio postmaster in Mengtze in Yunnan Province.

Alice Mary, the first Mrs. B-T, née Vale. B-T kept a copy on his study until he died.

B-T with Ann Amy Jane née Michie, his second wife, probably taken at their marriage.

Ann Amy Jane B-T in her fur coat — possibly purchased from looted goods following the Boxer Siege.

The B-Ts with sons from his first marriage, Raymond, aged around 15, rear, Leonard, aged around 18, front.

Picnic at Yellow Temple, near Peking 1900, probably taken just before the Siege:
B-T standing extreme right. Ann, shortest, fifth right rear row, looking directly at camera.

End of Siege, B-T seated first left second row, with flat cap. (Sir Robert Hart is third left rear row.)

Mukden, 5 Dec.

My very dear Daughter,

Your letter of 3 October came the day before yesterday. Thank you for news and for various items of information, which are interesting.

You must not be too hard upon us who go abroad, dear. Some times we can secure certain ends that way and the road looks easy when one is young. Now when all my looks are directed backward perhaps I see more clearly all that I have lost. But I do not repent. Up to a certain point I have done what I set out to do and I shall pass on leaving my deeds to bear what fruit they may.

I have written you asking you to try to keep Ray's things till I come home. I will stand all the expenses, dear, hire of room, storage, cartage and so on. Please keep a note of all such spendings and of all fees you have had to pay. You are not to stand any such things. We can get at grips with things

---

First page of letter from B-T to daughter-in-law Evelyn, written following his son's death.

Alexander Michie, Snr.

B-T, aged around 71, with grand-daughter
Joan, and Jock at Earlsferry, Fife. The B-T's
home 'Cathay' appears on left.

Newly engaged: Raymond (standing) with Evelyn Ellis,
Roy Suttill with Daisy Ellis in Inglefield garden.

B-T and new daughter-in-law in a 'droshky' in Mukden.

The Ellis family. Peg is centre first row, her daughters, Winnie end left first row,
Daisy end right first row, Evelyn front right, sons Bernard third left rear row,
Edward end right rear row.

10

Discord in Mengtze

Mengtze was to provide a most contrasting experience to Shanghai. It was also to prove a critical testing point in the lives of B-T and his wife. In terms of work, it helped to establish his reputation, but for domestic harmony and his marital relationship, his time in this peaceful place was to prove catastrophic.

Around the time that B-T went to Mengtze in 1906, wider changes were taking place in the aftermath of the Boxer collapse and the subsequent settlements with foreigners. This was a period of considerable administrative change in China, and the Customs Service was not unaffected. The Tsungli Yamen, which had been the office responsible for the ICMC, had already been replaced by the Waiwupu, the Foreign Affairs Department. In 1906, an imperial edict announced the appointment of a special commission to oversee the Customs; this was seen as a possible step towards eliminating dependence on foreigners. About the same time, Hart announced his intention to retire, something he had hinted at for years. This might have been somewhat unsettling for B-T, as he clearly got on well with him, though given Hart's age (seventy-one), retirement was hardly unexpected. The *North China Herald* published a special late news supplement to report these events, suggesting that Hart's brother-in-law Bredon would probably take over. Never reluctant to present its views, the newspaper dealt with the independence issue:

> That the Chinese will some day be capable of managing the Customs and
> Postal services as efficiently as now, we do not doubt; but that day is a long
> way off.

There was no objection to the arrangement for a special commission: 'the High Commissioner Tieh Liong and the Vice-Commissioner Tang Shao-yi are men of note and ability'; the writer considered that reference to them of issues by the Inspector may be preferable to 'the notoriously dilatory' Waiwupu.[1]

In many parts of China, small communities of expatriates formed synaptic links for extending and sustaining trade at numerous strategic points. The small Yunnan town of Mengtze in southwest China, close to the border with French Indo-

China (now Vietnam), was one such place. It had been opened for trade in 1887 under the French Treaty of Tientsin signed in that year. The Customs had opened on 1 January, 1890. New dwelling houses for Customs staff were built in 1894, and a new Customs house in 1895.

Mengtze, an islolated spot, would have not been without its dangers. For example, the new Customs house together with the French Consulate had been looted in 1899.[2] Even getting there, as with other remote places in China, had its problems. Another Englishman, who was to become famous as the plant-hunter 'Chinese' Wilson, went to Mengtze around the turn of the century. His diaries illustrate the hazards of the long and arduous journey, which B-T was to undertake just a few years later. These included passing through areas where epidemics raged, having boats capsize, and having person and property attacked by robbers.

Wilson went to the area on the first of his four trips to China en route for a remote Yunnan location, Szemao, to meet another ICMC employee, Dr. Augustine Henry. Henry was a medical officer who took up plant collecting and successfully sent many species to England; he also appears on the list of Customs commissioners for Mengtze in 1899/1900. Wilson's sponsors were especially concerned to obtain seed and data on the precise location of the rare *Davidia* (the 'dove' or 'handkerchief' tree, which has spectacular white bracts); Henry was alleged to know where to find it, but as it turned out his knowledge was vague. Wilson embarked on an arduous three-year expedition to find the tree.

To get to Mengtze, Wilson travelled via Hong Kong to Haiphong by sea, which took five days, and then by river overnight to Hanoi in Annam, where the French were intensifying their colonization of French Indo-China. There, he met a Frenchman taking up an appointment with the ICMC at Mengtze. After another five days by river steamer, they learnt that travelling further would be very unsafe for foreigners, as the French insistence on building a railway line to Yunnanfu (Kunming) had increased anti-European hostility. At Mengtze, another nine days distant, the Customs house had been razed to the ground, 'the Commissioner, his wife and members of his staff had escaped in their night-clothes pursued by a frenzied mob'. Wilson was also informed that four men had just been murdered on their way to Mengtze, so he had to wait some weeks before the route became safe. While waiting in the unhealthy small village located in the jungle, there were daily burials of people dying of an epidemic during the rainy season that summer of 1899. On reaching Mengtze on 1 September, he was greeted by the grim sight of five heads of rioters suspended in wooden cages.[3]

Taking a similar route, B-T and his wife arrived on 5 January 1906 into this unpromising situation, to take up his position as Acting Commissioner on 8 January. As expected, the journey had been arduous.[4] The previous commissioner, Neumann, had had to leave his post on medical advice, needing attention in Hong Kong for his deteriorating health; however, he did not survive the journey. The announcement of his death commented that his demise will be

> regretted by all in Yunnan, foreigners and Chinese. He was extremely popular and his hospitable home in Mengtze was open to all.[5]

B-T had his predecessor's reputation to live up to.

A major railway linking Hanoi to Yunnanfu was being built by the French, aided by Italians. Much later, in 1930, Edgar Snow regarded the railway as one of the engineering marvels of the Orient:

> It is a remarkable railway, conceived with such audacity as to leave you at the end of your trip breathless and admiring . . . The mountain locomotive puffs and snorts red cinders into the solemn woods as it digs deeper into the rocky heights. There is a moment of suspense when you cross a lank bridge with no guard rail, its legs resting on huge boulders, straddling a snarling stream a hundred feet below . . . It is a superb, daring exploit, this railway. The breadth of image behind it and the faith in its purpose reveal boldness and emprise.[6]

A few years earlier than Snow, in 1922, the novelist Stella Benson, the recently wed wife of James (Shaemas) Anderson who later became a Customs commissioner, gave an account of their arrival and life in Mengtze. Apart from the warlords and the bandits probably having further strengthened their position, Mengtze was likely to have changed little since the time that B-T was there.

Perry Anderson, son of James, describes the situation:

> Yunnan, famous for its natural beauty and hospitable climate, was a province of China whose remoteness and many ethnic minorities made its warlords virtually independent rulers. . . Banditry was rife around Mengtze . . . but politically the area was quiet.[7]

The spectacular setting as the Andersons arrive by railway from Indo-China is portrayed by Benson:

> Our train seemed to have reached the sky and ran mildly and austerely over sort of downs of grass and flowers, perforated with great gashes of bloodied earth, and suddenly we were looking from very high up over an enormous plain set in a ring of mountains like long red receding waves on a beach: in the middle of the plain, among crops and beside an indeterminate lake, was Mengtze, a round town set in trees.[8]

Mengtze was in the province of Yunnan on which Joy Grant, Benson's biographer, comments:

> In the 1920s it was still an industrial backwater, its hinterland home to tribes of shy semi-nomads, and infested with gangs of bandits who periodically

issued forth to plunder the villages and waylay, and sometimes capture and hold to ransom, the unwary foreigner. Mengtze, some fifty miles up the line from the frontier, served as a border post of the Customs; it was manned by five Europeans and a handful of subordinate Chinese.[9]

Benson's first impressions of the Customs staff compound had been encouraging:

> A fine well-treed compound full of birds and shade and the sweeping lines of eucalyptus trees and big rose trees, and rather dull flowers in pots. The birds are magpies and egrets and hoopoes and there are unseen birds singing constantly. The three houses . . . are built Chinese style with upturned wavy-tiled roofs and whitewashed walls and rough wooden pillars with a little blue and green painting beneath the eaves.[10]

Benson was not at all happy with the limited range of people she was to meet: two English couples and the small French community consisting of the consul, doctor, railway manager, schoolmaster, bank manager and their wives who provided an endless round of At Homes, teas, and dinners and constantly played cards, chess, and tennis. Even in that remote area formality was important, and social calls by the ladies demanded the wearing of hats and gloves.[11] Benson found the social atmosphere suffocating, and portrays a dismal picture of Mengtze and its pathetic shopping booths. But by 11 November she records 'I like being here'.

Another observer, writing at the time the Brewitt-Taylors were there, tells of 'a small club (the Cercle du Commerce) with a billiard table and tennis courts' enjoyed by the foreign residents, mostly French and Italians, then mainly engaged in the railway construction.[12]

The lifestyle must have been not too dissimilar for the Brewitt-Taylors, for B-T also refers to riding and walking, tennis, fêtes and other parties. But the couple appear to have enjoyed the place and its stimulating setting at 4,500 feet, at least B-T did, since the situation appealed to his retiring nature and was certainly preferable to the bustle of Shanghai. An early semi-official report in April 1906 reads lyrically:

> This place has a delicious climate and the feeling of peace after the noise of Shanghai is very refreshing. Our night noises are the bark of the occasional dog; our day, the chirping and singing of many birds. The customs compound is quiet and the birds are never disturbed; as a natural consequence the place is full of them.[13]

Threats from banditry were compensated by a general tranquillity.

In June of that year, it seemed that B-T would be asked to return to Shanghai to head up the Statistical Department. The importance of the post is partially demonstrated by the fact that it was the head of that department who had assumed the role of Acting Inspector General during the Siege of the Legations. Yet despite the seniority it would have given him, B-T was very reluctant to take the posting:

> Both of us are pretty well used to Mengtze now. You know we have a beautiful compound the envy of the whole place and we are able therewith to play the grand seigneur in graciously letting people into our 'park' as they call it.

Signalling the useful work he was doing, he refers to a party he gave to a visiting French governer general, letting his boss know the careful work he had put into it: 'I think it was a success . . . we took a good deal of trouble over the arrangements.' The following year, he recorded that the Empress of Annam (now central Vietnam and then part of French Indo-China) conferred on his wife a decoration called a 'kinboy', a medallion of thin gold, as a compliment to the hostess for the visit.[14]

B-T's wife also enjoyed Mengtze and her status there. Writing much later, she recalls the beauty of the place and their position:

> I was much more happy than before being chief's wife with every luxury and everyone paying me homage, of a large staff with many nationals and I was looked up to by the other people in the place, as my husband was a leader.[15]

B-T's June 1906 report adds:

> The weather is good and as we have forgotten the rough road up, so we think not of the rough road down . . . I should not care to go back to Shanghai. It is an expensive place, very distasteful to me, and my trip here cost me a fair amount.

Then, as if reminding himself that the Inspector General had a reputation for sometimes deriving satisfaction from demonstrating his powers to award and deny favours, he quickly adds:

> But I am ready to leave, as I have ever been, to obey orders and do my work as well as I can, without regard to my private feelings. ['What a fine fellow', I noted to myself as I read this in the archives.]

B-T had also heard of the possible new edition of a well-used Customs textbook and adds, in what today seems a somewhat obsequious tone:

> Finally, Sir Robert, if it be thought I am the man to attend the re-editing and the key, I can only say 'Here I am, send me.'[16]

B-T's responsibilities in Mengtze were unlikely to have been time-demanding, and he was able to focus on his literary and related work. The Customs publication referred to was the major *Textbook of Documentary Chinese; For the Special Use of the Chinese Customs Service*, which had originally been edited by Dr. Friedrich

Hirth. The first volume had been published twenty years previously, in 1885, and the second volume of vocabulary came out in 1888. Hirth was one of China's most eminent sinologists; he replaced Giles as President of the NBRAS in 1885. He resigned from the Customs Service in 1897, becoming a member of the Bavarian Academy until 1902, when he was appointed professor of Chinese at Columbia University.[17] The fact that B-T was granted the task of following him for the second edition was an accolade in itself, a tribute to the recognition of his mastery of Chinese. B-T's edition was more than a revision: it completely reconstructed and enlarged the work, and Hirth's title was slightly modified, B-T inserting 'Modern' before 'Documentary'. The work is cited as one of three important translations of Ch'ing documents.[18] He must have thrown himself into the work, which he claimed was done entirely in his own time, rising early in the morning for the task. His first volume, published in 1909, is divided into seven sections which include valuable and most interesting material on the working of the Customs and areas which impinged on Customs activities; the second volume, which was the Chinese key, was published in 1910.[19] The same edition was considered of sufficient worth to be published again in Taiwan sixty years later, in 1968, though at that time there was a good deal of republishing of books on China going on in Taiwan. This was B-T's last known published writing before he recompleted his more famous translation of the *San Kuo*.

His semi-official reports to the Inspector General give some indication of his work concerns in Mengtze. There had been a suggestion when B-T arrived that there might be a joint customs arrangement with the French as they were already highly prominent in the area.[20] But the proposal for a joint arrangement was seen as a potential source of trouble, and the idea was abandoned soon after B-T arrived, though it was resuscitated later. In February 1906, he expressed worries about the local price of salt, and later in the same month he drew attention to the need for repairs to the compound: the wood was needing protective paint and trees were growing too close to the walls, undermining the Customs house. Also, 'the magic of the lake was worn away by the feet of packs of animals who drink therefrom', so a retaining wall needed to be built. In April, he is pleased to report an increase in Customs income on the previous year, before his arrival: 'We have made a fine collection for the first quarter, an advance of 20,000 taels on the first quarter of 1905.' He adds without comment: 'The increase was chiefly in opium.'[21]

Yunnan was important for the export of tin, tea and opium. B-T was most concerned about the price of the last commodity, being so important for Customs revenues, than the morality of the trade; the dominant purpose of the Customs was to raise revenue, anything detracting from that was seen as a problem. B-T expressed his major preoccupation a little later that year:

I think the new opium rules will knock a very promising year's revenue to pieces, we have done well to date.[22]

Opium continued to feature frequently in B-T's reports throughout his stay in Mengtze, recording its vacillations as a revenue source. At the end of the following summer, after noting another fall in revenues from opium, he comments: 'I hope business will look up in the presence of a prospect of a favourable harvest.'[23] Nearing the end of his stay there, he closed an establishment used for the sale of illicit, that is, custom-avoided, opium. He also referred to arms smuggling, which he tried to put down but does not note whether he was successful.

Earlier in the year the Brewitt-Taylors arrived, an article appeared in the *North China Herald* on the progress of extending the railway line from Tonkin in French Indo-China to Laokai. The line was being extended from its then terminus in Yenbai for another ninety miles to Laokai. This was the most difficult portion of the line, and there had been considerable delays in building. The line ran through the valley of the Namti, a tributary of the main river, the Red River. Namti was 'the most unwholesome place in Yunnan', to which all approaches were unhealthy. Three thousand of the five thousand coolies employed on the project had died as well as over thirty Europeans. The correspondent thought that though it had been due to be completed in the April of 1905, it was unlikely to be completed for another five years; he complained that the French had insisted on an especially difficult location despite being advised of a preferable route.[24]

In June 1906, B-T decided to undertake a journey through the remote area, over a hundred miles away, in order to get a first-hand view of the railway-building problems. His report illustrates some of the dangers, inconveniences and sheer unpleasantness of getting around, demonstrating a certain humour as well as stoicism:

> Travelling in Yunnan one has to take food, cooking gear, bedding, and, in fact everything. The inns supply neither fire nor hot water: food is out of the question. The Red River craft are very rough and very flimsy-looking for the work they do, but they mostly get over the rapids without incident. In going down one rapid we bumped a rock heavily and had to run ashore and re-caulk ... The journey down was not unpleasant as the head breeze was cool and we made good time. Coming up the heat and damp were very trying. Heat and damp mean insects of all kinds ... You may be at dinner and a flattish pointed-headed creature alights on one of your precious loaves, precious because you never know how long the river journey will last ... . the aroma he gave the loaf is indescribable ... . I was very glad to get home again.

B-T also acted in the role of negotiator between the French and the local Chinese community. For example, had been looking at properties in Hokou needed for the extension of the railway, which may have required getting rid of a tree with its animistic connotations; building a small temple would have been 'a sop to the spirit of the tree', but the railway company treated this as an attempt at 'squeeze' and had to be persuaded otherwise.[25] The role of cultural intermediary could be an important function for Customs commissioners, conveying to foreigners Chinese attitudes and practices which were alien and difficult to comprehend. The Annam-Yunnan Railway, running 420 kilometres from Hanoi to Yunnanfu, was eventually opened in 1910.

Visitors to Mengtze were rare, and B-T gives accounts of a couple of odd travellers. One he describes as an Irishman, Crawley [sic], who having climbed in Mexico and the Alps, tried to climb Kanchinjunga in Nepal with his wife and baby. They failed. The Brewitt-Taylors gave him and his family hospitality, though B-T had doubts about this self-proclaimed mountaineer and writer: 'Altogether he is a queer man, such an one as is usually styled mad as a hatter.'[26]

His assessment was prescient, for the man turned out to be Aleister Crowley, an extraordinary personality who became notorious for his involvement with the occult; he was also an accomplished mountaineer.[27] Crowley later settled for some years in Sicily, until rumours of drugs, sexual orgies and magical ceremonies involving the sacrifice of babies culminated in his expulsion from Italy. B-T would not have known about him in 1906, though a series of newspaper articles after B-T retired brought Crowley the notoriety he craved. Crowley liked to be known as 'the Great Beast'. Whether he regarded himself as the devil incarnate is not certain, but he was a Satanist, dubbed 'the wickedest man alive' by the press. Several people associated with him died tragically, including his wife, said by Crowley to be an alcoholic, and their child.[28]

Crowley left a description of his visit to Mengtze:

> A French outpost with all the civilization, culture and cooking that heart of man can wish. The inspector of customs, Mr. Brewitt Taylor, very kindly asked us to stay in his house, though at first sight he could hardly believe that I was an Englishman. The journey had reduced me to rags; I had no chance of washing or trimming my beard; the skin on my face was torn by the wind. I must have looked simply frightful. (I still do.)
>
> We only stayed three days in Mengtsz in spite of the attraction of the little French colony. Everyone invited us everywhere, including a garden party where I played lawn tennis for the first time in ten years.[29]

Crowley's writing at this stage in his life did not obviously display the oddness that B-T discerned. He was about thirty years old when he went to Mengtze in 1906; he died, a heroin addict, in Hastings in 1947. It must have been an odd encounter: the reserved scholar-bureaucrat hosting the Great Beast-to-be.

Another unusual arrival given hospitality by the Brewitt-Taylors was an Englishman, Lorrimer. He was walking around the world for a wager, entirely on his own, and had arrived in Yunnan via India and Burma. He had come on foot all the way so far, and after Mengtze he was making his way to Haiphong and Hong Kong.[30]

Such visitors were obviously a welcome diversion for the small community. There were, however, other, more familiar diversions, for life in a small, socially intense community had the potential for a perennial problem: adultery. Benson comments on 'a customs colleague in the throes of a long-drawn-out affair with the wife of a French official, given to "amorous yap".'[31] B-T had to deal with a similar situation which took on more drama when another Frenchman, one of his staff, Noel, whose wife had fallen in love with another man, was arrested. Noel had decided to shoot them both but only managed to kill the lover. The wife took an overdose of morphine, but she survived the suicide attempt and gave evidence on behalf of her husband, who was eventually acquitted; they were required to leave Mengtze, and B-T heard later that they divorced.[32]

It was while B-T was in Mengtze that he decided to establish himself further in China, purchasing land in far-off Peitaiho [Beidaihe], a growing holiday resort for expatriates, with six miles of beach around two hundred miles from Tientsin.[33] In the 1890s Peitaiho's popularity increased, with its use as a welcome summer escape by British railway engineers building the line from Tientsin to Mukden: 'as a health giving, cool summer residence it is unsurpassed in China or Japan'.[34] But many houses there had been destroyed and looted during the Boxer Uprising,[35] so even a few years later, prices may have been low. B-T invested in three substantial plots bordering one another (Lots 31, 32, and 33) on 16 January 1906; he may have put this purchase in train earlier, giving power-of-attorney to a lawyer in Tientsin for the purpose. The plots were purchased 'in perpetuity' from Chinese owners. Whether he built any houses other than his own bungalow is not known. Much later, on 3 February 1915, he was to buy another plot in the same resort (Lot 84); this is especially interesting given his domestic circumstances at that date, for by then his wife had gone to Scotland to live. Ownership continued well into retirement, which suggests he was envisaging a long-term relationship with China, though he may have seen the enterprise entirely as a potentially profitable investment.[36]

Intermittent knowledge of B-T's personal life was provided by the regular semi-official reports written by commissioners; this was especially true in his early years as commissioner, when Hart was still Inspector General. For example, while in Mengtze, B-T relates that he received 'a wire' informing him that his elder son, Leonard, then aged twenty-one, was embarking on his career: 'my boy has started for Bangkok. His race has begun.'[37] Much more ominously, by the end of his first year in Mengtze, intimations are given of B-T's concerns regarding his wife's health.

'I and mine are well though the wife has been a little seedy just lately: the weather I suppose', he adds hopefully.[38] But he must have been sufficiently anxious to have mentioned this.

A few days later and sounding fine, B-T's wife writes a long, seven-page, well-expressed and confident letter to Hart while he is summering in Peitaiho. She refers to the visit Hart had received from his wife and daughter and expresses regret over news of his impending retirement: 'But what are we going to do? One cannot help selfish reflections, however genuine our sympathies with our friends.' She then requests a photograph of him to add to the one he gave her in 1892, fourteen years before. She goes on to describe something of the happy life she and B-T are enjoying in Mengtze, mentioning how the women run one another down:

> They don't get on very well among themselves, but we try to manage our intercourse with them all, by being friendly with all but not too much so with any.

This probably referred to the largely French community, for she complains of the tiresomeness of speaking French all the time. She also details the congenial English staff in the Customs, Saker and Wilson, and describes the active social round:

> Charlie and I have become quite gay here, and lead a life quite the reverse of the one we had in Shanghai. And one that suits me very much better. I am naturally fond of Society which my husband is not, but the pleasant life here — the relief from the strain and tension of Shanghai, and the comfortable surrounding and close contact with nature have opened out his heart like a Peitaiho sunflower turning to the light.
>
> We give tennis parties constantly, the grounds are so lovely, and dinner parties — all but dances (which I am afraid these floors would not stand the strain of!).
>
> Sometimes, only occasionally, as I see the sun set gloriously behind the wall of great mountains which surrounds our little basin-plain, I have a feeling of being left behind, and wish I could go with him [B-T on his official trips] and just look up my far away friends . . .
>
> Our two great fetes are over. The one for entertaining the Governor, whom we found charming — and the one for the fourteenth of July. You would be surprised to see how many people could be mustered on these occasions in our tiny community.

Ann signs off familiarly with her nickname, 'Birdie'.[39]

Those trips away probably explain how B-T was able to obtain the documents needed for his *Textbook of Modern Documentary Chinese* which were unlikely to have been available in remote Mengtze. He must have used the opportunity to ferret out and discuss what might be useful to include.

Despite the happy tone of Ann's letter, a month later B-T refers again to his wife's being 'a little under par'. By the end of the year, he admits to the problem having been more serious, though he tries to appear optimistic. He blames the Boxer troubles for the problem:

> I have had some private worries but they have pretty well disappeared. The worries of 1900 seem to have affected my wife more deeply than I thought.

He adds with fortitude, 'but this is one of the things one meets in the day's work'.[40] We shall see that the situation had already gone well beyond this. Yet given that there had already been some history of frailty as we saw earlier, it is somewhat surprising that past instances of his wife's mental instability do not appear to have had a serious affect on B-T. He may not have wished to admit to others (or even, perhaps, fully to himself) that there was a deep-seated longer-term problem. While the reports make no further reference to the situation, his wife's condition had already worsened considerably.

Psychiatric disorders, which is what this proved to be, were by no means rare among expatriate wives, especially in isolated outposts. A number of commentators have noted that conditions of life were likely to foster any predisposition towards mental instability.[41] Another commissioner colleague, Morse, thought his own wife's ill health was exacerbated by the Shanghai Mixed Court troubles of 1905, which gave rise to waves of anti-foreigner riots. Morse's wife probably suffered from a form of schizophrenia.[42] The Brewitt-Taylors were also in Shanghai around the time of the same troubles. The condition of B-T's wife could have been another factor in his preference for the serenity and isolation of Mengtze, in addition to simply preferring a quieter lifestyle.

Serenity, however, was soon to be shattered. One of the men Ann referred to in her letter to Hart as 'congenial' proved overly so. A deterioration in her condition was associated with a strong romantic attachment she developed with Richard Maxwell Saker, one of the young members of B-T's staff. B-T had arranged for Saker to sleep in his guest room while he was away on Customs business, to protect Ann from unsavoury characters in the locality. After returning, B-T began to suspect that a romance had developed, and believing his wife to have been unfaithful, he was, according to his wife, furious with jealousy: 'If you had not been ploughing with my heifer', he thundered at Saker with uncharacteristic crudity and display of emotion, continuing with more than a touch of hurt pride, 'you would not have guessed my riddle.' The 'riddle' presumably was his inability to satisfy his wife physically.[43] Saker resigned in October and left Mengtze;[44] the distraught Ann had to be hospitalized in the small local French hospital. There she remained, apart from a short break, for several months from around late autumn 1906 to May 1907, when arrangements were made for her to be accompanied back to Britain for more professional treatment. On arrival, she was received into the mental asylum, Bethlem, in London, where she spent a further seven months. Conceivably, B-T's practice of keeping his first wife's photograph on his desk dates from this time.

How far the relationship actually went between Ann and Saker cannot be known. But the sudden immediate resignation suggests guilt. Given the circumstances, one could understand Saker's sudden departure from Mengtze, but why resign the Service immediately rather than go to Peking to protest his innocence? Of course, there may have been other factors at work. Years later, Ann denied that the romance was fully physically consummated, despite B-T's obvious belief, according to her, that it was. The romance could well have been heightened on her part by being flattered by the flirtatious attentions of a much younger man, contrasting with her unexciting, older husband, and on Saker's part by the frisson of enjoying some kind of intimacy with the chief's wife.[45]

There is nothing in B-T's reports to the Inspector General which refers to his wife's hospitalization in Mengtze, or her return to Britain; nor, understandably, is there any hint that the illicit romances encouraged in the intense small expatriate community had affected B-T more intimately than he would have wished. All this must have been conveyed to Hart by other means and was likely to have accounted for the sudden departure of Saker, as well as the understandable absence of any of this in the semi-official reports. In the small, intimate society of Mengtze, rumours of the affair would have abounded; the stories would also have insinuated themselves into the wider world of the Customs, possibly even fostered by the young Saker's boasting of his conquest, unless he was too embarrassed by the affair.

What is extraordinary is that several years later, Ann was to reveal all this in a highly vivid account of her own early sexual discovery, her continued romantic obsession for Saker, and her obvious mental delusion. She is amazingly frank about how she feels about her husband, throwing light on their marital relationship. It is a remarkably explicit record in a period when insightful statements of this kind were rare. Knowledge of her mental instability and her romantic attachment in the expatriate world where respectability was paramount must have affected the Brewitt-Taylors and their self-awareness throughout the rest of their time in China. Compassion might have coexisted with malicious gossip, but I could find nothing about how the couple were actually perceived.

Ann was accompanied home with difficulty.[46] Now alone, B-T must have given considerable thought to his situation. In November of 1907, he anticipated his impending leave, and with it a change of post. Anxious to get away to see his family again, B-T was especially annoyed when his successor, Houston, decided to take a different route from the one that B-T advised, arriving in Mengtze a month late. He complained that if Houston had taken his advice, 'He could easily have been here by Xmas eve.' B-T's final report from Mengtze states with some irritation that he now expects to get away for home leave late in January 1908.[47]

Mengtze had marked a significant period for B-T. Temperamentally, he was well-suited to the location which he had initially enjoyed; he had also neared completion of his radically revised edition of the *Textbook of Modern Documentary Chinese,* which was to further enhance his reputation as a translator. However, his domestic life was shattered by his wife's perceived infidelity and the intensification of her mental instability. He must have made the journey home filled with apprehension.

11

B-T's Sons and the Ellises

Leave and Family

B-T's leave situation in 1908 is somewhat hazy, as he does not appear to have taken the normal quinquennial one-year leave. He returned to Britain in March, and soon after he arranged for his wife to be taken from Bethlem Hospital; on 1 April 1908 she was discharged 'well'. By May of that year, B-T was still in London, as he undertook some Customs work in the ICMC London office. He and his wife must have returned to China by the summer, for his younger son, Raymond, now a medical student in London, came to Peking to be with him in August; Raymond rather reluctantly also visited his stepmother in Peitaiho. Robert Hart had already left for England in May 1908, technically going on leave, but in fact never to return. Before leaving, Hart made various changes at the top of the organization, and it is likely that he had made it clear to B-T that in promoting him to the rank of full commissioner in the inspector general's office in Peking, together with becoming Co-Director of a new Customs College, he was to have a shortened leave that year. This could also have been a way of compensating for the long period he was away for his previous home leave when his wife was in hospital and her father died. Returning to China early enabled B-T to undertake preparations for the new college.

The period of leave could not have been easy for the Brewitt-Taylors. Outwardly, B-T would have been achieving considerable success in the Customs, with his full commissionership and being effectively director of the Customs College; of this he would have been proud. But his private world would have been clouded by his wife's mental condition, the niggling memory of her romantic attachment and the embarrassing awareness that both were probably public knowledge in the circles in which they moved.

The Brewitt-Taylor and Ellis Families

Back in London, B-T's sons had both attended the University College School in London's Hampstead, where Leonard, the elder son, before leaving school had become a close friend of another boy in the same class, Edward Ellis. Edward, six months Leonard's senior, came from a large, prosperous and lively family which was to become significant in B-T's personal life.

Edward's father, Henry Ellis, was the grandson of William Ellis, descendant of a Huguenot refugee. William Ellis had combined a successful career in marine insurance with a strong interest in education and had published innovative ideas which attracted attention.[1] The grandson, Henry Ellis, was apparently more interested in natural history, collecting butterflies, fossils (one of his finds, an ichthyosaurus, is still prominently displayed in the Lyme Regis Museum), astronomy and playing music than he was in the family business, and he was later to take early retirement to pursue his interests.

Edward's mother, Margaret Ellis, known as Peg, was a strong positive influence in the family She was the daughter of Henry Morley, an early pioneer in establishing English as an area of study in the universities. He became professor of English Literature at University College, London, the first British university to create a chair in English, and was said to be 'the foremost popularizer of English literature, particularly of Shakespeare, of the late Victorian era. Morely had high ideals, impressive teaching qualities, 'and the courage to introduce a great range of innovations'.[2]

For over forty years, Peg and her four brothers and sisters regularly wrote what they called a 'budge', a monthly account by each of their activities during the preceding month which they sent to one another as a means of keeping in touch. Peg's budges are in the possession of my wife; they make a fascinating historical record of domestic life in an upper middle-class family from 1900 to the early 1940s. They have been an important source for learning about the increasingly close contact between the Ellis and Brewitt-Taylor families.

Family life with the Ellises, unstuffy Unitarians, was lively, stimulating and warm. Their lifestyle was comfortable but not flamboyant; their dominant characteristic was their hospitable welcome and acceptance of people. To Leonard Brewitt-Taylor, with the loss of his mother and disrupted family life, the Ellis home became an idyllic haven. He does not seem to have visited the large family house, Inglefield, at Potter's Bar until after he and Edward Ellis had left school. Edward, especially interested in botany, went to an agricultural college, Cooper's Hill at Egham in Surrey, to study forestry. Leonard had wanted to attend the same college, but he had not done sufficiently well in his examinations to be admitted.

In the autumn of 1902, Edward having just started college, found no congenial friend among the students. His mother, Peg, wrote:

> I am most sorry that his old school-fellow, Brewitt-Taylor, did not get through.
> He is a thoroughly good young fellow and the two would have kept together.

Leonard Brewitt-Taylor's first visit to the Ellis family home in October of that year was to collect a prize that his brother, Raymond, still at the UCS, had won; the prize had awaited collection since the summer. Peg had been gardening and had been suitably dressed for that activity, with muddy boots on; Leonard arrived

> attired sprucely for making a call and I should think made a note that he needn't trouble to be very tidy another time. We had a good talk and he stopped for family tea.[3]

There were five children in the Ellis family: Edward was the eldest at eighteen years old, Bernard was seventeen and still at UCS, then there were the girls — Winnie aged fifteen; Margaret, known as Daisy, thirteen; and Evelyn, just eleven years of age. The girls were educated at home and developed into an attractive trio with wide interests; they were adequate linguists and talented musicians, giving local concerts with their father. Winnie, the only girl of the family not to marry, became a well-regarded amateur violinist, as well as something of a naturalist; her notebooks record birdsong in musical notation.

Leonard and Raymond Brewitt-Taylor

Having failed to get into the agricultural college, Leonard was studying Chinese interpretership through evening classes at King's College and was living with a German family to improve his German. It would appear that his intention was to join the Consular Service. He began to be a regular visitor to Inglefield. The following Easter, the Ellises invited him and his younger brother, Raymond, who was then fifteen years old and still at UCS, to stay for the holiday. Peg anticipated their visit:

> I hope the younger one will not feel too shy to enjoy himself. He is said by his brother to be very bashful . . . I asked them both because they must like to be together in the holidays, as they usually see each other about once a week. Their parents are in China.[4]

She need not have been concerned, for the following month she reports that after the visit, two letters of thanks arrived from the boys

> very characteristic of the two youths. They are the Polite Person and the Imp. The elder is six months younger than Edward, but he is a polished gentleman. The younger is a long-legged fellow of 15, bidding fair to beat his brother in height, though he is 5'11". The Imp was silent at first, but by degrees sly jokes began to break forth. He has roguish dark eyes with very black lashes, a funny mouth that seems made to laugh, and walks erect with his head held high.

Leonard's politeness rather bemused the somewhat casual family, but he was obviously attracted by their welcome warmth and soon became a frequent visitor:

> In the morning he read to me while I worked and after lunch we all played croquet not very scientifically as our tennis lawn is not very flat. I see he has been here three times this month.

Leonard enjoyed walking and cycling as well as chatting with Peg. Having lost his own mother when he was six, and having probably left home a couple of years after his father's second marriage, he would have been drawn to her friendliness. And she grew fond of him. In the autumn of 1905, she writes: 'I suppose Leonard will go to China very soon, and we shall miss him.' Edward, her son, had completed his forestry course and was preparing to take up an appointment in Burma. Leonard passed his Chinese interpretership examinations, but instead of going to China he took up a post with the Consular Service in Siam, and later that year the University College School magazine reports that he joined the Consular Service in Bangkok.[5] After passing competitive examinations on 13 October 1905, he was appointed a student interpreter, the normal route for anyone envisaging a career in the Service, and went to Siam on 17 November; the post paid £200 a year, plus quarters and passage, and he was required to devote himself to studying the local language. He resigned on 4 May 1907,[6] but stayed in the country, having found work with the Bombay-Burma Trading Company, mainly dealing in teak, which is likely to have suited his interest in forestry. Leonard may have gone to Siam instead of China to work in forestry and have easier contact with Edward.

With three attractive girls in the Ellis family, it would have been surprising if one of them did not appeal to this maturing, polite young man, and indeed family lore has it that Daisy, the liveliest of the girls, attracted Leonard's interest. Certainly, Daisy, when she was fifteen, records Leonard's frequent visits in her diaries (sometimes almost daily); they had long talks together: '4.30 Leo came. He up into nursery and we sat on sofa and talked, each with a cat, by firelight.'[7] By the end of 1905, Leonard was on his way to Siam. Daisy, by then aged around sixteen, and something of a honeypot for the buzzing boys that attended her at dances, was not at that stage ready for a serious relationship, though she enjoyed mild flirtations.

Raymond, Leonard's younger brother, then started going on his own to the house more frequently. 'He will miss his brother', writes Peg, 'who has always arranged everything for him'.[8] The budges give accounts of long cycle rides with Peg and the remaining son, Bernard, or with the girls, never with one only, and spending Christmas holidays with the family. In 1906, aged eighteen, Ray matriculated, having taken two shots at it, and went to medical school at St. Bartholomew's Hospital in London. While he and Bernard were at school at the same time, they were two years apart in age and not likely to have had much contact there. But during this post-school period, their friendship became closer; Bernard, the elder of the two, was articled to be a solicitor. They spent many holidays together, mountaineering in the Lake District and the Alps.

About this time, from about 1907, another young man, Roy Suttill, also started to visit the Ellis house. He came from Bridport, where his Unitarian family attended the chapel where Peg's sister's husband, Henry Shaen Solly, was minister. The Ellis and Suttill families had met attending the same chapel. Roy had just completed his studies at Oundle public school and had gone to London to take up articles in accountancy. He was another young man for whom Inglefield became a haven; an additional incentive, doubtless, was the Ellis daughters. If Leonard still had yearnings for Daisy from distant Siam, they were to be frustrated by this new arrival on the scene.

By the time B-T came on leave in 1908, both his sons were well on their respective ways to their careers. The boys must have known of Ann's fragility from her period in Bethlem; they were less likely to have known about her suspected infidelity.

12

The Customs College and Leave

On returning from a short leave accompanied by Ann, B-T took up his position as full Commissioner at the ICMC Headquarters, Peking. From the quiet backwater of Mengtze, he and his wife were now launched into the public eye of the capital in his new, prestigious role. They must have hoped that Ann had now entered a calmer phase. There is no record of her behaviour there, except her own later reference to oddnesses when in Peking.[1]

The ICMC was now under the leadership of Hart's brother-in-law, the Acting Inspector General, Sir Robert Bredon. Bredon was to be replaced by Francis Aglen within a couple of years, and Aglen, as we have seen, was not substantiated as Inspector General until after Hart's death. No regular reports from B-T have come to light for this period, as reporting was apparently only customary for commissioners responsible for ports and other out-stations outside of Peking.

The function of the new Customs College, of which B-T was Co-Director,[2] was the training of selected Chinese for senior positions in the ICMC, eventually providing

> a pool of well-trained graduates from whom, along with the most qualified of clerks, Aglen began to appoint a number of Chinese assistants.[3]

'Assistants' referred to the different grades of assistant commissioner. The Customs College provided a four-year higher education course, became a valuable avenue for a good career in the Customs Service and earned a reputation as a model institution for the training of civil servants.[4] The curriculum embraced law, history, economics and statistics, and the languages English, French, German, Russian and Japanese. Admission was highly selective, and its students came from all over China. Teaching staff were recruited from those holding office in the Customs and from Peking universities.[5] The college remained in Peking until 1935, when it moved to Shanghai and merged with another college established in 1930 for training certain Outdoor positions in the Service. By that time, the Peking Customs College had produced over six hundred graduates for the Service.[6]

B-T was appointed for four years. In support of B-T's nomination, Hart had described him as a man

> whose previous training and experience and sound Chinese scholarship marked him as eminently fitted to fill the post of Co-Director, who has to devote his full time to assisting both in the teaching and administrative work of the College.[7]

The following year, B-T wrote to Hart who was now back in Britain, knowing that Hart was likely to be interested in the college's experience of its first intake of students. He comments on their satisfactory examination performance, complains about the lack of accommodation and the anticipated intake of forty students in the coming year and addresses the students' behaviour:

> A year's experience have [sic] shown the young fellows to be well behaved and good tempered. They are about the same social level as our best Clerks and give little or no trouble. We had a few of the turbulent Young China sorts at first, but the troublesome fellows, all but two, have resigned and we were not sorry to see them go. They wanted to flit through the College and then take up positions as Deputy Commissioners and so on in the Service. The young fellows we have will doubtless benefit in many ways from their sojourn here and already I think I see an improvement in their appearance and general behaviour.[8]

This period was one of growing uncertainty following the deaths of both the Emperor and the Empress Dowager, with political change in the air. The reference to 'the turbulent Young China sorts' is interesting in revealing B-T's view of the emerging more politically conscious generation,[9] youths with optimistic expectations for their future; he was clearly not enthused. He then mentions arrangements for a long summer vacation of fifty days: 'this gives the Cantonese who can afford it a chance to go home. Half are from the south.'

Copies of all the set examination papers were also sent to Hart, apart from the Chinese exams, for which the questions were written on the board. These papers make interesting reading. Translation, arithmetic and science were straightforward enough. English and geography were the only subjects where the teachers had clearly made efforts to relate the content of their teaching to China. History stands out as being completely irrelevant when it could have been a valuable preparation. The examination paper focussed entirely on the Middle Ages in Europe, without even attempting to draw parallels with China, let alone use more appropriate recent political and economic history. It could be seen as a particularly literal example of the 'pedagogy of imperialism'.[10] The irony is that this college was supposedly a modernizing educational institution, intended to break with conservative tradition. It would be too much to hope that the students would have been rewarded with bonus points if they had the initiative to suggest Chinese parallels. One wonders whether this was a reflection of B-T's nondirective personality or the inability to get a suitable teacher. We do not have Hart's reaction to the examination papers.

Raymond's Visit to China

Shortly after B-T's appointment, his son Raymond, now nearing twenty-one years of age and a medical student at St. Bartholomew's Hospital, London, visited China during the summer vacation of 1908 to see his father. From China he wrote letters, now in family hands, to Peg Ellis, as well as to her seventeen-year-old daughter, Evelyn. For the lively 'Imp', Raymond, was not attracted so much by the spirited Daisy as by her shy, demure younger sister.

The journey to Peking via the Trans-Siberian Railway, opened in 1891, had not been a joy for Raymond. Northern China had been flooded, and it was necessary for the occupants to leave the train in order to cross the Lian River. Prior to that, they had experienced 'the most unpleasant part of the trip from Harbin', where the train changed, the Harbin arm only having been completed in 1901.

> The carriage was lighted [sic] by one small candle which shortly went out. We could not undress or wash all night and were devoured by mosquitoes. And just to see that we did not fall asleep the train was patrolled the whole night by an armed guard so that every 10 minutes or so a man came along with a lantern which he poked into your face and with him was a guard with fixed bayonets. This went on all night and they slammed the doors of course. I wonder whether they expect people to suddenly develop into murderous ruffians while they are asleep. At Quangtelengtze we got into a Jap train where we had cane chairs to sit upon. These got very uncomfortable after a very short time and got almost unbearable by the end of the day. They use very bad coal too and there was a constant shower of smuts all day. There was no dining car on the train and we therefore laid in some provisions. Some four pounds of dried figs formed our staple diet. I am fond of figs but when it comes to figs for breakfast, figs for lunch, figs for tea, and then again for supper I must confess I begin to wish for something else. Still with them and the bread we bought we got on very well.

Raymond and his fellow-travellers also had problems making the Japanese waiter understand about drinks, but eventually, having tried using English, French, German and Chinese, he went away and found someone who was able to interpret for them in German and

> got some iced coffee with very dirty ice which probably came from the river in the winter. Still we risked it.

At Mukden, where they had to change trains, they overnighted as was then customary. It seemed to Raymond to be an interesting city, and it looked imposing with its walls:

> On all sides it is surrounded by the characteristic Chinese graves which are scattered everywhere over the country as little mounds about 4-feet high.

He writes in August (in a hand very like his father's) that the heat in Peking was averaging 95 to 100 degrees during the day and 85 at night. He was to go to Peitaiho for a fortnight to join his stepmother who was staying at the bungalow they owned at Rocky Point on the coast. Peitaiho was about two hundred miles away, and though an increasingly popular resort for expatriates, around the time B-T owned his bungalow it was still a sleepy fishing village.[11]

Probably a little apprehensive about his stepmother's state of mind, Raymond was not particularly anxious to go to Peitaiho, as his father was unable to accompany him, being busy with college admissions and preparing for the inaugural term starting in October. But one advantage it offered, in addition to the sea bathing, was the opportunity to avoid the system of paying social calls expected in Peking which had cramped his time for sightseeing there:

> This is a dreadful place for people to be called on, every day so far I have had to go out in the afternoon paying calls. They have a system which I approve of here according to which people have a box outside their door in which cards are left. I do not mind that method of calling but unfortunately ladies and the tin gods in the city cannot be so treated and one has to go in. I suppose I must get used to this sort of game some day however [perhaps he was anticipating working in China?], but I shall be almost glad to go to Peitaiho to get away from it. Then in the evenings I am took [sic] to the club where I fail to recognize and remember the names of the people whom I am supposed to know.

In Peitaiho, travelling to and from the station was by walking, rickshaw or riding a donkey. The place being undeveloped, the last way, the one chosen by Raymond, could be hazardous especially if the rain had been heavy:

> There were still places where the mud and water came up to the donkey's knees and occasionally higher still. My donkey took it into his head to sit down in a moderately bad place and was unable to get up again. In the end I had to get off and then he added insult to injury by getting up with a splash and flinching his tail so that I arrived at the station in a very splashed condition.

Though born in China, Ray had not previously visited the capital except possibly as a child when his father was in Tientsin. Social engagements had prevented much sightseeing in Peking early on, but he managed to do some before the trip ended, and his descriptions of the Peking of a century ago are worth recording:

What I have seen is very fine. They are very fond of a rich red colour which with the sun on it looks very gorgeous. The Chien Men (pronounced Mun) [Qianmen, south of Tiananmen] which is the main gate of the City on the south wall is really magnificent with its red and gold and rich blue and green, and leading from it to the North are the roofs of the gates leading to the Emperor's palace which are all of a golden yellow. But there has been no rain for weeks and the city is full of dust. I have taken very few photographs as yet chiefly on account of this.' [He had risen at four in the morning] and went along the city wall for a couple of hours and saw the sun rise. In the day the wall gets almost red hot.

He would not have minded the heat, but the early morning was better for his father. He goes on:

You can find your way about Pekin [sic] very easily for all the roads run either N and S or E and W. Then there are the big gates to act as landmarks, and knowing that whatever road you follow you will come to a wall makes it a very easy matter. Taking a rickshaw you only have to learn the Chinese for N.S.E.W. and you can direct him anywhere.[12]

Later, Raymond responded to a letter from Evelyn which had criticized his spelling. Evelyn, though quiet and unassuming, had a sharp mind and liked precision; she could be quite caustic. Ray justifies himself, but not wishing to offend her, writes, 'I bow to your superior knowledge.' He then describes a visit to the Temple of Confucius, north of the Forbidden City:

I was fortunate in going there the day before the Emperor was to be present at the sacrifice and the musical instruments were put out ready for the occasion. This only occurs twice a year.

He goes on to paint a picture of the famous temple nearby:

The Lama Temple was very fine with numerous courtyards and marble staircases. In one of the buildings is a wooden Buddha 80 feet high. It seems that they give silk handkerchiefs to the Buddha and this one had over his right arm a long thin one presented by the Empress Dowager. I should think it was at least 90 feet long for it was doubled. Close to this large one was the deity with 1000 hands. I am not sure it was not a woman, anyway in the middle of each hand was an eye and the hands were arranged round the head in a ring.

The medical student adds: 'I wonder how the nerve supply of all of these arms is arranged for . . .' Ray then gives an account of a visit he made to the Forbidden City:

A couple of days ago I was wandering about trying to get some photographs of the forbidden city. I came to a place where a number of lotuses were growing and I tried to get down to them but one of the palace guards made his appearance and I was forced to depart. They allow one into the city to a certain extent but what you may not see is very strictly guarded . . . Not far from the grounds there is a very gorgeous Pailou which is an archway on the road. It is beautifully decorated with gilding and rich red. Pailous are used for the names of the streets and are pretty frequent in the city but are usually in bad repair.

After mentioning other places of interest and the thirty-foot-thick wall around the Tartar city, he concludes with a reference to the events of eight years earlier:

It is strange to see the effect of the Boxer troubles on the city here. Pekin seems principally to be a diplomatic city. I mean by that that most of the Europeans are connected with the Chinese or other governments. The legations are now practically forts and the space all round them is kept clear of houses for nearly 100 yards. It is certainly a very unfortunate state of affairs for China for it will be a very long time before the nations will consent to withdraw their troops. At present it seems an extraordinary state of affairs.[13]

In a separate letter to Evelyn's mother, Peg, he complains about the socializing — dining out or having people to dinner almost every night — but also mentions an enjoyable visit to the Ming tombs which he describes in detail. He records a strange sight from his stay in Nankow on his return journey:

[Nankow is] quite a little village but is evidently of some importance for the caravans to and from Mongolia all pass through it. Yesterday we passed some 80 or 90 men each carrying perched on their poles two eagles. As a rule one large and the other quite young. The big birds were fine brown birds with yellow beaks and the young were darker. I was told that every year these men took them to Mongolia but how they catch so many and what they do with them I cannot understand . . . There were also a large number of camels passing through all the time. They must find it rough going up the Nankow pass.[14]

The eagles were in fact used for hunting, like falcons.

The following year, in 1909, B-T visited the Temple of Heaven at the time of the Emperor's sacrifice, one of the most important events in the ritual year of the imperial calendar. He took photographs of the temple bedecked with decorations and drums, and then he had pangs of sensitivity over having done so. Over twenty years later, as we shall see, he was to donate these to the British Museum, revealing a disturbed conscience for having committed a sacrilegious act.

During B-T's final year in Peking, 1912 to 1913 he was appointed Acting Chief Secretary of the ICMC by Aglen, while C. A. V. Bowra was on leave. Bowra described the position of chief secretary as having the powers, but not the title, of a deputy inspector general, a number two to the inspector general;[15] he handed over the office to B-T in April 1912. The appointment could be seen as an expression of confidence in B-T by Aglen, coming at a time of uncertainty when the republican revolution had just taken place.

B-T combined the position with being co-director of the college, an arrangement which was then institutionalized by the chief secretary taking on the college responsibility ex officio; this arrangement lasted about ten years, until the student unrest in Peking in 1921, when it was deemed necessary to revert to having a full-time co-director. When Bowra returned from leave in 1913, the Chinese ministers informed him that they expected him also to combine the posts. This did not appear to have created difficulties between B-T and Bowra, for they remained on friendly terms, B-T loaning his bungalow at Rocky Point, Peitaiho, to Bowra for the summer of 1914. Later, Bowra was to stay with B-T in his commissioner's house at Mukden when he went there to meet his wife arriving on the Trans-Siberian train in 1916, surprisingly crossing Europe in the middle of the First World War.[16]

Yet, it is a little odd that despite these and other social occasions, and also having been at the Siege of the Legations together with B-T during the Boxer troubles, Bowra leaves no personal comments on B-T in his diaries, though he does comment on other senior members of the ICMC. This lends support to the impression that the obviously competent B-T was an amiable, scholarly administrator, a safe pair of hands rather than a colourful and charismatic figure; the kind of man, perhaps, who does not readily invite comment.

During the time B-T lived in Peking, the Ch'ing dynasty came to an end with the October 1911 Revolution, and the Republic was officially established on 1 January 1912. As has been observed, the speed of this change was 'seldom equalled by any other great revolution in the world'.[17] Yet, sadly, there is no record of B-T's view of that momentous event and its complex aftermath, as various personalities and groups vied for power. Bowra noted that there was 'no anti-foreign element whatever in the insurrection and no cause for concern as to its repercussion on the Customs Service'.[18] The Customs Service as a whole in fact survived the revolution well, though in many ports the local Chinese officials, as the imperial authority in the place, 'were either ousted, fled, or went over to the revolutionary party'. Aglen praised the revolutionaries for their lack of interference in the Service:

> It speaks well for the patriotic feelings of the revolutionary leaders and their sense of national obligation . . . In few countries would a matter of this kind be approached in such a spirit of common sense and sweet reasonableness.[19]

Of course, the Republicans needed the revenues from the Customs, a high proportion of which was still allocated for honouring loan debts and indemnities. Given the problems they faced, initially they could do little other than to leave the organization and its operations well alone. Many of the revolutionary leaders were familiar with the West, many having lived there, and were not virulently anti-foreigner, though they were opposed to the unequal treaties imposed by them.[20] Understandably, they wished to see more Chinese people in positions of influence.

At the college, the final examinations for the first intake had to be postponed because of the unsettled situation, and the diplomas were awarded in January 1913, 'rendering the recipient eligible for appointment in Government service'.[21]

Leave and Family Affairs

On 22 April 1913, B-T and his wife left Peking for his year of leave, taking the Trans-Siberian route.[22] Though much shorter than the sea route home, B-T could not have been looking forward to the confinement of the long train journey, for his wife's illness had worsened again, and she may even have required hospitalization in China before they left.

Earlier that year, in January 1913, Raymond, who had by now qualified as a doctor, had taken up his first appointment at the Dorset County Hospital in Dorchester. He wrote to Evelyn:

> News from China is rather bad as regards my [step-]mother. There are even talks of her requiring to go into an asylum again. She seems to be getting worse and worse and my Father finds it very difficult to put up with things as they are.[23]

In June that year, for the first time, B-T visited the Ellis family in Inglefield. He must have been made aware from Ray that his relationship with Evelyn was becoming closer. Peg describes the visit:

> He is an odd mixture of his two boys, but shortish and broad. He had Daisy and Evelyn to lunch one day and took them to the Academy . . . He is now in Scotland, where his wife has a house by the sea-side.[24]

The July budge relates that Ray and his father spent a day with the Ellises after a week's tour of Cornwall:

> The Polite Potentate from the East had a glimpse of a free-and-easy sort of household he is unaccustomed to. We now know where Leonard gets his ways from. Only Mr. B-T is a shortish, broad man with a round brown face and sad brown eyes. He feels being always parted from his boys very much.

Ray went up to Earlsferry, Fife to stay for a few days, and from there he wrote to Evelyn:

As for my mother she tries to be very nice. Too nice and therefore fussy . . .
She can hear but often asks suddenly what you are talking about and thinks
it is something different . . . You probably would not spot that she was mad
unless you knew . . . I am doomed to go out with her tomorrow for a drive.[25]

A couple of days later, he wrote again:

Just at the minute [she] has been shouting at no one — probably a "voice"
— telling it to leave off . . . I don't know how the servants stand her.[26]

In the July budge that year, Peg reported that Ray took a six-week locum
contract at the Royal Free Hospital in London, and then in the August report she
informed her siblings that Evelyn and Ray had become engaged:

For years she has been 'the one person in the world' to him — as he puts it
. . . She will make a home for one who has never had one to remember. His
mother died when he was quite little.

Peg obviously had the impression that the home provided by B-T with his
second wife had not been a sufficient substitute.

In September, Peg informed Evelyn where she is staying in Dorset that a box
arrived from Elie containing

three beautiful satin robes, each labelled for one of you. Win's is white
embroidered with white flowers, with a dark blue embroided border, and lined
with white silk. Daisy's is the blue she likes with butterflies and salmon azaleas
on it, lined with pink. Yours is pale blue with apple-blossom sprigs, lined with
old rose. Most lovely, what a beneficent Pa-in-law you are acquiring!

She also describes them in detail in the next budge and tells her siblings that Daisy
and Evelyn donned their new silk robes for a visit to a ball at the Trocadero, in
London's Piccadilly Circus.[27]

Later that year, in December, Evelyn went up to town for Christmas shopping
with her mother. They were to have tea with Mrs. Brewitt-Taylor, but she excused
herself as being too tired from shopping to join them, so 'poor Mr. B-T and a lady
friend of theirs entertained us'. But shortly after Peg eventually met Ann when B-T
brought her out to Inglefield:

The elusive lady did really come here on the 15th with her husband for tea.
I was the only one at home, which just suited her. We got on all right, so
that we are now friendly. I believe she was afraid of me. She is a bundle of
nervousness, though plump and homely to the observer. I felt sorry for her.[28]

B-T again joined the family, without his wife, when they all went to the
Alexandra Palace, where Winnie and Daisy were performing in the *Messiah,* and

a couple of days later, in between their shopping, he entertained Peg, Evelyn and Daisy for lunch and tea. He had wanted to take them to the ornate Hotel Cecil in the Strand (the home of his father-in-law, Alexander Michie, who had died there a decade earlier), but that was not convenient

> so he had to content himself with Fuller's in Regent Street, — quite nice enough, too, for homely people! We went to his hotel for tea when the shopping was done. He is the impersonation of gentle kindness. Evelyn and Daisy will both have excellent fathers-in-law.[29]

In March of that year, Roy Suttill had, unexpectedly it seems, proposed to Daisy after asking permission from her father, and they had become engaged.

While B-T was on leave, Leonard was able to arrange his leave from Siam; he visited Inglefield in a motor car on 3 February 1914, just after arriving in Britain. He and his brother went up to Scotland to be with their father as he prepared for his journey back to China; whether Leonard was nursing any disappointment at Daisy's engagement is not known. On 21 March 1914, Peg reported:

> Papa B-T came to say goodbye, Leonard and Ray were with him. We have an excellent photo of Papa B-T taken at the Army and Navy Stores. He left for China on the Monday. He is a very nice man.[30]

B-T must have been well pleased that his son was to be married into such a warm and welcoming family.[31]

Mrs. Brewitt-Taylor did not return with her husband to China. B-T, anxious about her health, but doubtless relieved at not having to face the demands and embarrassment of his wife's behaviour, left Britain in March 1914. At the end of May, Evelyn and Ray went up to Scotland to visit the stepmother. Evelyn records in her diary that 'Mrs. B-T talked all evening about her head creatures' and was 'bad' enough to stay in bed for the following several days.[32] In July 1914, Leonard went to Elie to say goodbye to her before returning to Siam in August.[33] Though ambivalent in their feelings towards her, the young men obviously behaved courteously; she had mixed feelings about them.

Ann's condition worsened, and she was admitted to the Royal Edinburgh Asylum in spring 1915 at her own request. She was to remain there for over four years, until June 1919, when B-T returned home on leave again; she was then discharged 'without improvement'. Further stays continued to be necessary for some years after B-T retired.[34] She never again returned to China.

13

Alone in Foochow and Mukden

On returning from leave B-T spent nearly two years in Foochow, and then in Mukden, in the far north-east of China. Reports from both areas reveal more about his work, but Mukden also proved highly significant for his personal relationships. It was while researching his posting I discovered much more about his wife, her mental illness and their marital relationship.

B-T's leave had been a mixture of strain at coping with his wife, pleasure at being with his sons again and meeting his future daughter-in-law, Evelyn, and the Ellis family. On returning to China, B-T was posted in May 1914 as Commissioner in Foochow. It must have been a strange experience returning (for the second time, for he had been there for a short stay in 1897–98), now alone, to the place where he had first worked in China as a young teacher in a far less exalted position. Then, he was also happily married to his young bride, who distressingly died after child-birth just over a year before he left Foochow to join the Customs Service in Tientsin. He was probably relieved not to be accompanied by his unstable wife offering such a contrasting experience of marriage.

When I visited the Second Republican Historical Archive in Nanjing, B-T's semi-official commissioner's reports for his time in Foochow were not available, but since then more reports have been uncovered as a result of a project widening accessibility to Customs material. They throw more light on the kinds of concerns B-T encountered at work.

The Service had become responsible for the Native Customs earlier in the century, and B-T reports the problems experienced by a station collecting dues from junks. These are hailed to hove-to from a Customs sampan, which then determines whether any dues are to be levied:

> If the junk disregards the hail, she is allowed to proceed, and the matter is supposed to be reported to the Head Office. Pursuit is seldom made as our staff cannot overtake a well-manned smuggler. Seizures seldom occur as junk and sampan owners . . . rely on their superior speed, and the fact that their vessels, which bear no distinguishing names or numbers, can mingle in a

crowd of similar craft within a few hundred yards of the station and so escape detection.[1]

The potential for bribery is obvious. He also reported problems in collecting dues on 'sea-blubber', a jellyfish netted in large quantities and imported to Foochow, supplying 'the poorer classes with much food, and though very cheap, is esteemed by them as a delicacy'. Collecting fees for this foodstuff was onerous for the station. B-T suggested that it would be more efficient if the station were to be closed down, and the Foochow Head Office organize patrols directly.

While in Foochow, B-T received another Chinese brevett. This award related to another interesting episode in China's history. Sun Yat-sen, who had led the Republican Revolution in 1911, was only president briefly, being replaced on 10 March 1912 by Yuan Shih-k'ai, noted earlier as an anti-Boxer Ch'ing governor. He enjoyed ritual and ceremony, especially when he was the prominent figure at an event. As put by Reginald Johnston, tutor to the last Emperor (P'u-yi), he was 'not superior to the little vanities of ordinary humanity'.[2] His delight in ceremony caused him to revive old customs,[3] coins, decorations, etc., in anticipation of restoring the monarchy with himself as head of a new dynasty; his planned enthronement, scheduled for January 1916, was aborted, and he died shortly after in June that year. One of the medals which he had struck was the Chia Ho, or 'Order of the Precious Crop', which he introduced in 1915. B-T was one of the early recipients of the new award, which was issued to him on 23 June 1915.

Shortly after B-T took up his post, the First World War broke out in Europe; it was to have its repercussions in China and personally for B-T.

During the war, Customs expatriates on both sides were generally loyal to their country of origin, and many young men of the appropriate age group left China, volunteering for their country's armed forces (in the Consular Service the situation was rather different, for until China entered the war, Consular officers were not allowed to join up).[4] There was, however, concern in the Customs Service about the problem of securing British recruits and especially about being able to maintain the international balance. As Paul King, then in the London office, put it:

> The international features of the Service would have been obscured by a too great preponderance of recruits of neither Chinese nor Western provenance, and the valuable balance of East and West in its ranks might have been irrevocably lost. Luckily, however, it was early recognized in the right quarter that there were British trenches, impalpable and invisible, but still real, to be held elsewhere than on the actual battle fronts.[5]

Despite the warfare between the expatriates' home countries, there were many individual examples of cordiality between colleagues of rival nationalities, especially when a son was lost on the battlefield.

Events in Mukden

B-T remained in Foochow until March 1916, when he was posted to Mukden. The area's Treaty Port status had been established over the period from 1903 to 1907, when it was being opened up to foreign residence and trade. A British Consulate was set up there in 1906 and at nearby Antung (Dandong) on the Yalu border with Korea in 1908.

When C. A. V. Bowra had been the Customs Commissioner in Mukden sometime earlier, in 1908, he opined that it offered 'a very trying time for a lady'; his wife found her stay by far the least agreeable of her China experiences.

> Beyond a few English and French missionaries who for many years could not venture out of their compounds without being robbed, the only foreigners the natives knew were the Russians and the Japanese . . . both of whom were loathed.[6]

It is doubtful that the situation would have changed much in the intervening years. However, B-T's lady was not with him to suffer Mukden; she was having a different kind of trying time elsewhere.

Mukden was in the highly sensitive area of Chinese Manchuria, which had been under the influence of Russia until the Russo-Japanese War. The area saw a good deal of conflict in that war, and with victory in 1905, Japan acquired rights in southern Manchuria formerly enjoyed by Russia, occupying Mukden (after bombarding it during the Battle of Mukden) and controlling the railway from there up to Changchun. As we saw earlier, Korea had already become a protectorate of Japan, which thereby extended its influence across the Yalu River.[7] Thus, the whole region was coming heavily under Japanese influence. That the area was highly sensitive politically could be seen by the fact that Mukden had several foreign consuls with the status of consulate general, which carried more extensive staff, being more important than a consulate. In 1913, Britain had eight consulate general offices in China, one of which was Mukden; Russia also had one of its eight consulate generals there, as did Japan; the United States, with five such offices, also had one in Mukden.[8] For the consulates in Mukden, it was especially true that the office was

> a political post whose object was intelligence-gathering; similar political posts aimed at monitoring other nations' interests were opened elsewhere in China in the early twentieth century.[9]

Particularly since the Russo-Japanese War of 1905 and the opening of several ports and inland markets to foreign trade, the Chinese government required the Customs commissioner to be a man of some standing or seniority.[10] B-T's appointment to the post is a tribute to Aglen's respect for him.

Bowra described the house used by the commissioner, which became B-T's home. It was a Chinese traditional residence, consisting of a central building with two wings — a low bungalow on three sides of a courtyard with a small garden and stables at the back. The central portion had two large rooms, used as drawing and dining rooms, and in the wings there were bedrooms and bathrooms.[11] So, it was quite useful for receiving guests who changed trains at Mukden.

Work at Mukden was light, normally only occupying the mornings, leaving afternoons free for riding and making useful social contacts, as well as other diversions.[12]

G. E. Morrison, the former China correspondent of *The Times* who became political advisor to President Yuan, knew B-T well: they had experienced the Siege of the Legations together back in 1900 and kept occasional contact with each other. I searched the records to see whether there had been any correspondence between them, and whether Morrison made any comments on B-T in his diaries. One casual comment led to an extraordinarily revealing seam of discovery.

Morrison had written to B-T in 1916 asking if he could stay, and B-T replied with a welcome, regretting that his best guest room was occupied as he had his son, Leonard, staying with him from Bangkok:

> However as you seek privacy rather than comfort I shall expect you unless
> I hear to the contrary. I shall doubtless be at the station to meet you next
> Sunday.[13]

Morrison arrived on the Tuesday and spent a couple of days with B-T before travelling on to Mongolia and Japan. He records in his diary having lunch with B-T and Leonard, discussing the political situation locally and in Siam, whose king is described as fat, flabby and nervous, 'who knows not women but is believed to be addicted to other joys'. They also discuss B-T's domestic situation, with his wife in Scotland, for in his diary Morrison quotes B-T's statement that his 'wife is now in Morningside Lunatic Asylum', and that her brother, Alexander Michie, is 'mad as my wife, but now serving in Dover'. The diary entry proved to be most significant in leading to a full revelation about B-T's wife's mental condition and their marital relationship. It will be apparent later why B-T's frank phrasing, openly expressed to a friend, carried such a bitter tone.[14]

B-T's reports while in Mukden to Inspector General Aglen were available in the Nanking archives; they were usefully revealing both about B-T and conditions generally. Frequent references were made to the local political situation, especially to the hostility between the different Chinese factions in the area, and the recurring attempts by the Japanese to deepen their local influence. Despite being allies of China, expatriate nationalities were also rivals and had to be watched, particularly given Japan's highly sensitive relationship with China. Changes in the weather and the resulting effect on crops are chronicled, as well as the generally unhealthy conditions. At one point half the foreign community was down with dysentery, and B-T notes, using the 'colonial' terminology current at the time, that 'I hear the natives also suffered from that and other intestinal troubles'.[15] B-T, now approaching sixty, several times complained of being unwell during the time he was there, but he recovered sufficiently to go riding with the U.S. Consul General. Borderlines between work and leisure were not well defined, and this excursion hinted at how he was using his time: maintaining contacts and hopefully picking up useful snippets of information.[16]

Examples of the perennial problems of fraud and severe forms of punishment are noted in the reports. As the year 1916 neared its end, there had been a bad case of embezzlement in a local bank, and on the order of the governor, five men had been shot, and the chairman of the Chamber of Commerce was imprisoned.[17] Another report related an unfortunate local accident which had involved Customs staff. As Mukden commissioner, B-T was also responsible for a Customs language school; a student of the school was out shooting snipe and one of his bullets grazed the temple of a local child — the student sent the child a toy and three dollars. Fortunately for the student, the police were conciliatory;[18] in the eyes of the police, foreigners probably tended to be less sympathetic to locals, and accidents of this kind might have been completely ignored by the offender.

Travelling in the area was something of a trial, and occasionally meeting dignitaries at the train station at inconvenient times was a burdensome expectation: 'It is no joke to meet the train . . . due at one in the morning and generally late', B-T wrote. He continued, 'Of course I shall go [to meet Madame Sze, an important person] for the sake of the good name of the service,' adding prudently, 'and one never knows when a good turn like that makes for our advantage'.[19] Aglen approved his courtesy — noting his recognition of the intention behind the point being made: 'It will be appreciated.'

The major aim of the Customs language school was to teach Chinese to new, promising expatriate Customs staff, ones who were especially being groomed for promotion. Aglen was particularly concerned about standards of Chinese in the Service and had tried to improve the levels by stiffening examinations.[20] B-T's first report is annotated by Aglen expressing the hope that he 'will take the greatest personal interest in the school and help the students as much as possible'. After this, B-T's reports almost invariably contain some comment on the school.

References in the reports to numerous dramatic incidents provide evidence of the hostility felt towards the Japanese. A bomb in Japanese Manchuria and more local occurrences in Mukden chronicle the friction existing between Chinese and Japanese; these include a bomb in the local Japanese bank and an assault on a Japanese policeman. B-T also reported an invasion by Mongols which had fizzled out, as well as 'the evil doings of the Redbeards'.[21]

After China's entry into the First World War in 1917, and with the war in Europe showing few signs of abating, the British consul invited all British of military age to consider volunteering for action. Some of the students of the school were unwilling to continue with their studies, and B-T, doubtless uncertain about this potential loss to the Service, had to ask for guidance.[22] Keeping the school going at all became increasingly problematic as numbers dwindled, down to one or two, and even none at one point. On one occasion he had problems with a teacher who wanted to leave. B-T tried to induce him to stay by

> placing my little villa [at Peitaiho] at his disposal for the summer, free of all cost providing they would not advertize the fact abroad.

The teacher accepted. But one teacher did resign a year after B-T took up office, stating, 'the whole spirit of the place has changed . . . if the place were under my control I would close it'.[23] What underlay this statement is not clear: it may have been the problem of obtaining good teaching staff, the paucity of suitable students or a reflection on B-T's style.

Despite the evidence of Aglen's confidence (illustrated by the appointment of B-T as Acting Chief Secretary and the Mukden posting), B-T's relationship with Aglen, who could be a prickly character, was not as confident as it had been with Hart. When B-T complains to Aglen that the school is too far away from the office for efficient control, the Inspector General notes curtly that B-T's predecessor maintained excellent control and did not find the school too distant.[24] Perhaps B-T, now in his sixtieth year, was beginning to feel his age, particularly after nearly forty strenuous years in China and his domestic strains. A few months later, the persistent B-T tried again when the lease on the commissioner's house was due to expire, suggesting that the new building could incorporate both a commissioner's residence and a school, so that when the commissioner had to make a visit 'he would not have to travel two miles over roads such as I do not wish to describe'. Aglen responds with a threat:

> I am sorry that you find things so difficult. I shall attempt to send you somewhere where you will not have to go so far for your work.

There may, of course, be a more friendly interpretation of what appears to be a rather sniffy response, and it might be thought that Aglen may simply have been trying to offer sympathy, except that he adds a note 'your predecessor managed very nicely' which, though he crosses it out, is still clearly to be seen on the report. Aglen had clearly learnt Hart's technique of using the threat of transfer as a weapon of control, creating anxiety even among senior staff. B-T replies speedily to the threat of leaving:

> I should be grateful not to be transferred if it can be avoided. My leave is due in the Spring of 1919, and I must go home if I can get away.[25]

Ann's continued hospitalization and other domestic concerns with his daughter-in-law pregnant, explain the imperative phrasing. The fact that the war was still raging when he wrote did not affect his expectation of being able to return home. Generally, the tone of his letters is very respectful, and when he makes an error in stating the salary level of one of his teaching staff, he apologizes profusely:

> To my profound regret I have made a serious mistake . . . I am very sorry for the error which I pray you will excuse.[26]

There is confirmation here of some uncertainty he felt in his relationship with Aglen.

It seems that B-T was away from Mukden for several months in 1918. His temporary replacement, Hansen, appears to have been on more intimate terms with the Inspector General, addressing a letter 'Dear Aglen', and he echoes more forcibly B-T's earlier complaints when he protests that the change between the

> nice clean healthy surroundings at home and this awful place is almost too sudden . . . Have you been here? Less said about housing arrangements and surroundings and immediate neighbourhood the better.

He also refers to his Chinese being too poor to help the school and ends, dangerously, 'I cannot think that you will keep me here permanently.' Later he writes, 'if only the nasty smells around here would also freeze, the cold would be entirely welcome'. By spring 1918, the school's student population was down to only one at most.[27]

Evangeline Dora Edwards

Life in Mukden was not unrelievedly lonesome. One personal relationship which B-T formed here lasted until the end of his life. His wife away, B-T must have been pleased to form a friendship with a young woman who had kindred interests in Chinese literature.

Evangeline Dora Edwards was born in 1888 and was therefore about thirty years younger than B-T. The daughter of Reverend John Edwards, she went to a small private school in Camborne, Cornwall. She set out to be a missionary, undertaking a preparatory course at a missionary college, probably following a teacher training course. Evangeline left for China in 1913, and on arrival she immediately enrolled at the Peking Language School to study Chinese. Within two years, in 1915, at about twenty-seven years of age, she became Principal of the Women's Normal College in

Mukden, a college for the training of teachers, and completed the Peking Language School's Diploma in Chinese by part-time study. She left Mukden and returned to Britain in 1919.

Whether there was anything more in the relationship other than a friendship born from common intellectual interests in Chinese, and their possible loneliness is not known. The conditions were suitable for fostering closeness, but there is little to suggest anything improper: B-T's position and his sense of propriety, together with her position and upbringing, may well have combined to inhibit that. There was also the age difference, though a nearly thirty-year gap between close friends is not unknown. We are also given to understand from B-T's wife that he was not oversprung sexually, despite several conceptions, though different partners can have different effects. Whatever the nature of the relationship, the friendship was doubtless welcome, especially as the relationship with Ann was somewhat precarious, experiencing as she was a long sojourn in an asylum. As will be seen later, the relationship between B-T and Evangeline was far from a passing one and continued long after they both left China.

In November 1918, B-T notes the peace rejoicings without comment; as will be seen in the following chapter, he had just recently experienced another emotional loss, which cast a poignant shadow on the celebrations.[28] His last report from Mukden was written on 12 April 1919 just before going on home leave. This was the year that Evangeline also went home; perhaps they travelled together. There was much to anticipate — financial and other arrangements and the pleasure of seeing family and especially his new grandson for the first time, but also apprehension over how he would find his wife.

14

Family Affairs and the First World War

The war in Europe, though distant, was to have a personal and sad impact on B-T. His son Leonard returned to Siam from leave just about the time war was declared, and he stayed there with the Bombay-Burmah Trading Corporation throughout its duration.[1] According to Leonard's daughter, Joan, he was in some kind of local volunteer militia, but it is possible that his poor eyesight would have precluded him from joining the war in Europe.[2] B-T's younger son, Ray, however, was caught up in the exhilarating patriotic fervour experienced by many young men. As early as 14 August 1914, immediately after the declaration of war, he went to Woolwich to volunteer for the Royal Army Medical Corps (RAMC), which his future mother-in-law, Peg, thought was likely to be safe enough, unless the Germans failed to respect the conventions of the Red Cross.[3] He was commissioned, and after a week of training in Woolwich was sent to France; he experienced the terrible hardships that winter in Ypres. For his work during that period he was recommended for a decoration and was mentioned in dispatches for joining in with the stretcher bearers to bring in wounded under fire. After a spell of home leave, he went out to Mesopotamia, where poor hospital conditions coupled with a difficult climate, and in 1916 he contracted malaria and was sent back to England to work in a civilian capacity. In January 1917, he married Evelyn Ellis, in Hampstead's Rosslyn Hill Unitarian Chapel,[4] and they had a long honeymoon in Wales. He could have remained in civilian life, but after a period of working in hospitals in Britain, he volunteered again to serve in the RAMC, and he rejoined in May.

B-T must have written to his new daughter-in-law about his concerns over something happening to Ray. In July 1917, he wrote to Evelyn from Mukden in terms which today would be regarded as somewhat didactic and sexist; the letter also conveys something of the life he led, and the activities expected of a Customs commissioner:

My very dear Evelyn,

I wrote you the other day telling you certain things which I hope you have read, marked, and inwardly digested. For the moment, as you see, I am writing Ray to the care of your mother . . . I shall not be glad to hear what the new address is unless it is a good one, conveniently near you, for you deserve some good luck you poor little woman . . . And when you have a little leisure your newly acquired relation this way would be glad of a letter . . . Half the year is gone as you see, and we are getting an undue amount of heat. A hundred and one yesterday in the shade and I had to go to a frock coat function where many men and women were assembled. It was grilling hot and I did not enjoy it a bit. But that is how the world wags you see. I am gitting [sic] old and am, quite vainly supposed to lend distinction to a sort of official gathering and so they try to kill me off by inviting me to such deadly gatherings, knowing well that custom and etiquette forbid my refusal. I simply had to go yesterday and the strain of the heat I feel sure aged me several months. Heat is not so bad when you can dress according to common sense. When you cannot it is deadly. That is a father in law growl dear, and it does not mean very much . . . Your very affectionate father, C.[5]

Ray returned to France in September, when Evelyn was at an advanced stage of pregnancy. A son, named Edward Gordon, was born on 15 December 1917. On the same day, Peg sent a telegram and a letter to Ray at the front announcing the birth of his son. Other letters soon followed recording that Evelyn had been sent by B-T's wife, Ann, (who was still in hospital in Scotland) what then would have been quite a substantial cash present, '£25 and a sweet little rose-scented sachet'. Peg also received a nice letter from Ann: 'the little grandson is a pleasure to her evidently'.[6] This first grandchild of B-T was born just a few days after his sixtieth birthday.

Deaths from the War

The grandson was named after Evelyn's brother, Edward Ellis, who had become the immediate family's first casualty. Edward was on his way home from Burma for a year's leave when war broke out; he volunteered for service (despite a recent operation) and joined the Royal Naval Division of the Army. He held a commission, had been mentioned in despatches at Gallipoli and was awarded the Military Cross for bravery in January 1917. In the following month, February, at just thirty-three years old, he died soon after being severely wounded in the head, back and foot at Thiepval. Edward had been a close friend of Leonard and was the initial link between the Brewitt-Taylors and the Ellis family. Evelyn and Ray heard the news while on honeymoon in South Wales; it must have cast a deep shadow over their early days of marriage.

Further sadness was to follow. Bernard Ellis, the surviving son of Peg and her husband, had become a very close friend of Ray. He was a solicitor, and having been in the Royal Naval Volunteer Reserve, he joined the Royal Naval Division of the Army and was commissioned. He was awarded the Distinguished Conduct Medal early in the war and later served in Gallipoli; he also received the Distinguished Service Order for bravery in action in January 1917. After his promotion to commander of his battalion, he was wounded at Wimereux in March 1917 by a bullet in the base of his neck, and his eyes had to be treated for gassing. Following an operation for the bullet wound, he contracted pneumonia and died in April 1918; he was thirty-two years old. His mother, Peg, together with his wife, Marjorie Blumenfeld, whom he had married in 1915 and who had already lost her brother in March 1917, went to France and were with him when he died.

Meanwhile, Ray received frequent news of his new son (known as Teddy); there are many letters comparing in a friendly competitive way Teddy's progress with that of Margaret, the first of Daisy and Roy's children.[7] Margaret had been born the year prior to Teddy, and was one of five to be born to Daisy (quirkily repeating the same demographic pattern as her mother, Peg — three girls and two boys; it was the same pattern as that of Peg's parents and coincidentally the same as that produced by B-T's parents).

Ray was then a captain in the Field Ambulance Service, which involved constant work under shellfire; he had been awarded the Military Cross for searching for a missing stretcher-bearer for two hours under heavy shell-fire, at last finding him in a shell hole and assisting to carry him back. Throughout nine days' fighting, he was constantly going forward under fire searching for and bringing in wounded.

Shortly after this, on 22 August 1918, at just thirty years old and less than three months before the war's end, he was killed outright by a shell. B-T was distraught.[8]

The devastating effect of the war on the family can be seen by the extent of the bereavement suffered. B-T had lost a son, and the Ellis parents lost both their sons and a son-in-law. For the Ellis daughters, the war meant that they lost both their very close brothers and Evelyn a husband too; the Brewitt-Taylor boys had experienced the loss of both their close friends before Ray himself died. A devoted family, the war was a highly personal watershed. Throughout her long life, Daisy, and doubtless her sisters too, shed a quiet tear every Armistice Day anniversary. She had been particularly close to Bernard. Her husband, Roy, who had served in the Pay Corps and had experienced service in Gallipolli, was the sole survivor of those in the family joining the forces.

Letters from B-T before and after his son's death reveal the depth of his feelings as well as his generosity. They show his ability to express emotion while still reflecting the widely held patriotic sentiments. Given the conventions of the period, his use of 'C' as his signature to his children is interesting:

My very dear Son,

A month from today and your second birthday at the front will be upon you.

This should reach you about that time and I wish you many, many happy returns of the day. You know you have all my best wishes for success and happiness and I hope there is something better for you in the coming year than there has been in the past. You have the comfort of knowing that you realized where your duty lay from the first and required no urging. You saw the position at once and had not to be awakened from a slothful dream. And when you read this more than a year's work will be behind you: sacred work for the country and all that it represents and the protection of those worth fighting for. God bless you my son and may you be kept as in the past, fit and well and able to play your part.

The best and very best of good wishes. Your loving father, C.[9]

Though no year is given, this letter was likely to have been written to Ray in 1915, the time of his second birthday at the front. Ray must have been sufficiently moved by the letter to have kept it. The date would account for the fulsome patriotism somewhat more widespread at that stage in the war — one wonders whether B-T felt quite the same way after Ray's death. When G. E. Morrison sends his condolences to B-T, he simply responds, 'Yes, my son has gone the way of thousands of young men.'[10]

Another letter, written in December 1918, after Ray's death and just after the end of the war, was partly in response to some kind of expression of sadness by Evelyn about B-T's being so far way. The letter also conveys something of his motivation as a young man for social improvement. B-T is rather unhopeful about his own prospects for survival, for to suggest at the age of sixty that he would probably reach the end of his life well before Teddy was likely to go away to school seems unduly pessimistic. He was probably feeling low after a recent bout of influenza which he had suffered in Mukden, likely to be a strain of the infamous deadly Asian flu which also rampaged Europe about that time (he reports the high number of deaths of those attacked locally). His pessimism is understandable in someone who frequently experienced the deaths of family and colleagues, for in at least two appointments he had replaced staff who had died in service:

My very dear daughter,

Your letter of 3 October came the day before yesterday. Thank you for news and for various items of information which are interesting.

You must not be too hard on us who go abroad, dear. Sometimes we can secure certain ends that way and the road looks easy when one is young. Now when all my looks are directed backward perhaps I see more clearly all that I have lost. But I do not repent. Up to a certain point I have done what I set out to do and I shall pass on leaving my deeds to bear what fruit they may.

I have written you asking you to try to keep Ray's things till I come home. I will stand all expenses, dear, hire of room, storage, cartage and so on . . . you are not to stand any such things. We can get at grips with things in the spring when I come home for I received a hint that I shall get away.

Then we can settle things better. I shall see you, and we can do in 10 minutes as much as reams of paper leave only more obscure. But my dear, I want to set your mind at rest a little about material things, alas! such a minor matter. You have a pension for yourself and Teddy £124. So long as I remain in this service and on pay I will make that up to £300 at least. I won't say any more than that. Then Teddy's little belongings will remain at interest till he has to go to school. But probably some years before that, for it is long to look forward to, you will succeed to what my boy would have had of mine. Though that is not much as wealth goes, not worth mentioning as a mainstay of life, yet it should always keep the wolf some distance from the door.

The 400 was to be the first instalment of the price of a practice [for Ray]. Now it is yours . . . You may deal with the 400 as you like, but don't skimp yourself. You must remember that sudden needs arise and always try to keep something in hand to fill them.

And there's Len [Leonard]. I may tell you one day what he proposed. I think you will find him a kind brother although, like me, he walks in distant places. We three were such good friends you know, and you came in. And he loves you as I do.

Good bye, my dear daughter, Yours always affectionately, CBT[11]

The letter conveys B-T's mixture of generosity and prudence. While the sums mentioned were not a fortune, they would secure a very comfortable lifestyle. Evelyn also had a legacy from which she received interest of about £80 a year. To give some idea of monetary values at the time, an income of around £400 a year was about the average sum someone in the managerial class could expect and around twice as high as the incomes of the highest-paid skilled workers, the 'aristocrats of labour', such as railway engine drivers and compositors.[12] Even in the high peak of basic wages for hand compositors in London in 1920, the rate did not exceed £5 weekly, and then it fell somewhat in the early 1920s, by over ten per cent, and remained at £4 9s. until the Second World War;[13] on this many compositors purchased their own house. A few hundred pounds could procure a considerable range of housing.[14] When Evelyn's sister Daisy and her accountant husband Roy bought their house in Edgware, a substantial property in a respectable suburb of London, upgraded from their first home in Whetstone, they paid £950 in 1925. B-T was thus ensuring that on the income his daughter-in-law Evelyn was likely to receive, she and his grandson would be able to maintain a pretty good standard of living, especially as she lived with her mother who was herself quite comfortable.

It will be noted that there is an expectation that fees would be afforded to send Teddy away to school. In 1928, Teddy did in fact go away to a preparatory boarding school, Fernden, in Hampshire, and then on to Bryanston, not the cheapest of boarding schools, in 1932, at the age of fourteen. This was possibly paid for by B-T and his son Leonard together, for Teddy thought that the latter, his uncle, also 'had a hand in it'.

The letter to Evelyn also contains something of B-T's warmth; one has a sense that under the controlled distance he generally displayed, he had a fund of feeling for those to whom he felt attached. He found expressing emotion at a distance easier than in person.

Marriage of Leonard

The following February, 1919, B-T received a visit from his son Leonard, who brought with him his recently acquired wife. At the age of thirty-four, Leonard had an unexpected and whirlwind romance. He had been in Japan and Hawaii, possibly on teak business, and decided to take a holiday in San Francisco. On the boat voyage there, he met an American, Margaret Elizabeth McGee, who was about two years his senior; they married in early January 1919 at Sutter Creek, California.[15] She was returning home after spending 'a happy year in Japan teaching the violin under the auspices of the YWCA'. She hailed from California, where her family settled as pioneers during the Gold Rush in the 1840s; her father was an attorney in San Francisco. According to Joan, one of the two daughters Leonard and his wife adopted, her mother alleged that B-T was 'horrified' that his son was marrying a California girl because his only experience of Western ladies on their own in the East was 'the hard boiled lady-of-the-town type one could pick up in any Shanghai bar . . . Somehow,' Joan writes, 'I doubt that he had more than misgivings, knowing Leonard, who was quite shy and very proper.'[16] It was also Joan's mother who confirmed that her husband, Leonard, had 'feelings' for Daisy Ellis. Joan writes: 'I remember Daisy very well and understand his admiration.'

Continuing the story of Leonard and his wife's trip to meet B-T, Joan writes:

> In order to win CH's approval they made a detour up through Korea to Mukden . . . and he took her out in that droshky to see the sights — all bundled up against the cold.

They certainly would have needed insulation going around freezing Mukden in February. The 'droshky' refers to the horse-drawn carriage shown in a photograph. Joan adds: 'They both [that is, her father, Leonard, and grandfather B-T] must have been devastated by Raymond's death.' Another reference to the marriage is found in one of Peg's budges:

> Of outside news a big piece is that Leonard was married on Jan 3rd [1919] to a Margaret McGie [sic] of California. He met her on the journey there from China. He had to have his holiday and could not come to England. So after a time with his sorrowing father, he went to California for the climate to finish his leave. And lo! Miss M. McGie was on her way home from Japan . . . Leonard has given me no idea of her at all except that her ideals are the same as ours.

Peg adds, with characteristic humour, 'That, naturally, sounds all right.'[17]

Certainly, Elizabeth, as she was known in a family full of Margarets, appears to have fitted in with the Ellis family very well. They all met at Inglefield when Leonard ('not changed a bit except in appearance, being thinner and rather bald') came home, it seems partly for work purposes, in the autumn of 1921. Then, when the couple went home on long leave in the summer of 1924, they saw a good deal of the family. By then Peg, together with two of her daughters, Win and Evelyn, and Evelyn's son Teddy, were in Bournemouth, where they had moved in September 1922. They had left their large Inglefield home in Potter's Bar to live in a somewhat more modest, though still very substantial, small villa. Leonard and his wife visited regularly, taking a flat near the family for a couple of months, and the family engaged in various activities together. Win, the violinist, introduced Elizabeth to playing together in local groups. Not being able to have children themselves, Elizabeth and Leonard eventually decided to adopt two girls.

On 19 April 1919, B-T left Mukden to go on home leave. This was just prior to the anti-foreigner (and especially anti-Japanese) May Fourth Movement student and worker demonstrations which followed the 1919 Peace Treaty. The treaty transferred German concessions in China to Japan, which the new China highly resented. Mukden being a politically sensitive area, it would have been interesting to have known B-T's thoughts, if expressed, on any demonstrations that occurred there.

15

End of Career

Final Leave

B-T was now entering the final stage of his life in China, and his leave of 1919 proved to be his last. He arrived back in Britain at the end of June 1919, going directly to Scotland to see his wife and take her home from hospital, despite there being no improvement in her condition. He went south during the summer and included Lyme Regis in his travels, where he probably stayed with or visited Peg's husband, Henry Ellis, known as 'Pope'. Pope and his wife lived amicably apart in their latter years. There are no comments on how he and B-T got on: Pope had a reputation for being difficult with people and was reputed to be something of a recluse. Yet, he had engaged sufficiently in public life to become mayor of Lyme Regis.

As already noted, B-T and Pope shared an interest in astronomy, for B-T it stemmed from the days he studied and taught navigation. Pope, a serious amateur astronomer who had lectured and written on the subject, was elected a fellow of the Royal Astronomical Society in 1898, and he was also sometime treasurer of the British Astronomical Association.[1] He kept his own powerful twenty-inch telescope in Lyme Regis, which sparked a rumour during the war, when he had only recently arrived in the town, that he was a German spy. He must have enjoyed showing the telescope to B-T. They would have also taken the opportunity to discuss the financial situation of Evelyn Brewitt-Taylor, Pope's recently widowed daughter, and their joint grandson, Teddy.

For the first time, B-T was able to see his grandchild, the now eighteen-month-old Teddy, who, he said, was 'perfection'. Evelyn took Teddy up to Earlsferry to visit them in the autumn, reporting home that she went for walks to the sea:

> Grandma has come with me both afternoons so far, I hope she won't always. We don't see much of Grandpa unless we seek him out in his den at the top of the house.[2]

There are other letters referring to her stepmother-in-law which frequently comment on her mental imbalance; they confirm the hospital's view that there was no improvement in Ann's condition. One letter from Peg to her daughter Win paints the picture: they are

> living on the edge of a volcano . . . Mrs. B-T gets wrong if she is over-tired. Mr. B-T retires to his den . . . He's given Teddy a wheelbarrow which is Teddy's joy. [The barrow is still in the family.]

Later, Peg wrote:

> Fortunately so far [Ann] has only erupted in private, to her unfortunate spouse . . . B-T adores Teddy, they are both great friends.[3]

Final posting and Leaving China

When B-T returned alone to China, the twin themes of his leave — enchantment with his grandson and concern over his wife's condition — must have remained with him.

On returning, he was sent to Chungking (Chongqing), on the upper reaches of the Yangtze River in Szechuan (Sichuan) province, taking up his position on 27 April 1920. It seems rather odd that given that he had only a few more months of employment left with the Service before retirement, other arrangements for his final leave were not made. But it later came to light that he had actually only applied for retirement from the Service on 26 May, just a month after his posting to Chungking. Sadly, the resignation letter was missing from the files, as this may have provided his reasons for so doing.[4] The domestic situation back home might have been a motive, in particular the condition of his wife, though there was also his widowed daughter-in-law and grandson. Another powerful factor was very likely to have been the promulgation in 1920 of a new Customs pension scheme.[5] The scheme was widely welcomed in the Service, as it had the effect of increasing pay, as well as 'contentment and hope', and a number of senior staff retired to take advantage of the scheme.[6] Satisfaction was thus provided for those retiring, and the vacancies which became available gave hope to younger staff.

Chungking had remained something of a backwater until industrialization began at the end of the 1920s, receiving a major boost when the Kuomintang made the city its wartime capital during the Japanese occupation. It was opened as a Treaty Port in 1891, and when B-T was there it was still a small, rather isolated place. Sanitary arrangements, for example, were somewhat primitive. Even three years after he left, a missionary family, albeit one with the luxury of a refrigerator, took their water supply from the Yangtze 'in which people washed, dropped their rubbish, defecated and died'; the water had to be 'not only boiled, but also strained through gravel, sand and, finally, charcoal'.[7]

Other conditions were also unappealing. Chungking in the summer is known as one of the three furnaces of China (the others being Nanking and Wuhan) with temperatures reaching forty degrees Celsius or more. Before air-conditioning was widespread it would have been most unpleasant for living and working, especially for an aging Westerner. One Consular officer living there in 1913, just a few years before B-T arrived, was of the view that without exception every officer stationed there had made every effort to escape as soon as possible,[8] so summer in Chungking too might have been a subsidiary circumstantial factor encouraging B-T's resignation.

B-T's commissioner's reports, presented in a regularly ordered sequence (local politics then Customs affairs including staffing, weather, crops and health), reveal some of his major preoccupations. This was the period when the warlords held sway in China and the society was in turmoil and deeply demoralized. To many, there was little distinction between common bandits and warlord troops.[9] He had problems with soldiers who had damaged property, the river had to be cleared of bandits and he had to close a Customs property which had been rented out as a teahouse and had become disreputable, though in what way was not disclosed.[10] Opium, so important for Customs revenues, continued to be a problem. There is a close relationship between the activity of the military and its price:

> The opium question is becoming a greater worry every day. I hear that the price is down to less than a dollar a tael [approximately an ounce in weight] and our total highest rewards — for seizure plus information paid to ships' officers — amount to 90 cents; concealment is also on the increase.[11]

B-T was very much aware that the military, under local warlords, controlled much of what went on and were instrumental in bypassing the collection of dues: 'under their influence the traffic in opium goes merrily on' bringing down the price to 80 cents a tael.[12] The following month, the price fell again. 'What affects us most', he writes, 'is military action'; this made the collection of revenue difficult and encouraged illegal trading:

> The city is full of it. The local price is 50 cents or less a tael. Opium is moved by military escort and army expenses met by its sale.[13]

A few years earlier, shortly after the Revolution, the Republicans had tried to suppress the use of opium, even that locally grown. But with the widespread usage, this proved to be extremely difficult, given 'the many highly respectable opium smokers all around us'.[14]

Apart from opium, the armies had other means of securing income. One of the leaders demanded two million dollars from the city

> threatening that if the money is not forthcoming he had a list of rich men of
> the place and he would seize them. Kidnapping and holding to ransom seems
> a common trick down river, people here fear lest they may fall victims.

The commander was eventually beaten down to $800,000.[15] B-T's final report is devoted entirely to military matters, which obviously dominate his thoughts. 'We are now really in the hands of brigands and the future of the place seems a dark one.'[16]

Stella Benson, the novelist who we met in the chapter on Mengtze, arrived in Chungking towards the end of B-T's stay there. She was chaperoning a married friend romantically attached to Shaemus O'Gorman Anderson, one of B-T's staff. Stella and Shaemus themselves formed a sympathetic relationship and were later to marry. When Stella needed a typewriter, Shaemus took her to his office one Saturday morning, where she 'burbled to his boss, a rather smug, fussy elderly man called Brewitt-Taylor'.[17] As Stella's initial comments on people were frequently critical, changing her view on closer acquaintance, it is difficult to know what weight to put on this assessment, though it could be significant that B-T did not appear to have attended any of the many dinner parties held for the visitors.

On 1 November 1920, he handed over control to his successor, E. G. Labas. Labas's first report comments on B-T's demeanor:

> I took over on the 1st and Mr. Brewitt-Taylor left on the 2nd looking very
> well. He has been quite cheery during the time I have spent with him, but on
> his departure felt a little sad, I think, at the idea of leaving China.[18]

After forty years, most of his working life, this was hardly surprising. There would be few regrets at leaving the unpleasantness of Chungking. But this was the country where he had made his home and still possessed property, where he had immersed himself in its language and culture and where he had achieved considerable success in his career and writings. Here, both his sons were born, and he had brought up his family in their early years. He had also experienced the sad loss of his first love, had tried to come to terms with the madness of his second wife and had learnt of the death of his son. It would have been strange indeed if leaving China had been without melancholy for B-T.

The voyage home was very likely to have been made by sea, for not only would the Trans-Siberian Railway have been in the grips of winter, the aftermath of the Civil War in Russia would have made a train journey perilous. The period between B-T's departure from Chungking and the date of his return home was long enough for him to have travelled by ship. There would have been plenty of opportunity to reflect on his time in China and to brood over the prospect of returning to live permanently with his periodically demented wife. One wonders how he intended to occupy himself in retirement, and whether, especially given the properties he still owned in China, he had intentions to return.

16

Retirement and Publication of the *Romance*

At the end of December 1920, at the age of sixty-three, B-T returned to Britain to join his wife in her house in Earlsferry, Elie, Fifeshire, Scotland;[1] there he lived throughout his retirement, though according to his will never really regarding it the place he would have chosen to live. He made frequent trips south, about four times a year according to his wife, to see friends and relatives. He went mainly to London, Bournemouth, as well as Portsmouth, and usually on his own.[2] Peg Ellis's letters reveal his movements and the close contact he was pleased to maintain with his deceased son's family, providing as they did a rare source of personal warmth and welcome.

He travelled south to visit the Ellises in February, very shortly after his return, and would have stayed longer if he had not promised his wife that he would return by a given date. At Easter, Evelyn and Teddy were due to see B-T in Scotland, the first of what became regular yearly trips to be with him around that time. But they had to keep putting off going that year, as Ann had had a 'very bad turn lately' and then had to go into a home in Edinburgh for a 'rest cure'.[3] In September 1921, Peg writes to her daughter Winnie that Evelyn, staying at the Earlsferry house 'Cathay', is 'having rather a rough time, I fear. Mrs. B-T is not allowed to see women and children.'[4] The sight of women and their children seemed to have triggered unhappy memories for Ann of the loss of her babies and allegedly destabilized her. Ann spent another three months in the Edinburgh Asylum then was discharged without improvement, still having hallucinations and delusions.

The following year, in February 1922, Ann had recovered sufficiently to join B-T on a visit to London:

> Grandpa B-T came to town for a week *with his wife*, who was unusually well. I went to tea with them . . . Grandma was most amiable and nobody would have guessed how dreadful she can be.[5]

Later that summer, Ann was in the asylum again. According to the hospital notes, she was being more frequently violent towards B-T, suffering outbursts of temper at night, battering doors and screaming; this continued throughout her two-month stay in hospital.

At that time, Peg and her two daughters were still living in Inglefield, which was proving difficult to sell. In this post-war period, people were reluctant to take on large houses, as servants were increasingly hard to find and expensive. They had first looked for a smaller house near Peg's daughter Daisy, then in Whetstone, Middlesex. They then decided to move to Bournemouth to be near one of Peg's sisters married to a Unitarian minister there, Rev. Henry Shaen Solly, whose father was referred to earlier, regarding the First Opium War. They found a suitable house, Branksome Lodge, far smaller than Inglefield, but still substantial, to which they moved that autumn, 1922.

During May of that year, Evelyn and Teddy went to tea with B-T at the Kingsley Hotel,[6] which he frequented on his trips to London:

> It was to meet a Miss Edwards, a professor of Chinese at the School of Oriental Languages, a friend of Grandpa's. Not very amusing for Teddy on the whole.[7]

Evangeline Dora Edwards had only recently become a lecturer at the school, in 1921. B-T had continued contact with her after their friendship began in Mukden and was obviously keen to introduce her to his intimate family. Teddy was only four years old then, but he does remember meeting her when he was around sixteen. Given that his memories of the whole of that period are rare, especially over details, it is surprising that he remembers her and readily recalled the name 'Dr. Edwards'. For that name to have registered, either he met her several times or he might have heard references made about her by the adults around him; perhaps something was said that caused the name to be significant to the teenaged Teddy.

On the same trip, B-T spent the whole day in the garden at Inglefield and returned the following day. He clearly found the family's welcome, in particular that of Peg, as congenial as had his sons just twenty years before. Now, he had the additional interest of a grandson. In October, soon after the move to Bournemouth, he visited them both before and after going to France to visit Raymond's grave. At Christmas he went again, taking a meccano construction set for Teddy. 'I think he likes Bournemouth', Peg wrote of B-T.[8]

The following year, May 1923, he again went to France, this time with Evelyn, to visit the graves, not only of Raymond but also of Evelyn's brothers, Edward and Bernard. B-T's knee was presenting a problem, so they could not walk enough to get warm — 'it seems to be sinovitis' (appropriate enough for a sinologist!), an inflammation of the knee.

That Christmas a slight disapproval was expressed by Peg, ever critical of indulgence, when Grandpa B-T insisted on presenting Teddy, whose birthday was around that time, 'a sugared cake'; later, she speaks of his spoiling Teddy more than she does, then tries to excuse him: 'perhaps he would not . . . if he were with him more'.[9] She had been more approving of B-T's brother,[10] who had given a box of Anchor building bricks to Teddy; they were popular with the boy, being 'brought out daily', but the approval was largely because they were made in Germany. Peg's social concern overcame any possible anti-German prejudice that might have remained from the level of family bereavement suffered in the war: she felt that the misery experienced by post-war Germany should be alleviated not just by sending cash relief, but by trade between the countries. 'Surely it is better to encourage commerce', she commented.

When Evelyn and Teddy next went to Elie, they were unable to stay in the house because of the condition of B-T's wife, and he arranged rooms for them and for Leonard and his wife who were due to come on leave from Siam:

> He cannot safely have them at his wife's house, she would become distraught by the prospect, probably. So a family party will be achieved this way.[11]

They went on 5 June, 'when the doctor pronounced all safe'.

B-T continued to make frequent trips to Bournemouth, where he could spend more time with his grandson: 'Teddy and he are excellent friends, birds of a feather.'[12] Teddy was also shy, sensitive and undemanding. References to Evelyn visiting B-T in London are frequent. They went to concerts and enjoyed meals together: 'salmon and chicken are luxuries we never taste . . . except when Grandpa B-T takes them to lunch anywhere', writes Peg.[13] Frugal over food, Peg ensured that in the Ellis household food was something to be eaten not fussed over, and rarely even discussed.

There is a curious allusion to B-T's having sailed for China at the beginning of May 1924, for when Evelyn went to Elie in early June she saw him everyday. He certainly could not have 'sailed'; that would have taken far too long: the direct route by steamer taking about thirty-two days in the mid-1930s, and if via Canada somewhere between twenty-nine and thirty-four days. Long-distance air flights to the Far East did not really develop until the 1930s, with refuelling stops every five hundred miles; flying would have been so rare to surely have been remarked on by Peg.[14] So in 1924, the trans-Siberian train route would have been the most probable mode of travelling quickly if not very comfortably; this is the way mail would have been sent. Even if B-T had gone then, it would have been an extremely brief visit, perhaps in connection with the *San Kuo* publication which was to come out the following year. More likely, he may have intended to go but cancelled the trip because of his wife's illness.

Something of B-T's feelings of sadness and frustration is occasionally expressed in family letters; after Evelyn and Teddy's Easter 1926 visit to Earlsferry,

Evelyn, who was fond of B-T, was 'loth to leave the lonely Grandpa'.[15] When later that year she went up to London in order to spend a few days with him there, he was irritatingly summoned back to his wife. 'Quite unnecessarily',[16] Peg asserts dismissively.

The *Romance of the Three Kingdoms*

Five years into B-T's retirement, in December 1925, his translation of the *San Kuo Chih Yen-I* as *Romance of the Three Kingdoms* was published in Shanghai by Kelly and Walsh. We have seen that various other works of his had been published well before this, his last being the revised edition of *Textbook of Modern Documentary Chinese,* Volume 1 in 1909, and Volume 2 in 1910. Apart from his *Chats in Chinese,* there is no evidence of other writings since the destruction of the complete draft of the *San Kuo* during the Boxer troubles, so for fifteen years he seems not to have published.

The long delay in publication given the speed at which the first draft was produced could be attributed to a number of factors. The shock of losing the first draft after so much effort might have caused at least the temporary abandonment of the endeavour by a lesser man, but this does not quite fit with what we know of B-T's stolid single-mindedness. He had obviously been keen to revise the *Textbook* — as we have seen he put himself forward for that task. He probably saw this book as being more relevant and beneficial to his career than redoing the *Romance*. Career progression to commissioner rank took place immediately following the Boxer episode, and his new responsibilities, in which he would have wanted to excel, may well have led to writing taking less of a priority. Every job change, and there were several in the years before his retirement, meant getting to know a new area and new colleagues within and beyond the Customs, learning to deal with new authorities and local powerful figures and generally establishing a social presence; these were all in their different ways time-consuming. Then there were family concerns, especially the demanding burdens of his wife's disorder, which must have been extremely disturbing until he learnt to adjust, working out strategies for survival by a combination of judicious handling and withdrawal.

In October 1926 Peg informed her siblings that B-T had sent copies of his capacious translation to the family:

> Grandpa B-T has sent Evelyn his two volumes of translation of an old Chinese romance, historical. He has had it published in China.

He dedicated the work 'To the memory of my son Raymond'.

The first edition's first printing carried the statement that it had been 'Especially prepared for the use and education of the Chinese People'; thus, the initial perception of the publisher was that the level of English literacy among Chinese at the time was sufficiently high to aim at the Chinese market. Within four years of the book's publication, the same publisher decided to bring out a cheap edition of the work, noting:

> The Standard edition of this translation of China's most famous historical novel . . . is fast becoming out of print. The price of this Standard edition, it was realised, was above the purchasing capacity of the average Chinese reader, and therefore, in view of the ever-increasing desire on the part of the latter to embrace Western learning, it was thought that a cheaper edition might meet with the support of Chinese friends who would be interested in reading in English what most of them have already read in their mother tongue.[17]

Conceivably, the unintended delay in publishing the work had provided an opportunity to tap a new audience. For following the May Fourth movement, a more positive attitude to popular culture emerged; it came to be seen as more creative and vital than the sterile classical works of 'high culture'. Though the translation seemingly ran counter to the Chauvinistic strand of the movement, the publisher may have thought that the widened interest in traditional vernacular novels could attract Chinese who also enjoyed reading English.

B-T's translation was the first attempt at a complete translated version of the *San Kuo,* written some six hundred years previously and attributed Lo Kuan-chung (1330–1400) but probably extensively revised by many hands and voices.[18] By producing the first full version in English of any of the major Chinese traditional novels, B-T pioneered the introduction of China's popular traditional novels to the English-speaking world.

B-T was well aware of the limited view of fiction as literature held by Chinese traditionally, and he quoted from another foreign scholar right from the beginning of his preface to justify his translation:

> A. Wylie,[19] in his invaluable *Notes on Chinese Literature,* says, 'Works of fiction *par excellence* are not admitted by the Chinese to form a part of their national literature. Those who have imbibed European ideas on the subject, however, will feel that the novels and romances are too important as a class to be overlooked. The insight they give in the national manners and customs of various ages, the specimens which they furnish of an ever-changing language, the fact of this being the only channel through which a large portion of the people gain their knowledge of history, and the influence which they must consequently exercise in the formation of character, are reasons too weighty to be left out of account, notwithstanding the prejudices of scholars on the subject. Foremost among these in popular estimation is the San Kuo Chih Yen-i.'[20]

The quotation goes on with a description of the novel. While laudable to quote another authority at length to justify oneself, this practice also seems characteristically self-effacing of B-T. More important, the reference gives a major clue to why B-T undertook the translation: to provide a complete example of a neglected genre to the English-speaking world, a genre that was generally more accessible than was classical literature, which had been the focus of the early sinologists. By his work, B-T was in the vanguard of the second wave of expatriate sinological pioneers.

So this was B-T's major explicit justification: novels and romances were too important a class to be overlooked. One can only speculate why he chose the *San Kuo*. Perhaps he did so because it was the most influential of the major novels; the possible urging by Giles would have helped; and the language of the edition he used for his translation would have been an additional challenge, a successful translation likely to enhance his reputation as a scholar (he would not have originally anticipated such a long haul to publication). One wonders, too, whether within the seemingly gentle translator there lay a yearning for adventure, expressed in the battles of the *San Kuo*, and, indeed, in his initial decision to go to China.

The importance of the *San Kuo* has frequently been emphasized. A recent edition regards the *Romance* to be 'China's greatest classical novel . . . fundamentally about people [in it, we] see our own strengths, weaknesses, wisdom, folly'.[21] Another edition of the translation has an introduction by Roy Andrew Miller, which summarizes the work as a popularization of events which took place in the period from AD 220 to 265. The main outline, he asserts, is historically correct, with real chief characters but with most of the incidents and anecdotes, fictional elements result from centuries of accretion:

> The book is . . . a historical romance of major proportions, a fascinating novel, whose chief theme is the nature of human ambition.[22]

Numerous other attempts to distil its essence have been made. One in particular lays emphasis on the concern with righteousness expressed in different ways. The novel's glorification of traditional behaviour, friendship, brotherhood and loyalty has had an immense exemplifying influence on Chinese secret societies still prevalent today.[23]

A recent contemporary novel has another take on the *Romance*:

> There is a saying, 'If you are old, you don't read The Three Kingdoms. If you are young, you don't read The Dream' . . . Because the Three Kingdoms is all about plotting and scheming. Old men are already shrewd, they don't need to read something that makes them even more so. The Dream is all about romance and when you are young you are already romantic enough.[24]

Several book reviews of B-T's translation have been effusive in their praise. The earliest found was by an A. J. Bowen:

> Mr. Brewitt-Taylor, formerly of the Chinese Customs Service, has placed the West under great obligation by this translation of a very distinctively Eastern work. Throughout the entire Orient, 'The Three Kingdoms' is widely-known, not only by scholars and general readers, but also by the illiterate, for its marvellous adventures and stirring battles have been told in countless tea shops and way-side inns by matchless storytellers from the time of our own great story teller, Chaucer, to the present day . . . The San Kuo is undoubtedly the most popular of all of China's many novels. . .
>
> The translator has done a most excellent piece of work. It is a real translation, and not an extended summary. It gives you the author's exact words, in so far as they can be expressed in idiomatic English. But better still, the way of saying it in English preserves very well indeed the tone and spirit and the movement of the original — a task by no means easy of accomplishment, a success which few translators of Chinese achieve.[25]

Another review, in the *Journal of the North China Branch of the Royal Asiatic Society,* appeared under the initials 'E. M.' The only member of the society then with those initials was E. Mengel, who around that time was Superintendent of Chinese Telegraphs in Yunnan. The piece contains the following:

> The English reader will be furnished with all that is necessary to understand the thrilling events of this most interesting period in Chinese history. To be unacquainted with these events is really to lose much of the materials that go to fill the popular mind with the romance of the country. The tales from this period supply the storytellers with their stock in trade. It is known how they keep an audience attentively listening, in some busy corner, for a long time with recounting the valiant deeds of a leading actor in these times long vanished. Many of the popular plays in the theatres are founded on some episode from the San Kuo Chi . . .
>
> At the same time he [the reader] will be getting acquainted with some solid facts of Chinese history, the knowledge of which will help him to understand many allusions in Chinese books. The romance is founded on fact. But in the romance there is much extension of fact . . .
>
> The volume before us contains a wealth of material not only of descriptive history, but of ample stuff to help the humanitarian, the psychologist, and the pathologist of the human passions to enlarge the subject of their studies . . . we are introduced to the inner working of the human mind in its plans and schemes! How it is often governed by selfish ambition and directed by subtile and crafty policy to gain personal satisfaction. At the same time we are made to feel that the finer emotions of love and self-denial are the common heritage of ancient folk as well as the modern man . . .

> Mr. C. H. Brewitt-Taylor undertook a great task. We are glad that its magnitude did not daunt him but that he has brought it to a completion. The work is magnificently done.

Then, almost sounding as though the reviewer expected the public to do penance for B-T's herculean labours, he wrote:

> The public should show its appreciation of the noble effort by reading the results of so many years labours, and thus not only show its gratitude but at the same time enrich their own minds with this wealth of Chinese lore.[26]

The reviews acknowledge B-T's qualities of hard work and meticulous persistence; even more, they are a tribute to his scholarship and feel for language. Others have rated his translation as 'brilliant' and 'masterly'. He must have been well-satisfied by all the acclaim.

Writings Post–*San Kuo* Publication

Few other writings by B-T have been found since the publication of the *San Kuo*. It seems difficult to believe that the known withdrawals to his den in Earlsferry produced nothing further, but it could well be that retirement with his wife was highly stressful, never knowing when she might erupt.

The year of his death was to see the publication of *The Dragon Book,* an anthology of Chinese literature by Evangeline Dora Edwards. This book was designed to recall 'the ancient spirit of old beauty and serene detachment' of old China, and it contains a number of quotations from B-T's translation of the *San Kuo.* Evangeline also records her thanks to B-T for suggesting a romantic poem with a light humorous touch: 'The Small-Footed Maid', possibly written by a Mr. E. C. Baker. The poem is something of a spoof and must have amused B-T and Evangeline. The following couplets indicate the flavour of the piece:

> But fairer by far was the small-footed maid
> > Who sat by my side in the sandal-wood shade, ...
> And dearest I thought her of maids in Pekin,
> > As from the pagoda she bade me chin-chin. ...
> And soon the most beautiful girl in Pekin
> > Fell asleep in the arms of her own mandarin.[27]

It has been suggested to me that the poem does not strictly belong in a serious anthology, and perhaps it was seen by them as a rather naughty inclusion, suggesting perhaps a little frisson or private joke between them; though it should be noted that there are other light-hearted pieces in the anthology, for example, one in pidgin English by H. A. Giles.

In terms of major work, the *San Kuo* was B-T's apotheosis, and it may be that he felt anything else he produced would do little to enhance further his reputation or, more particularly, his personal satisfaction. After a demanding life, and a trying wife, he was emotionally drained and tiring, feeling his years as he approached seventy.

Additional Translations of the *San Kuo*

Following B-T's rendering of the *San Kuo* into English, translations into other European languages appeared: German in 1953, Russian in 1954 and French in the early 1960s.[28] There had already been translations into Far Eastern languages: Manchu, Japanese and Siamese.[29]

But for seventy years, the only full translation of the *San Kuo* into English was that of B-T. There have been numerous editions since it was first published in 1925. One in 1959 by the Charles E. Tuttle Company in Rutland, Vermont, has had multiple reprints, the most recent in 2003. Likewise, another publisher, Graham Brash in Singapore, published the work in 1985 and has found it sufficiently popular to have repeated reprints since.

In 1991, a new, complete English translation of the *San Kuo,* undertaken by the American sinologue Professor Moss Roberts, was published. The only acknowledgement to B-T made by the author is brief:

> A word of recognition is also due to C. H. Brewitt-Taylor, whose 1925 translation of *Three Kingdoms* I read long before gathering enough Chinese to confront the original.

The only other reference is to his disagreement over the interpretation of the *yanyi* in the title, which B-T translates as 'romance'; Roberts deliberately does not use this 'because it denotes a world removed from reality', preferring 'historical novel'.[30]

Roberts argues that the *San Kuo* has two aspects: the historical is Han; its literary aspect, Ming. Others have also pointed out that in the Confucian tradition, history and literature are not generally seen as separate fields:

> The historical novel *Three Kingdoms* . . . has shaped the thinking of the Chinese people about the issues of war, politics, and history, perhaps more than any other single work. It is also a major literary masterpiece that influenced the development of drama as well as the novel in China.[31]

B-T was well aware of the difficulty of how to describe the work, for a review he wrote in the 1880s contains a full discussion of the very point Roberts takes issue with.[32] B-T argued in some detail a century earlier that it is neither a romance nor a novel, not even an historical one; he preferred to call it an 'historical drama not written for the stage',[33] a clumsy description he was to jettison in favour of the more simple 'romance'. He does not justify his choice of title when the book is eventually published thirty-five years after the review. Chinese speakers I have discussed this issue with are of the view that 'romance' is an acceptable translation of *yen-i*.[34]

The publisher's blurb to Roberts's new translation refers to its being a 'readable translation . . . the early English version [being] turgid'. A review of Roberts's translation avers the novel's 'indelible position in the Chinese heritage' and goes on to describe B-T's translation as complete but faulty. The reviewer states that Roberts provides in his 1991 edition a complete and authoritative translation which 'perfectly captures the feeling of the original text'.[35]

Not all sinologues share these views. A contrasting view has been presented by John Minford:

> *The Romance of the Three Kingdoms* is, to me best translated by C. H. Brewitt-Taylor, though there is a recent one by Moss Roberts.[36]

He and another British sinologue who had compared the two translations and were familiar with the Chinese version were asked separately how they thought they compared. Their verbal assessments coincided: their view was that Roberts's version was both more complete ('everything was there') and more scholarly, with very useful annotations, but they considered that B-T's translation better captured the flavour of the original and was more concise and stylistically superior; B-T caught the essence more. The verdict of each was the same: 'he has not been superseded'.

17

Final Years

The Customs Service experience had a powerful effect on its members. Many, including B-T, retained a strong identification and interest in the Service well into retirement and old age. In response to a letter from B-T, Maze, a former commissioner colleague who had become Inspector General, wrote a long letter castigating Aglen, whom he eventually replaced, for his policies of trying to act independently rather than serving the Chinese government. Maze encloses confidential material about the affair which Maze had written, asking B-T for his comments and to share the contents with another former colleague, William MacDonald, who had retired to Inverness and with whom B-T retained contact, sending newspapers from China to each other. MacDonald was to ensure that the material was returned to Maze, marked 'personal'. Maze strongly reviled Aglen's attempt to get a recorded minute changed (to suggest he retired from office rather than being dismissed) as being 'not merely childish but stupid, and is evidence of senile decay'. He also criticizes those who sent Aglen a letter of condolence; B-T had been one of the co-signatories.[1]

B-T replies with spirit. He did not think his signing along with others was 'presumptuous and meddlesome'. He had done so from his experience of Aglen who, as far as B-T was concerned

> did nothing that might compromise the Service at any time, never showed any tendency to self assertion or independent action. He always insisted upon his position as Servant of the Government . . . It may be that habitual approval wrought some sort of change, but I saw no such tendency. While I was in Mukden there was never any opprobrious or contemptuous reference to the powers that were . . . Of course the Service has been an anomaly ever since it was created, but it has been a stout staff for China to lean on during the dangerous period of renewal of contact with the outside world.

B-T added, 'Long may you live, and the Service endure!'[2] The letter, reserving judgement on Maze's vituperation, is a rare expression by B-T of a personal view. Given that by all appearances B-T had not got on all that well with Aglen when he was Inspector General, a sense of fair-mindedness is displayed by B-T. Not long after this correspondence, Aglen himself died, in 1932, aged sixty-two.

B-T's assertiveness may reflect his advanced years — he had nothing to lose from speaking as he felt; whether he would have done so while still in office is more uncertain. However, there is no doubt that B-T felt proud of the Service and of its value to China. He excused his lack of writing to Maze for some time: 'I have little or nothing to do. I fear I must confess to laziness and perhaps weakness of purpose.'[3] Approaching seventy-five years, B-T was withdrawing from his wider interests. His remaining years were mainly concerned with family, domestic matters and tidying up his affairs.

Sadly, he was to experience yet another loss, that of his remaining son, Leonard.

Retirement and the Death of Leonard

Following marriage, Leonard seems to have returned more frequently from Siam, either for leave or business. He, together with his wife and daughter, Joan, saw a good deal of the Bournemouth family, and they all, including B-T without his wife, spent holidays together. In January 1928, B-T's grandson Teddy, aged ten, left home for preparatory boarding school in Fernden, Hampshire, after which, in 1932, he went to Bryanston. His uncle, Leonard, was involved in the choice of Bryanston,[4] which confirms Teddy's impression, referred to earlier, that Leonard possibly contributed to the costs of his education — fulfilling his intention to help in some way as indicated by B-T in his letter to his daughter-in-law soon after the death of Raymond.

Later in 1928, after a spell in a nursing home in Siam, Leonard was ordered on medical grounds to return to Britain for good. His illness is unclear, but he had to retire early, at only forty-four years old. Peg reports him being depressing; nervy, grumbling and shivery, and that winter he went on his own to the south of France to recuperate.

Earlier, Leonard and Elizabeth decided to adopt a baby. B-T was apparently happy about that and was to treat all his three grandchildren equally when he made his will. However, according to his granddaughter Joan he apparently did not want them to adopt boys, as this would 'confuse the line', so two girls were adopted. Joan, who had been born in Romford, Essex, in 1924, was adopted around 1926 when adoption had only just become legal under the first Legal Adoption Act, 1926. A few years later Leonard must have recovered sufficiently from his illness to contemplate increasing their family by another daughter, Nancy, born in Manchester in 1930; they adopted her probably sometime in 1931.

But soon their family life was to be severely disrupted again, for only a couple of years later, on 14 May 1933, Leonard died. As Peg reports to her siblings:

The first part of May was made sad by Leonard's illness and death on the 14th. He was Edward's age and almost like another son to me. Inglefield was nearest to home to him when he was growing up. Poor old Grandpa has had many sorrows. I hope he will find Teddy always a source of happiness.[5]

A memorial seat to Leonard is still to be seen in the crematorium in Woking, Surrey. The cause of his death is unclear, but it appears to have been a cancerous blood condition. He was only forty-eight years of age at his death. B-T must have found it grievous to have outlived both his sons.

Elizabeth, Leonard's widow, was 'very thin and desolate', according to Peg. Characteristically non-traditional; Peg was pleased to report that she had not gone into traditional mourning attire: 'Elizabeth, I am glad to say, has not gone into black.'[6] Shortly afterwards, she took her daughters, Joan and Nancy, to live in Bournemouth, where she would be closer to Peg and her family.

Leonard's will dated from December 1929, soon after his retirement from Siam. Following the adoption of his second daughter, he added what reads like a rather confusing codicil in July 1931. But the will is interesting in that it reveals continued contact with his uncle, Herbert William Taylor, the brother of B-T, and his family: a bequest initially for B-T (and if he were not alive, for Teddy) would, if they were both to predecease Leonard, go to Herbert William's family, which suggests some attachment felt by Leonard for that part of B-T's family of origin.

The death of his son prompted B-T, then aged seventy-five, to make his own will — somewhat late for a prudent man of some financial substance. He signed this will in London on 23 June 1933; the date suggests that the will must have been drawn up shortly after Leonard's funeral. B-T had probably come down for the funeral, and the loss of his surviving son must have propelled him to discuss his own will with his London solicitor.

B-T also decided then to begin to put his affairs in order. He had retained his four properties in Peitaiho, China, the three purchased in 1906 when he was in Mengtze and one in 1915 when in Foochow. Perhaps these purchases were made simply as investments, but there may also have been some sentiment involved and even a vestige of hope that he might return to live or spend holidays there after retirement. Whatever the motivation, he had now decided to divest himself of the properties he still possessed. Via a solicitor acting with power of attorney, he managed to sell three of his four lots on 3 May, 1934 to another expatriate, a Mrs. Clive Jackson; the record does not show how much they were sold for, so there is no way of assessing their success as an investment.[7] But property values were likely to have been detrimentally affected by the Japanese occupation of Manchuria since 1932. A letter to Elizabeth in 1934 relates his preparation of papers for the sale: 'I am very busy copying deeds relating to the Peitaiho bit: [and] have been copying Chinese all the morning.'

Donations to the Brtish Museum

Shortly before this time, he corresponded with the British Museum, having sent the institution some materials, including certain very valuable items.

He wrote to Lionel Giles from his home in Earlsferry, Fifeshire, on 1 January 1930. Lionel was the son of his old friend and mentor Professor H. A. Giles, and he had become Keeper of Oriental Printed Books and Manuscripts at the British Museum; like his father, he had also been in the Consular Service, and he followed his father in becoming a China scholar. His brother, Lancelot, had also been in the Siege of Peking, though there is no reference to B-T in the diary Lancelot kept of the period. B-T wrote to Lionel:

> My dear Giles,
>
> A happy New Year to you and yours!
>
> I wonder if you would care to place the enclosed on record in your Department.
>
> In April 1909 I went into the T of H in the late afternoon, I think on the day before the Emperor was going to sacrifice. I took these photographs and afterwards I felt somewhat ashamed of having do [sic] so and so to speak suppressed them. I gave a set to my companion, a colleague, and another set to Sir Robert Bredon [then Acting Inspector General] or his wife. So you see they have had a very limited circulation. You mayn't find them very interesting. To me they are.
>
> Yours very sincerely,
>
> C.H. Brewitt-Taylor

One senses that through the years he had retained a feeling he had been intrusive, or worse sacrilegious; taking photographs in the Temple of Heaven, could have affected the propitiousness of the occasion. The episode is another demonstration of his cultural sensitivity or even perhaps superstition.[8]

B-T must have been going through some of his old materials, for later in the same month, on 30 January 1930, B-T sent the museum the three volumes or sections (*chüan*) of the very famous *Yongle dadian*, the importance of which was referred to earlier. The volumes dealt with military matters, inscriptions and architecture.

Correspondence retained by the museum (and now located in the archives of the British Library) reveal that the volumes were originally intended as a loan to the museum; they were sent particularly for Giles to look at in connection with some work he was engaged on, and B-T intended to have them back when Giles was done with them:

Dear Giles,
I have posted to you the three volumes on loan to the Museum and please send me a note enabling me or my representative to reclaim them. We will allow you plenty of time to examine them at your leisure.
Never mind the postage.
May they be full of interest to your special studies.

Yours very sincerely, C.B.T.

At the end of 1930, B-T decided to give the volumes to the museum:[9] 'It is now my desire to present these three volumes to the British Museum if the authorities will accept them.' The authorities did: in the museum's internal formal request that the donation be accepted, the trustees were informed that the gifts 'are of considerable value'.[10]

Among the correspondence, there is a letter from B-T written on 4 January 1931, containing the following:

Dear Giles,
Found! [referring to a mislaid receipt for the volumes.]
Now you can destroy this receipt and therewith all the evidence that the three volumes of Yunglo [a shortened form of the Wade-Giles transliteration, *Yung-lo ta-tien*] ever belonged to me.
Best New Year wishes to Mrs. Giles and to yourself.

Yours very sincerely, C.B.T.

By placing the volumes in the public domain, he may have thought he could divest himself of having been involved in an unsavoury episode. He was obviously sensitive about the evidence connecting him with the volumes and the post-Boxer looting — unaware that the British Museum would be likely to keep all records of this kind.[11]

Declining Years

B-T and Teddy continued to get on well together; B-T had accompanied the family when they visited Bryanston School before deciding to send his grandson there, as they liked its new methods.[12] B-T is also said to have initiated Teddy into golf during visits to Earlsferry, the golf course opposite the house where he lived in Links Road providing a convenient incentive.[13] Teddy, not a games player, did not keep it up, and he did not think his grandfather was particularly good at the game either.

A letter to Elizabeth, most affectionate in tone, written early in the year 1934, displays B-T's awareness of his age and feelings of physical vulnerability. He wrote:

> Dearest . . . So far as health is concerned you need not worry about me, my
> dear. I am a little below par but free from all untoward symptoms . . . [but] a
> 'cold' might do anything to me. I am rather old, you know, dearest . . . I should
> like to join you at dinner this evening and look at you before you run away.
> [Elizabeth was staying at the Waldorf Hotel, London before leaving to take
> a short trip to the States to see her mother.] . . . Now I can hope only to meet
> you and you will write me and keep me up to date.[14]

From 1934, B-T began travelling to London less frequently. Evelyn's sister,
Daisy, and Roy, well-established in their Edgware house, received a sudden,
unexpected visit from him on 23rd February 1934. He, along with all who met
her, was attracted by the beautiful, spirited Daisy, whose welcoming warmth, like
her mother Peg's, characterized her life. She was surprised but not alarmed: 'I was
cooking a plebeian scrambled-egg supper!', she exclaimed, 'luckily he is a small
eater, so he seemed satisfied'.[15] What induced him go there without giving any
warning, which was rather surprising for him, is not clear. Perhaps he wanted to
say something, but changed his mind, or maybe he just felt lonely and wanted to get
away from the impersonality of his hotel; Daisy had a lively family of five young
children, and he was especially fond of Margaret, the eldest.

The last record of a visit to London is in the winter of the same year, when
Evelyn went to stay with B-T at the Kenilworth Hotel.[16] Following that occasion,
Evelyn and Teddy continued their regular trips to see him in Scotland around Easter
time, staggering their visit with that of Elizabeth and Joan and Nancy, who went
there later in the summer. B-T particularly wished for Daisy's daughter, Margaret,
then aged eighteen and attending Harrow Art College, to accompany Evelyn on the
Easter visit in 1935. Peg records that he was unwell and

> is to have his leg x-rayed to see if the bone is joining up . . . I hope seeing the
> trio will cheer him up and bring variety to his days in bed, lying flat. He has
> not much strength.[17]

B-T's strong liking for Daisy's daughter, Margaret, also known as Barg, or 'B',
and Teddy's senior by a year, is confirmed by Peg. She writes that B-T has treated her
like 'an adopted grand-daughter for a long time'.[18] Margaret, when asked about her
memories of him when in her eighties, did not remember much apart from visiting
B-T at his home in Scotland. But she did recall a visit B-T made to her in hospital,
when she was recovering from an operation on her eyes. They were bandaged and
she could not see. B-T brought her a chrysanthemum and got her to feel the texture
and shape of the flower. The flower is doubly significant, being both evocative of
China and associated in Chinese medicine with improved vision. For Margaret, then
about eleven years of age, and already showing promise of the professional artist
she was to become, that touching incident revealed his fondness, a kindly sensitivity
and an aesthetic appreciation.

A similar demonstration of this, his capacity to communicate with children despite a distant reserve, is contained in a charming little letter to his granddaughter Joan, the daughter of Leonard and Elizabeth:

> My Dear Joan,
>
> Not long ago I took Jock [his dog] on the sands at low water. By and by he came running back to me and looked as if he wanted to whisper in my ear. So I bent down low, nearly to the sand and I heard him say, quite low 'Just now I met a small crab just on the edge of the water and he said, "Hello Jock! How is Joan?" "Who are you?" I replied. And the crab said, "You don't know me again then? I am the crab that Joan caught and kept all night in her pail. She was a kind girl to put me back on the shore. Some wee girls put crabs in the grass and they can't get to the sea again."' So that is what Jock came to say. And I send my love and Jock a kiss.
>
> Your loving grandfather, C.B-T

Joan's mother was sufficiently touched to keep the letter to her daughter, who in her eighties had it still.[19]

Death of B-T

The 1937 Easter visit was the last Evelyn saw of B-T. Teddy was by then a first-year undergraduate studying electrical engineering at Imperial College, London, and living with his aunt Daisy in Edgware. Evelyn and Teddy travelled up to Scotland by Teddy's car, taking Margaret with them, and stayed at a house, also in Links Road, close to B-T. In a letter to her mother she reports:

> Nothing has been seen of Grandma yet by any of us except glimpses in the distance. Some of us go to see Grandpa twice a day but she avoids us.[20]

The following year, on Friday, 4 March 1938, just prior to Evelyn making her usual spring visit, B-T died from 'uraomia, pyelitis and chronic cystitis' (kidney disease and inflammation of the bladder). He was eighty years old.

But the family had not been told; perhaps his widow was too distraught or confused. One of the maids realized this and had the initiative to telegraph Elizabeth to inform her about the funeral arrangements. Peg records that

> at 11 p.m. we heard that Grandpa B-T had died that morning. Evelyn and Elizabeth went next day to Daisy's for the night, collecting Teddy who travelled with them to Edinburgh by train on Sunday.

Scotland in the 1930s was a difficult place to travel on a Sunday, and there was no transport on to Elie. They could not get there till Monday morning and were only just in time for the funeral.[21]

Surprisingly, apart from a brief notice of B-T's death in the local paper in Elie, the only obituary that could be found was in one of the reports of the Royal Astronomical Society:[22]

> CHARLES HENRY BREWITT-TAYLOR, late Commissioner to the Chinese Customs service, died on 1938 March 4 at his residence, Cathay, Earlsferry, Fife, aged eighty years. He was born at Kingston, Sussex, 1857 December 11, and spent most of his active life in China. For many years he resided at Foochow and taught navigation and astronomy at the Imperial Arsenal there. During the hostilities of 1884–5 his house was wrecked in the bombardment by the French fleet. In 1891 he was appointed to the Imperial Maritime Customs, being afterwards attached to the Chinese Post Office; while Postmaster at Shanghai he was responsible for the building of the new Post Office. He was in Peking during the siege of the Legations in the Boxer rising of 1900, when his translation of a long Chinese novel was destroyed and had subsequently to be rewritten. He published a work on *Problems and Theorems in Navigation and Nautical Astronomy,* and edited and enlarged a second edition of F. Hirth's *Textbook of Modern Documentary Chinese;* in addition he made various translations from the Chinese, including the novel in two volumes mentioned above, entitled *San Kuo,* or *Romance of the Three Kingdoms.*
>
> He married, first Alice Mary Vale, who died in 1891, and by whom he had two sons, both of whom predeceased him, one being killed in the Great War; and secondly, Ann Michie, of Tientsin, who survives him with two daughters.
>
> He was elected a Fellow of the Society on 1885 May 8.

B-T's will is revealing in a number of ways.[23] First, it gives his address as The Royal Societies Club, in St. James' Street, London; this club was formed in 1894 for 'members of learned societies, universities and institutions, or well-known persons in the spheres of literature, science and the arts'.[24] There is no evidence that he actually stayed at the Club, preferring the Kingsley and Kenilworth hotels in Bloomsbury, closer to the British Museum and SOAS. Perhaps he was put off by the architecture![25] Given that by then he had been living in Earlsferry in retirement for the previous seventeen years in addition to the years it was his home when he went on leave, providing the club address seems strange; he states that he is 'temporarily residing' at Earlsferry, Elie, 'on account of the health of my wife' — the unnecessary wording suggests some resentment at having to live there, or perhaps an expectation that his wife might die first and that, if so, he would probably leave Earlsferry, hence the Club address.

Second, among the pecuniary legacies, he leaves his brother Herbert William Taylor of Carew Lodge, Carew Road, Wallington, Surrey (the address Herbert had lived at for nearly forty years), £2,000. So, as was seen in the case of Leonard's will, he must have continued contact with his younger brother and family, for the wife [Ada] or two daughters was to receive the legacy if Herbert predeceased B-T.[26]

Another somewhat surprisingly important beneficiary was Evangeline Dora Edwards of SOAS. He left her an initial £1,000, plus a further rather more valuable residual financial legacy, in addition to much of his Chinese collection.

Provision for a very comfortable annuity of £600 was made to his widow, which was to be rescinded if it were to be vested in any other person for any reason [perhaps if she were no longer able to deal with her affairs], in which case the public trustee, who was to be the executor, would have discretion about how much she required for her maintenance; she would have no claim on the capital fund which was to be set up by the trustee to provide the income. The residue, after providing for the fund for his wife's income, was to be divided among the residual legatees: Elizabeth and Evelyn were to have seven-fifteenths each of the residue, and Evangeline was to receive, in addition to the bequest of £1,000, the remaining one-fifteenth. When the income to his widow ceased, Elizabeth and Evelyn were to share equally all the ultimate residue of the estate, i.e., any capital remaining from the fund set up to provide the income. Elizabeth was also left 'my brown coat lined with fur generally called Chinese sable', and Evelyn 'my long robe of Chinese pattern lined with fur generally called Lynx'.

Evangeline could also have

> such of my Chinese Dictionaries and Chinese books and books relating to China and Chinese subjects as she may wish in addition to the pecuniary legacy.

Teddy was left 'my case containing my medals and decorations and those of my late father'; B-T added somewhat oddly, 'but if my said wife should wish to have the use and enjoyment of such case and the contents thereof during her life she shall be at liberty to do so'. This does suggest some kind of continuing fondness or at least their shared memories of China. She apparently did not take advantage of the opportunity. He also specifies that his wife could have 'the use and enjoyment' during her lifetime of 'certain Chinese curios, clocks, embroideries, books, pictures and other like articles', which would be indicated by his wife and for which the public trustee was to make an inventory, for after her death these would become part of the residuary estate. Teddy remembers going up to Scotland 'to collect something' after Ann's death.

The sums involved were not inconsiderable at the time, for the probate value of the estate exceeded £43,000, today worth anything between fifty to a hundred times as much (depending on the index used), that is, between at least two to four million pounds. B-T retained interests in China at a fairly late stage in his life, as the public trustee had to have contact with the authorities there. We have seen that B-T had kept his Peitaiho property well after retirement. But the largest plot (Lot 31), which, as we saw earlier, he had been unable to sell, had to be valued for probate purposes along with various deposits, stocks and bonds, some of which had become worthless,[27] for the Japanese invasions in the 1930s would have affected values. What became of the land is not known; perhaps a moderate fortune awaits an enterprising descendant of a beneficiary!

B-T made no distinction between his 'natural' and adopted grandchildren, who inherited their respective mother's portion should she predecease them before B-T died. This level of equality between birth and adopted family was not always so readily acknowledged at that time.[28]

Aftermath: Subsequent Lives of B-T's Relations and Friends

Family was of considerable importance to B-T. His initial experience of family life was limited, his father's early death being followed by a long period in boarding school and work in London. Given his wife's mental frailty, and the loss of both his sons, B-T's emotional bonds were strongest with his daughters-in-law and their families, and the rare friend. Given their significance for him, it is worth sketching what happened to those closest to him following his death.

After B-T's death, there appears to have been no further contact by his family with his widow, Ann. She, it is worth noting, also had little experience of family life. The realities of Victorian and Edwardian family life were often far removed from the ideal image that is commonly held of the past, which tends to ignore the unsettlement of early death. Ann's mother had died when she was a baby, few of her early years were with her father and she seems to have had an assortment of carers; her brother appears to have become an alcoholic, and she nearly died in childbirth or miscarriage. For some years, she lived apart from B-T, remaining in Britain while he was in China, and spending years in asylums. Her last recorded stay in an asylum was for over two years, from 1927 to 1929,[29] well before B-T died. She wrote a tranquil letter in 1930, though we know from family letters that her mental condition remained precarious, and she had bouts of distress when the babies of others were around.

Ann eventually died from a heart attack at the age of seventy-nine, after the Second World War, on 29 April, 1947. In a hard-to-decipher, scrappily written will, witnessed in November 1945, she leaves all her possessions to her brother, Alexander Michie, who had also worked for the China Customs, his wife, Kathleen, and their daughter, Kathleen Joyce, all of whom are also named as her executors. Her beneficiaries lived in Modica, Sicily, though it appears that her brother may have predeceased her. She still lived in Cathay, Earlsferry, at the time of death.[30] A former neighbour, obviously a young boy at the time, remembers that she was known as 'Mrs. Michie' which may have been due to her insistence (an indication of her identity) or derives from the residual collective memory of the Michie family by Earlsferry residents. He recalls her as 'a bit strange', and that she went out in 'a flimsy dress and headscarf, festooned in large beads'. He also recalls B-T, 'a heavily built man'; the husband and wife 'kept to themselves'.[31] The net value of her estate was over £11,000, the property (which seemed to consist of two houses at either end of a plot connecting Links Road with the High Street, Earlsferry), being valued at £3,250.[32]

Peg, with her welcoming acceptance of those who came to her in need of contact, provided a home that B-T's sons could come to when they were in London for their education. This welcome extended to B-T himself, and the family always seemed pleased by his visits. The 'Polite Potentate from the East' is how Peg first saw him, appreciating his courteous reserve and generosity. A public-spirited woman, she was active in the Liberal Party and the Temperance movement. Her commitment to the latter might appear to some as countering the picture of her as a warm, tolerant person, but her motivation was concern with the effect of drinking on family life and on increasing poverty. She would not have been pleased had she known that one of B-T's major work preoccupations was the loss of revenue to the Customs Service from opium's declining price and illicit sales, and she would have regretted the absence of any moral concern over the trade itself (which probably affected many Chinese as deleteriously as did drink on the impecunious natives of Britain). Peg died the same year as B-T's widow, in 1947. She was aged eighty-eight.

Evelyn and Winnie continued to live in the large house in Bournemouth, rather silently, for with age Winnie's oddness of character increased, and they did not get on well together. Later, when Daisy and Roy retired to live in St. Agnes, Cornwall, the Bournemouth sisters decided to go there too, and each separately bought herself a small bungalow; but Winnie did not like living there — 'the hedges in Cornwall are too high', she would say, 'You cannot see over them' — and went to live near her nephew, Teddy, in Great Malvern. She never married and was the first of the three sisters to die, in 1973 aged eighty-five. Evelyn, who was very attached to Daisy, continued living near her in St. Agnes; she died in 1977, also aged eighty-five. Her son, Teddy, married in 1945, having met his wife, Nancy, where he worked in the Royal Radar Establishment. He is now ninety (in 2008) and they have two adult children. Colin (a physicist working in the same establishment) was interviewed by the famous sinologist, Joseph Needham, when he applied to enter Cambridge; Needham, recognizing his surname, asked Colin whether he was related to the translator. Frances is a music teacher, choir conductor and organist. She was written to by the Thai father of one of her overseas students after he realized her surname was familiar; he had originally read the *San Kuo* in Thai and then in English:

> I enjoy reading the lengthy volume again and again . . . a great work that your grandfather [actually great-grandfather] had contributed to English literature, and that you should be very proud of.[33]

Daisy, the most outgoing of the sisters, followed Peg's pattern, both in having three daughters and two sons and in keeping a warm, open house, especially attracting those in need of support. She was widowed in 1975 when Roy died. The last of the Ellis children, she died in 1978 when working in her garden, having just reached the age of eighty-nine. Of her five children, Denis and Erica have died; the others, at the time of writing, happily flourish: Margaret, who knew B-T best, being ninety-two in November 2008; Rab, eighty-nine; and Charmian, eighty-five.

Elizabeth, Leonard's widow in San Francisco, died about 1960 aged around seventy-seven. Her younger daughter, Nancy died in the United States just a few years ago; Joan, now eighty-four years old, still lives there.

Apart from family, the only very close friendship of B-T's that we know about was that with Evangeline Dora Edwards. She died in 1957, just reaching sixty-nine years of age, and only recently having retired from SOAS two years earlier, in 1955. At the time of B-T's death, she was a reader in Chinese and Acting Head of the Far East Department. On her return to England and a lecturership at SOAS in 1921, she had vigorously pursued her qualifications, taking a bachelor's degree at the age of thirty-six in 1924, her master's the following year, and in 1931 she was awarded a Doctor of Literature by the University of London for her work on T'ang dynasty literature. She was appointed to a readership in that year and promoted to the chair of Chinese in 1939. In 1951, towards the end of her career, she became the Acting Head of the recently endowed Percival David Foundation. Professor Edwards retired in 1955 and lived in Cornwall, the county of her youth. On her retirement, she gave a number of items, including books and prints, to the school. These included a volume of the great Chinese encyclopaedia, the *Yongle dadian*.[34] Conceivably, she could have picked it up when she lived in China, but given the rarity of the volumes and the brief time she was there, it is much more likely that she was given this by B-T. If so, he may have done so at the time he gave his copies to the British Museum in 1931, or even before, for otherwise he might have given it with the others; by then, he clearly wished to disassociate himself from having owned them.

An obituary by Professor Walter Simon, who replaced Edwards as Head of Department, is appreciative:

a rare combination of kindness and firmness she commanded universal respect and admiration. Her personal interest in the welfare of staff and students won her innumerable friends.

At the memorial service, the school's director was even more glowing:

> To all who knew her a very dear friend . . . She was a delightedly sincere, tolerant, and gracious lady . . . She flinched from no task, no enterprise, however severe . . . Above all, Eve Edwards had a genius for loving friendship, a capacity for creating, sustaining, and releasing kindness . . . [a] tranquil happy person.[35]

Obituaries tend to eulogize, and her colleagues' views are somewhat tempered by a more critical account which appears in a study of the man famous as the tutor to the Emperor Hsuan-t'ung (the reign title of P'u-yi), Sir Reginald Johnston, who immediately preceded her as Head of Department. According to this study of Johnston, he himself had not contributed much to Chinese studies, using his position to take long unauthorized leaves visiting China to be with the deposed emperor. Of Dr. Edwards, the author writes:

> By all accounts a capable, energetic and important administrator and organizer within the School. She was also strict and ferocious in dispute and tenacious when it came to bettering her position and her salary — although the problems she faced as a woman in such an environment might well have stiffened her manner. Although her academic reputation is now negligible, her institutional legacy can be found in the Percival David Foundation, whose creation she oversaw when shifted sideways out of the Far East Department to make way for Walter Simon . . . a far better scholar and teacher.[36]

A large, traditional Chinese painting that she donated to the school still hangs outside the senior staffroom of SOAS.

Whether B-T was attracted to Edwards's 'loving friendship', ability to release kindness or relative tranquillity compared with that of his wife, we do not know. Yet despite her strictness and reputed ferocity, this formidable personality was not without humour and an appreciation of the romantic. In a lecture on 'International Understanding in Relation to China', she argued by way of analogy that if understanding between two people is to be real understanding, it must be a two-way affair; neither should assume that 'the other person will take the initiative and set himself to understand us'. We must 'quite deliberately reveal ourselves to him . . .When a young man is interested in a girl', she explained, 'his first concern after what may be called the initial shock is to understand her'.[37] The reference in the lecture was to 'a young man', which would have eliminated B-T as the one that sparked any flutter she might have felt, for there was an age gap between them of 30 years — though she might have just been putting potential gossipers off the scent!

To suggest that the relationship of B-T and Edwards went anything beyond the close friendship of two expatriates with a common interest in Chinese culture and literature when they first knew each other in Mukden might be going too far. Given his sense of propriety and loyalty, and the possible continued affection for his absent wife despite the problems caused by her illness, intimating a closer relationship would be speculative. Yet given the circumstances, a strong emotional attachment is not inconceivable: with the deterioration in his wife's condition closer feelings might well have developed. Certainly, the relationship must have been affectionate as well as intellectual for it to have matured to the extent that he took members of his family to meet her; he was happy not to keep their friendship hidden. The fact that he left her many of his Chinese materials would be explained by their close intellectual companionship. But she was the only financial beneficiary outside the family; to leave what in those days were fair sums of money to someone in a well-paid and secure position does suggest some warmth in their relationship. They may not have been lovers, but they were certainly close, affectionate, kindred spirits.

18

The Man and His World

The Man — An Appraisal

What kind of conclusions may now be drawn about B-T? So-called facts often wrought from faulty memory are hazardous enough in contributing to biography; understanding and interpreting individual personality, as well as trying to summarize the life of someone not directly known, compound the problem. It may also be more difficult to depict a 'good' man, unless clearly a saint, than one whose negative characteristics lend colour to his personality, making it easier to capture. The sketch in this chapter may be firmer in tone than the material warrants, but though perhaps not entirely accurate in the detail, the broad picture it presents of the man is probably not far from the reality.

Photographs of B-T reveal little. He is usually formally dressed in well-tailored suits of good material, with white cuffs, in the contemporary custom revealed below the sleeve. He is groomed well, hair carefully brushed, and has the H. G. Wells/ Somerset Maugham moustache characteristic of the time. His direct gaze expresses resigned sadness, noted early on by Peg, and a quiet dignity. There is rarely any projection of personality, but that too was typical of photographs taken then, when the sitter was exhorted to keep still.

That he was able to rise socially from a poor family reflected the fact that the class structure at the time was by no means rigid, education often being the means by which social mobility was facilitated. B-T was able to achieve this change of status through his attendance at the Royal Hospital School; as did his brother. His sisters' educational experiences seem to have been more limited, girls then being generally expected to have less education than men, which was particularly true for the social layer B-T initially inhabited. It could be argued that the sense of social marginality B-T is likely to have felt enabled him to appreciate the contrasting culture of China. The argument could be extended by hypothesizing that social or cultural marginality could well be a factor in those who, through background or personality, stand outside their world of origin and are thus able to appreciate or empathize with different cultures. Scratch an anthropologist, sociologist, or especially a Western sinologist, and one might well discover marginality![1]

Marginality often leads to political or social radicalism. B-T never displayed any signs of such attitudes. He appeared to be rather conservative, apolitical in his views and tending to the conventional.

Undoubtedly, his humble origins influenced his determination to succeed and may have encouraged, if not a driven personality, then at least an ambitious one; his achievements were aided by characteristics which included persistence, conscientiousness, dedication and a capacity for hard work. He had a single-mindedness that enabled him to switch off intrusions. These traits were probably accompanied by an unthreatening personality and a quiet confidence, one that was never overbearing or pretentious. Feelings of social marginality could well have been especially powerful during his early years in China, mixing, as he and his working-class first wife did, with colleagues from a higher social background. This sense of marginality could have encouraged his interest in the challenging minority appeal of mastering Chinese, providing a focus for an identity which initially may not have been fully realized in his work.

Some impressions of the man are revealed in B-T's reports and letters, for example, his concern with corruption in Swatow, his sensitivity over status in his Shanghai posting, acting as a cultural intermediary between the French and Chinese in Yunnan, his apparent light-touch as Director of the Customs College and the Mukden language school.

He refers to being able to 'play the grand seigneur' in Mengtze and to his being 'quite vainly supposed to lend distinction to a sort of official gathering' in Mukden. These self-denigrations have an element of the tongue-in-cheek about them, but they can also be read as a quiet satisfaction in looking back to what he had achieved and how far he had come from his early deprivation.

Some of the qualities he displayed, for example, his purposeful concentration and ability to withdraw, probably enabled him to cope with the stormy life with his second wife and the demanding situations produced by her mental illness. But even during marriage with his first wife, these characteristics of purposeful concentration were evident, in his early mastery of Chinese, his translations and his published writings. These achievements he combined with full-time employment — though contemporary practice probably meant that the time required for his teaching and administration was not too onerous. His mastery of the language was almost certainly aided by the practice common then of having a private tutor to teach him; one wonders whether that relationship continued in any personal way beyond the functional. This would have been rare if so, for a Chinese tutor would generally at that time have been treated as a kind of superior servant.

Even among senior staff members in the Customs, where knowledge of Chinese was encouraged, most were only moderately competent. Only a few became distinguished sinologists.[2] B-T was one of those few. H. A. Giles, Professor of Chinese at Cambridge, claimed to have urged B-T to master Chinese and was to name him as one of the new wave of sinologues. B-T's literary work gave him 'a deservedly high reputation as a Chinese scholar'.[3] His writings also expressed the man himself to be less an intellectual, more a scholar. His bureaucratic career as Commissioner of Customs, together with his knowledge of Chinese and his writings, epitomize the characteristics of the 'mandarin-scholar'.

In that tradition, B-T was not given to a great deal of physical activity, though he appears to have engaged in a little tennis and horse riding in China, and golf in later life in Scotland, at which he did not excel but undertook for the exercise. There are, however, hints of physical courage in the special mention by MacDonald, the British minister at the time of the Siege of Peking, and his voluntarily taking a hazardous journey in the jungles of Yunnan. During retirement he did some woodwork, and as a change from paperwork in his 'den', he relaxed in a workshop in the garden. There, for example, he made a small nine-drawer chest, still in use by his grandson Teddy's wife.

From the occasional insights we have of B-T, it would seem that his ambition was not at all motivated by a desire for a flamboyant lifestyle; frugality was one of his characteristics. There was a need for financial security and perhaps social prestige, compensating for his humble origins. His correspondence frequently reveals a carefulness with money. That he was prudent is apparent, and he was able to accrue a useful amount of savings, despite considerable expenses, such as boarding school for his children, help for his widowed daughter-in-law Evelyn and the additional costs involved in his wife's mental health problems (though his wife was the owner of their retirement house). Money and security were important motivators, but so was a sense of personal fulfilment, achieving the Confucian model of scholar and competent bureaucrat.

B-T does not appear to have had any religious inclination, the only reference to such matters being his attending a Unitarian service once with the Ellises, and a sardonic reference to non-comprehensible actions by authorities in one of his commissioner reports: 'However they are a law to themselves and to him [lower case] who shall be nameless.'[4] His second wife comments on his weak interest or regard for religion.[5] Whether or not the absence of God in his life could be attributed in any way to the Confucian tradition, he certainly would not have also imbibed its popular association with ancestor worship.

B-T demonstrated administrative skills quite early in his career. Soon after becoming an acting commissioner, a rank reached unusually quickly, he was seconded to be the District Postmaster in Shanghai. Shortly after this, he was in line to become the Statistical Secretary of the Customs in the bustling city of Shanghai, a position of considerable standing in the Customs hierarchy. But he eschewed this, preferring to exercise his more mandarin-style talents in a Yunnan backwater, and volunteering to undertake the editorship of an important Customs publication. This clearly reflected his personality and predilections. He was also chosen to be the first co-Director of the Customs College, an important post which he held for four years, coterminously acting for a year in the prestigious post of Chief Secretary of the Customs.

B-T had an eye for detail and appears to have had some aesthetic appreciation, likely to have been enhanced by an understanding of Chinese artistic culture. This is instanced by his choice of Chinese robes for the Ellis sisters, each reflecting her individual taste in colour. Another example of his sensitivity was bringing a chrysanthemum to the young Margaret Suttill's bedside for her to feel when she was temporarily unable to see following an eye operation.

His sensitivity was paralleled by a strong desire to be disassociated from any impropriety. One example of this was his carefully worded apology for recording a wrong salary figure; another was his wish to divest himself of any association with the probably looted volumes of the *Yongle dadian*. His continued embarrassment over taking the photographs of the Temple of Heaven around the time of the emperor's sacrifice also demonstrates a cultural sensitivity. After forty years in China, he would have captured more than a flavour of prevailing delicacies and superstitions.

An area of exception to this quality of sensitivity might have been in his attitude to women. His second wife hints at this and instances his sister's view that he did not know how to treat his wife. Despite his sensitivity, perhaps there was a blind spot causing him to be unaware of what was going on, his concern for detail missing the broader picture. This could explain his apparent non-realization of something critical happening to his second wife, though he did stand by her, notwithstanding their stormy marriage and her extremely demanding illness.[6]

Apart from his early publications and the occasional letter,[7] in which he infrequently does express an opinion, he rarely revealed himself in his writings: for example, there is no considered explanation of how he decided to choose the *San Kuo* to translate. It could, of course, be argued that the translation of China's 'most famous historical novel' needed no further justification than his quotation of Wylie in the preface that 'the novels and romances are too important as a class to be overlooked'. This is a persuasive argument. But why the *San Kuo*? Was it because of its importance in Chinese culture or was it to him a special challenge, compared with the other novels? Perhaps the adventures described and qualities stressed in it appealed to the young, gentle, unobtrusive romantic — he was after all sufficiently adventurous to be attracted to work in China and had his share of adventure there. The *San Kuo* is very much regarded as a man's book, dealing with stratagems for successful outcomes and stressing manly qualities such as chivalry, heroism and loyalty. It is tempting to speculate that the bookish young man, deprived of a father figure through his own father's frailty and early suicide, unconsciously found role models in the *San Kuo*.

It would have been interesting to know how B-T regarded earlier partial attempts at translation of the novel. Rarely is the context given for his other main writings: he selected most interesting material for his edition of the *Textbook of Modern Documentary Chinese,* but no clear reasons are given for what is included. He expressed himself well and had a good turn of phrase, yet the absence of elaboration, apart from in reports to superiors, somehow seems characteristic. It sits with the impression he conveys of stoical distance, the air of a calm somewhat weary resignation, appraising the world with a detached dignity. Yet, as we have seen, when the dignity was pricked, for example by his questionable status when district postmaster in Shanghai, or his presumption of being cuckolded in Mengtze, out of that gentle sadness a roar could spring.

B-T experienced considerable sadness in his life. We do not know how the young boy felt about his father's suicide, but he was certainly affected deeply by his later losses: that of his first wife, whom he loved and lost in early adulthood; and both his sons, initially by geographic absence through education and career, and then by their deaths. These losses were compounded by the mental instability of his second wife, from which they both must have suffered for most of their life together.

While B-T appeared aloof, to his friends and certain close relatives, at least, he was kind, gentle and loyal. He seemed to be untouched, uninvolved, dispassionate, yet he was able to express in writing an emotional warmth, tenderness and capacity for affection he was less able to display in personal contact. His letters, for example, indicate an underlying strength of feeling, using 'my very dear son', as well as 'dearest' in addressing a daughter-in-law, and signing off with 'Your ever loving father' — perhaps searching for an emotional connection which his childhood lacked. His letters also reveal a quiet ironic humour and generosity. He was regarded with respect and affection by his sons and their families, who were well aware of some of the difficulties he faced. But even to those with whom he was intimate, he was distant, not revealing much about himself. He was especially reticent about his family of origin and his early life, adopting the hyphen in his name to distance himself from them as well as to lend his name some distinction.

In his inner world, there may have been something of the amused romantic, evinced perhaps in his relationship with Evangeline Edwards. This may be hinted at in the poem 'A Small-Footed Maiden', chosen on his suggestion for her publication *The Dragon Book*.

The quality of distance in BT's personality was likely to be encouraged by working in a large-scale bureaucracy with its need for formality in relationships and to have been reinforced by short-term postings. Seeming self-sufficiency could well be accompanied by a craving for affection and the need for the demonstration of personal warmth beyond the more formal relationships offered by work.

Given the Brewitt-Taylors' social position, life in China would have precluded the possibility of social withdrawal as a means of coping with Ann's bizarre behaviour. B-T's status demanded entering the world of social engagements and expatriate clubs, a life in the public eye and subject to its tongues. In retirement, his reclusive disposition would have been more of a protection, but his last years would still not have been tranquil: life with his wife must have been trying even for a patient man. He was ambivalent about being in Earlsferry; while he enjoyed living in a peaceful place close to the sea,[8] he resented being cooped up with his mad wife, far from family and friends. Family became increasingly significant for him, a safety line to a more personal world and a foil to his domestic situation, which could not have been easy to bear.

B-T seems to have been liked and respected by colleagues, but his unobtrusive nature is reflected in the fact that comments about him are exceedingly rare. There are no references to him by fellow commissioners, such as Bowra, who knew him well and left detailed memoirs. Bowra borrowed his holiday home and stayed with him in Mukden, but he never comments on him as a person, just referring to him, for example, by his initials and listed among those attending social functions, yet he comments about others on similar occasions. Michie, B-T's father-in-law, makes no observation on him in any of his expansive letters, even when he is staying with the Brewitt-Taylors, nor does Addis when the couple have dinner with him — though he does comment on B-T's wife. Morrison, who knew B-T in the Siege of the Legations during the Boxer troubles and stayed with him in Mukden, makes no personal reference to him in his diaries. Other diarists of the siege, such as Lancelot Giles, scarcely make reference to him, apart from the loss of his possessions. One feels that here was someone who was liked, sensitive, competent, loyal and wise, unthreatening, discreet and cautious, but who otherwise had a somewhat unobtrusive personality, without strong colour or, despite evidence of independent thought, stated opinion. B-T did, however, have the capacity to get on well with people regarded as difficult: the wily Hart, the critical H. A. Giles and the forthright Evangeline Edwards. Though not a dynamic personality, he was well-regarded, sensible and reliable, 'a safe pair of hands'. Given his achievements and his forty years in China, some obituary notice of him in a journal or English newspaper published in China would have been expected, but none could be found.

One academic has usefully distinguished three types of identity possessed by the British in China: British, imperial and local;[9] these identities were ever-present, though at different times one group could predominate more than the others. There are other ways of distinguishing different expatriate groups, which could co-exist with these identities. For example, expatriates could be classified in terms of their different levels of involvement with Chinese people and culture. There were those who settled in the country, sometimes for multiple generations, who remained aloof from the local Chinese as much as business interests allowed; as far as they could, they maintained their original lifestyle and interests and were often scornful of those who learnt Chinese and were appreciative of the local culture. These expatriates, who tended to be those with strong commercial connections, were probably the majority; they can be called 'cultural and social isolationists'. At the opposite end was another group, very small in number and mainly found among the missionaries, who tried to distinguish themselves as little as possible from the locals, sometimes adopting Chinese dress and occasionally even the pigtail queue (either out of overidentification or as an attempt not to be conspicuous, especially in remote areas); these could be called 'cultural assimilationists' — almost 'unilateral assimilationists', as they tended to be derided by Chinese. Then there were those who maintained their expatriate lifestyle, as far as they were able, yet though largely embedded within the expatriate community, were highly engrossed by sino-culture, often becoming scholars in Chinese literature, history, philosophy, religion or the arts; they were in the main the more intellectually or aesthetically inclined administrators and teachers. These expatriates could be termed 'cultural empathizers': whatever their original motives for being attracted to China, they often became important conduits in bringing China to the West. Within this classificatory system, B-T fitted the last category.

Sadly, we know little of his personal and professional relationships with Chinese people; the occasional reference by him to 'natives' was characteristic of the speech of most expatriates at the time and did not necessarily carry disparaging overtones. In a period when Europeans often displayed their feelings of superiority, one wonders whether his early expression of disdain for novice expatriates who tried to intrude values at variance with those embedded deep in Chinese tradition persisted.[10] Certainly, as we saw in Mengtze, his knowledge of Chinese customs and attitudes would have made him a valuable mediator with unsympathetic foreigners. This 'cultural mediation' must have been important in the Customs Service, trying to effect understanding between alien cultures and facilitating solutions to difficult problems. Despite his appreciation of Chinese culture, his contacts would probably have been similar to those of many of his expatriate colleagues, whose intimate relationships with Chinese were infrequent.[11] Many expatriates had racist feelings of varying degrees, as did the Chinese. Had B-T been racist at all, his expression of it would have been polite and understated, what can be called 'genteel racism',[12] rather than blatant, though probably he would have been horrified at the accusation.

While there is no evidence of any long-standing personal relationship between B-T and any Chinese person, many aspects of his personality would have been appreciated by Chinese people: his courteousness, politeness, consideration and dignity, as well as his knowledge of Chinese language and interest in Chinese culture; his familiarity with the highly regarded astronomy and mathematics would have enhanced his standing. He was also familiar with China geographically and socially; he worked in many of its contrasting regions — cities on the Eastern seaboard, the capital, the lush south-west, as well as the harsher north-east. In his role as an oral Chinese examiner, he visited staff throughout the Customs stations.[13] Further, he would have worked with or met others with a variety of experiences of life in different parts of China. Over his many years operating at commissioner level, he would have known the Chinese supervisors of Customs who would formally hold a corresponding position and also had contact with many local official and other dignitaries, as well as his own staff. From all this, B-T would have built up a range of knowledge of Chinese people and about China and its development.

Throughout his forty years in China right up until his retirement in 1920, a period which witnessed considerable change, B-T worked in Chinese institutions run by foreigners, in particular, the Customs Service, which was throughout the period one of the most important organizations in China, economically and politically. As a senior member of a significant organization, which underwent change in its relationships with the Chinese authorities, as well as being someone closely immersed in Chinese culture, he clearly knew China well. He surely would have held interesting views of China and Chinese people. Yet of these, we have scarcely a comment. Several major events affected B-T directly (for example, the destruction of his Foochow home and place of work in the 1885 Franco-China War, the Siege of the Legations, which might have exacerbated his wife's illness, and during which B-T's possessions including his manuscripts were destroyed, and the 1911 Republican Revolution), yet we know nothing of how he felt about them. It is almost as if he was unaffected by the larger canvas, dealing with day-to-day Customs affairs as they arose and otherwise absorbed in his translations or his domestic travails. His attitude to opium was characteristic — he displayed satisfaction when prices were high and Customs revenues increased and was dismayed by the possibility of a downturn — after some price fluctuation, he comments in Mengtze, 'I hope business will look up in the presence of a prospect of a good harvest.'[14] Not a hint of opprobrium, though this was similar to the attitudes of many foreign operators in China other than missionaries. He had a job to do as a bureaucrat, and the expression of judgement was not for him: it was the pragmatic rather than the moral imperative which was more important for the Service. Any references he might have made to significant events would probably have been confined to their effect on the organizations he served.

Certainly, China gave B-T a great deal. He achieved what he set out to accomplish, and his material rewards were considerable: a good income and economic security. China also provided an interesting and varied life, and most important an identity, especially as a sinologist. It is difficult to gauge the strength of any altruism in his attitude, any feeling of helping a developing country, initially through his teaching and later by providing China with resources through Customs revenues and by creating a pool of Chinese administrators through his directorship of the Customs College. But a purely materialistic stance of simply doing a job for its financial benefit would not be sufficient to explain his continued involvement in Chinese culture, both before and after retirement. Further, the fact that he retained property interests in China for so long after leaving may not have been simply an investment decision; it could also express some level of commitment and identification with a society he was so immersed in culturally and perhaps even a hope that he might return there. Other main players in his life, including Hart, the Michies (father and son), Evangeline Edwards and the Giles family, were all involved in China and generally appreciative of Chinese people and culture. He kept contact with several of the friends he made during his life in China, persisting well into retirement and old age, buttressing a sense of identity.[15] This contact between certain 'old China hands' (especially former Customs hands) suggests the existence of a group who combined sharing the special experience of living and working in China with their scholarly and intellectual interests, a community of interest which continued long after they ceased to live there.[16]

B-T was proud of belonging to the Customs Service and believed it to be of considerable value to China ('a stout staff for China to lean on'), aiding the country's transition towards becoming part of the modern world; he would have seen himself as a servant of China rather than 'empire'. China both provided opportunity and gave identity. While not likely to have been his intention, to have contributed to introducing China to the West with his translation was a way of paying China back.

His work in China was acknowledged, and he was awarded a number of Chinese honours: the Order of the Double Dragon, Third Division, Second Class in 1886; the Button of the Third Class in 1891; and the Order of the Chia Ho (Precious Crop), Third Class in 1915. He also received the British Medal with Clasp, Defence of the Legations, having had a special mention in despatches for 'distinguished conduct' during the siege, though it is not clear whether this was for any particular action. As was customary for British personnel working in China, he applied for and received permission from the British Crown to wear the Chinese decorations on formal occasions.

High rewards for the expatriate were not without cost: disease, miscarriages, a high rate of infant mortality, the prospect of a wife's death in childbirth and other health problems. Few escaped suffering these from time to time, or other stresses which arose from family separation, physical discomfort and danger. Even domestic arrangements could be uncertain and trying, despite the relatively lavish help available; travel too could be uncomfortable. B-T experienced all of these.

What effect did the drama of Ann's illness have on B-T's life and work? This proud man would have felt demeaned by possibly being cuckolded, especially by a young member of his staff, with all the ensuing gossip that was doubtless put about regarding the situation and its causes. His sensitivity would have been exacerbated by embarrassment at his wife's public behaviour during her phases of mental disorder. It is difficult to assess whether these bouts disturbed his concentration or increased his capacity to withdraw and focus on his studies. We saw that even in his happy first marriage, when building his career and with all the preoccupations of family life, he displayed an ability to focus on his study of Chinese, speedily becoming recognized as a sinologue. He remained with his second wife after retirement: Was this out of loyalty, even love, or at least a residual affection, despite her exasperating behaviour (his letter to his daughter-in-law referring to their happy memories of San Francisco is suggestive)? Was it due to the need to provide support, or simply lethargy, convenience or even the economic inducement of the reduced expenditure in sharing the same home? Perhaps there was an element of them all in his staying with his wife. One also wonders whether the memory of his father's episode of strangeness and suicide smoothed his reluctant acceptance of his wife's condition.

Any attempt to summarize a life is bound to be simplistic. What stands out in B-T's life is its combination of public success and private sadness. The 'polite potentate' achieved considerable satisfaction in his career and through his scholarship yet experienced deep and lasting sorrow in his personal life.

Reticence about himself is the one quality of B-T's personality that stands out. B-T was and remains tantalizingly elusive. This quality pervaded his life even in death. Apart from the paucity of obituaries, there is another curiosity. My intention to photograph his gravestone with its inscription was frustrated: there was no gravestone to be found. Despite evidence in the County of Fife records locating his and his second wife's graves in the Elie churchyard, there are no headstones. Neither the long-standing firm of undertakers nor the local monumental masons had records of the burial or of gravestones being ordered, though B-T's grandson, Teddy, recalls the coffin being lowered into the grave in the rain. There are just two grassed mounds in the registered locations for him and his wife. At B-T's death, Ann was probably incapable of dealing with the arrangements, one daughter-in-law was soon to go to the United States, the other possibly insufficiently worldly to consider whether anything needed to be done, or perhaps she assumed his wife would make the necessary arrangements and did not wish to intrude. The grass mounds add a poignant flavour to a life which has been so surprisingly unremarked. At first I felt thwarted, yet on reflection it seemed appropriately symbolic. The absence of a gravestone reflected the elusiveness and the unobtrusiveness of the man, giving an especial literalness to the phrase 'his secrets went with him to the grave', that is, until partially unearthed by this study of his life.

The China Context

This account has tried to relate one man's life in China to what was happening in the country at the time. It has attempted to demonstrate how the interaction of events and trends was significant in providing opportunities as well as presenting problems for the individual.

The forty years of B-T's career spanned a momentous period in China's history. Following the Opium Wars and the opening of the Middle Kingdom to the West, the country was in a semi-colonial situation; while to some extent it may have been able to play off the different powers against one another, it was also highly dependant on them. This was especially true for Britain, whose presence in China for the majority of the period was the most powerful.

During B-T's period in China, from 1880 to 1920, major events took place. These include the battles with France in the mid-1880s, followed by the more significant 1894–95 Sino-Japanese War, the effect of which was shattering to China's confidence; this also led to further humiliation as the West forced China to make more concessions at the end of the 1890s around the time of the aborted attempt at reform. The period also witnessed a major expansion of the Treaty Ports and further intrusion by foreigners — French, German, French, Japanese, and Russian, as well as the British. The foreigners' demonstration of superiority 'carried the seeds of its own destruction', as the swing of the dialectic produced both anti-monarchist and anti-foreigner movements. The Boxer troubles were a manifestation especially of the latter, and, although it was put down, the pendulum of the dialectic swung even further when the indemnities imposed by the foreign nations generated a hostile reaction. The anti-monarchy climate culminated in the 1911 Republican Revolution and the unstable period which followed. Although the monarchy was abolished, foreign presence and influence, though challenged, remained until the 1940s.

China's history is, of course, not just a series of events; it is an amalgam of a variety of trends, interconnections, situations and reactions that can loosely be called 'processes'. Among these, as already argued, the interplay of three processes — foreign domination, internal dissent and modernization — directly affected the foreigner in China. The Taiping and other revolts revealed the vulnerability of the Ch'ing dynasty. Witnessing Western superiority in ships and arms, reformers were gradually able to encourage modest changes along the road of modernization, and the help of foreigners was reluctantly sought in doing so. The term 'modernization' is a highly relative one, but the germs of China's transformation began to be spread during this period, consciously characterized by Self-Strengthening, as the authorities struggled to respond both to internal dissent and to Western power. The heightening of anti-foreigner sentiment as a reaction to foreign domination was expressed in the Boxer episode; further internal dissent eventually led to the fall of the monarchy and the establishment of the Republic on 1 January 1912. The Foochow Naval Yard School, part of Self-Strengthening, provided B-T's first work opportunity in China. A modern Customs service had resulted from that triad of strands, arising as it did from internal dissent, foreign power and determination to trade and the need to modernize. It demanded able staff. The foreigner-led Service became the avenue for B-T's main career, satisfying his ambitions as a successful administrator and enhancing his reputation as a Chinese scholar.

In recent years, historical analysis of China has been dominated by the role of Western imperialism: this has been the major hegemonic explanation. There is no quarrel here with the central validity of imperialism's significance in China's development, though discussions on its effects have varied in their level of sophistication. But as has been argued earlier, imperialism is by no means the whole story. First, it should be said that not all foreigners operating in China would have seen themselves as 'agents of empire'. While it could be argued that however they saw themselves, directly or indirectly they were agents, it needs to be stressed that expatriates in China were by no means a homogenous group: they had different perceptions of their roles and their attitudes and relationships to Chinese. Second, imperialism takes a variety of forms and has many shades. Any imposed presence in a foreign land is a form of belligerent arrogance, but it can still have benign effects. Third, and most important to emphasize for this study, there were those who, going to China with a personal agenda, for individual self-interest, became appreciative of Chinese culture and its language. They were small in number, but this study argues that they should not be overlooked.

While in many of their activities in China these expatriates were consciously or unconsciously examples of what has been called the pedagogy of imperialism,[17] the pedagogy was not always one-way — they were not always only bringing foreign lessons to the East. Through their disinterested scholarship, they taught Chinese lessons to the West, introducing knowledge of Chinese culture in areas such as philosophy, literature, art, architecture, horticulture and landscaping (and later, but by no means less importantly, in culinary appreciation — though this was largely brought by Chinese themselves as migrants). These expatriates were thus important conduits for disseminating knowledge and understanding of Chinese culture more widely. B-T was one of this minority, choosing in his *Romance of the Three Kingdoms* to bring to the English-speaking world one of the most famous examples of China's traditional novels, the first of the most popular traditional works to be fully translated.

There is an interesting question of how B-T was personally affected by his *Romance*. He must have spent the best part of forty years, on and off, close to its events and characters, from his early writings in the 1880s to the full translation's publication in 1925. His thinking was likely to have been permeated by the Buddhist-Daoist traditions underlying the story and the period it was set in. Certainly aspects of his personality accorded with those traditions — the sense of acceptance, resignation and slight aloofness engendered by coming to terms with the world, characteristics valuable for coping with his domestic turmoil. Yet his working life demanded action and ambition, qualities abounding in the *San Kuo*. There is a dualism in these contrasting elements of a kind familiar in Daoism.

This dualism is also to be found in an apparent irony in B-T's choice. He lived through and indeed participated in far-reaching changes in China, on which he makes little recorded comment; yet, it was the *San Kuo,* detailing significant events in the third century, that he chose for his major literary effort. Here was a man highly involved in China's modernization but drawn to an early example of traditional culture. In a sense, he underlined that culture by bringing, more fully than hitherto, one of its major products to the attention of the West. He chose the *San Kuo* early in his career; by the time he was preparing for its publication he would surely have developed a deeper awareness of the symbolism of the choice and the inevitability of change. He could hardly have avoided noting to himself the underlying parallels between what he saw of change and volatility during his period in China, the unpredictability experienced in his personal life and the theme of the *Three Kingdoms,* expressed in the stirring opening words of his famous translation: 'Empires wax and wane; states cleave asunder and coalesce.'

Appendices

Appendix I: Alexander Michie, Snr.

Apart from obituaries and a partially inaccurate reference in the *Dictionary of National Biography,* surprisingly little has been written about Alexander Michie, B-T's father-in-law. Yet he was highly prominent on the China scene, and during his last few years there published and edited the *Chinese Times* in Tientsin, a paper which, as will be shown later, had a fine reputation in the East. He had been born in March, 1833 in Earlsferry, Fifeshire, Scotland, the son of a weaver, also Alexander Michie. According to his daughter Ann B-T, Michie's father had treated Michie's mother badly, and left her to go to America with another woman.[1] On his death, his widow, Ann (nee Laing, the daughter of a joiner), married a seaman, George Thin. Initially there was some uncertainty whether George Thin already had children, or whether the two sons he had were a product of this marriage. Later it was established that the sons were indeed parented by George and Ann. Both the Thin sons, George born in 1838 and Robert born 1843, graduated in medicine, the former, according to a Michie's obituary, practised in London as the 'greatest living authority on skin diseases'.[2] By the Census of 1881, Dr. George Thin and his wife, Robeina, three years his senior, were living with two living-in servants, in the fine location of Queen Anne Street, St. Marylebone, London, later they moved round the corner to Harley Street, with an additional living-in servant. Whether or not George was 'the world's greatest living authority,' he was certainly highly successful.

Michie, a strong personality, initially had a career in business. He went to school in Kilconquhar, Fifeshire, and received a commercial training in Colinsburgh, working as a banker's clerk. In 1853, when he was still only 19, he went to Hong Kong and by the age of 24 had become a partner in Lindsay and Co., a firm engaged in the China trade, and was sent as their representative to Shanghai. When the fortunes of that firm waned, he joined Chapman, King & Co., then had a partnership with Dyce, Nichol and Co., and later held an appointment with the prominent firm of Jardine, Matheson. He also became chairman of the powerful Shanghai Chamber of Commerce.[3] Michie's position in the expatriate community was outstanding: he was sent on various trade missions to places little known by Europeans, and was said to have had a role in drafting the Treaty of Tientsin, later ratified in the 1860 Convention of Peking. He was sufficiently well-regarded to participate in discussions with the Taiping rebels in 1861,[4] remaining with them for about three weeks as their guests. He was also said to have been 'an intimate friend of Gordon,' who had led the army which helped defeat them. By 1862, still with Lindsay as their representative in Shanghai, he was elected to the Shanghai Municipal Council, which ran the International Settlement there.[5]

In 1863, when he was 29, Michie returned to Britain for a few years, deciding to take the overland route via Mongolia and Russia. The journey took four months, rather than his expected three, and he arrived in Britain around December 1863. The account of his experiences was published the following year and include his thoughts on China's relationship with Europe and its need to modernize.[6]

According to the DNB, on 16th December 1866, Michie married Ann, the daughter of Charles Morley Robison of Forest House, Leytonstone, Essex. Ann was 25 years old, the eldest of five children of Robison a silk merchant; she had been born in Norwich and was not in gainful employment. The business was sufficiently successful for both her brothers to become silk merchants, according to the 1861 Census. One of the brothers later lived in Japan where Michie visited them in the 1890s. The family was also likely to have had trading connections with China, which could explain why Michie, who was also familiar with the silk trade, knew them. If the date of the marriage, given in the DNB without stating where it took place, were correct, she would have been heavily pregnant, as the Shanghai papers announced the birth of their first child there in January, 1867. None of the local English papers in Shanghai and Hong Kong records the marriage, which was unusual especially for a prominent resident, I thought this may have been explained by embarrassment inhibiting publicizing the event. Perhaps, I argued, Michie had already gone to China before Ann Robison realized her condition. But somehow it didn't ring true, and further searches were carried out in case they had married earlier in Britain. There were no salacious explanations for the late date, just that the DNB was out by a year: the marriage had in fact taken place in the City of London in December, 1865, before they left for China in 1866.[7] Their first-born was a son, Alexander Michie, jnr. This was followed about a year later by a daughter, Ann Amy Jane, who was born on 21 February, 1868, also in Shanghai.[8] But on the 8 March, just a couple of weeks after the birth, just over two years after their marriage, his wife died, almost certainly from the birth. Her death was regarded as

> the great tragedy of his life ... he worshipped his wife's memory and his life for 34 years may be said to have been a long silent embodied grief.[9]

Michie's daughter Ann and his son were sent home after the death of his wife. His half-brothers, the Thins, had come out to China, taking up medical posts there probably on Michie's suggestion. George Thin practised in Shanghai for seven to eight years, from around 1866 to 1874 This is where he gained knowledge of tropical diseases before developing his interest in dermatology.[10] George was well regarded in the expatriate community. Charles Addis sought his advice on the medical aspects of taking opium,[11] and Robert Hart requested Campbell, the London secretary to the ICMC, to arrange for Thin to see his son, James, when he had a breakdown in 1901.[12] His younger brother, Robert, had also come out to China to practise medicine after taking his Licentiate of the Royal College of Surgeons in 1865, but in 1867 Robert Thin died in Shanghai.[13]

Michie continued with his involvement in public affairs; the same edition of the NCH which noted his wife's death also records Michie's election as Municipal Councillor. In February the following year he was selected by the Shanghai Chamber of Commerce to be a member of a small expedition up the Yangtse to the province of Szechuan to assess which ports would be most desirable to open up for trade, Michie was described as 'an enterprising traveller, and well acquainted with the value of teas and silks'.[14]

For the following few years, Michie remained active in Shanghai. He, together with his half-brother George Thin, served on the Committee of the Northern China Branch of the RAS, becoming Vice-President. In addition to his membership of the Municipal Council, he was a member of the Chamber of Commerce; he also spoke frequently at meetings of Ratepayers, an organization of those who paid a household tax.[15]

Reports of Michie in the *North China Herald* cease from early 1874. That was when he probably returned to Britain again, partly to see his young children, now aged six and seven. His brother, George Thin, also left in the same year, and were likely to have returned together. Michie remained in Britain for some years. In the 1881 Census, an Alexander Michie is recorded, born in Scotland, whose occupation appears to be stated to have a Colonial and East connection (the entry is not very legible), and boarding in St. Pancras, London; he is described as a widower. He is likely to be our man, being exactly the same age, and known to be living in London at the time, working in the City,[16] where he helped to found the Eastern Agency.[17] The children by then would have been aged 13 and 14, and must have been staying with family, at boarding school, or otherwise being cared for. There is a reference in the 1881 Census to a fourteen-year old Alexander Michie 'scholar and boarder', living in Streatham, born in Shanghai, who would have been exactly the right age; he was probably attending a small private boarding school. But the whereabouts of his sister is not known as she is not recorded in the Census for that year, neither in England and Wales nor Scotland; it is conceivable that the thirteen-year-old was then receiving part of the Continental education she was known to have had.

Alexander Michie, then returned to live in China, moving to Tientsin in 1883, as Jardine Matheson's agent in northern China.[18] He also engaged in journalism. From 1886 to 1891 he published and edited the *Chinese Times* the stated purpose of which was 'the spread of information about foreign countries among the Chinese and about China to foreigners'. The introductory leader emphasized that it had no cause to advocate, though its sympathies were with those 'who had the responsibility of affairs'.[19] Though Michie identified strongly with China he was not a man to mince his words when moved to criticism. In one of his editorial leaders he makes the scathing comment, that the Chinese are 'endowed by nature to dissimulate'.[20]

His final editiorial in 1891 is a sad comment on how he then perceived the outlook for China, and contains a rationalization for the role of the foreigner:

> Of real policy we never see a trace in China. Either there is none or the various agents counteract each other. Nothing is done but stampede under the influence of panic. Having no guiding principles … there remains nothing for China but to be squeezed into such shape as the hard bodies she meets with determine. Other hands must mould her, since she is not capable of moulding herself. Nor is it easy to perceive any escape from this destiny, unless it is in the personal ascendant of the Emperor. He alone wields the authority to silence clamour, neutralize opposition, and lead the state into the paths of pleasantness and peace. Will he? Having no desire to be written down 'pessimist' we leave the answer to the ingenuous reader.[21]

Yet the paper established a fine reputation, confirmed by a later assessment that it 'may well be the best English-language newspaper in nineteenth-century China.'[22] This view would have been endorsed by Paul King, who also became a Customs Commissioner. King knew Michie in Tientsin during his posting there in the 1880s and thought very well of him:

> Alexander Michie held a high place in the Tientsin of that day. A merchant, but ever of a literary temperament, he found an outlet for expression in the Chinese Times. … the columns of [which] bear witness to his facile wit and inimitable style … We all loved him, and those of us who could write were eager to do so under his direction. … and as Viceroy Li Hung-chang was behind the paper and his policy was undoubtedly the soundest of the kind in the China of his day, one felt one was writing to order in a good cause.[23]

Whilst the meaning of Li being behind the paper is uncertain, as will be seen he trusted Michie and was comfortable in providing useful contextual information and thoughts he felt able to reveal.

In 1891 Michie retired from the paper, returned to London and wrote various books and articles on China and the Far East. He not only wrote about the region but possibly, it has been hinted, also engaged in political advice if not intrigue: Hart and his London secretary, Campbell, refer to him in slightly critical tones in their correspondence, noting that he dined in the Junior Carlton Club with a number of M.P.s in 1898.[24]

After retirement Michie made a couple of extensive trips to China, one was to marry off his daughter to B-T in 1894, remaining there to cover the Sino-Japanese War for *The Times*. He was also nominated by Li Hung–chang to go to Japan with Detring, Customs Commissioner in Tientsin and B-T's first Customs chief, in an attempt to re-open communications in 1895, but the Japanese insisted on a high-ranking Chinese doing so.[25] In 1901 Michie returned to China again, this time to visit his daughter then in Swatow following a very stressful time in the Siege of the Legations. During this trip Michie also visited his aging friend, the formerly powerful Li Hung-chang who was to die a few months later. After an hour-and-a-half's discussion, Michie got up to go, but was begged by Li Hung-chang not to hurry away as it was a 'positive relaxation to be able to converse freely with one who had no demands to make upon him'.[26]

Michie himself was not to survive long. He had been back to Earlsferry to look at designs for a house which his daughter was planning to build; he also met a cousin whom he hadn't seen for forty years, who had asked Michie for his advice on writing a history of the small town. On his way back to London he had fallen ill on the train and was taken to the room he lived in at the Hotel Cecil, where on 7 August, 1902, he died. The following brief outline of his career in *The Times* contains extracts from his obituary:

> Few names are better known both to students of Far Eastern affairs at home and to British residents in the Far East than that of Mr. Alexander Michie, whose death occurred on Friday last in London at the Hotel Cecil after a brief illness. He was born in Earlsferry, Fifeshire in 1833, and went to China at the age of 19 to join the then important firm of Lindsay and Co. in Hong Kong. 'At the early age of 24, having done valuable work in connexion [sic] with the opening of the new treaty ports in the north of China, he became a partner in the firm and its representative in Shanghai.' One of the leading spirits of the British community, he did important work 'in the stirring days of the Taiping rebellion in carrying orders and despatches during operations in the Yangtze Valley'. In 1863 he travelled home through Siberia and had a book published the following year by John Murray based on his experiences: *The Siberian Route from Peking to Petersburg through the deserts and steppes of Mongolia, Tartaary, etc.* He was chairman of the Shanghai Chamber of Commerce's mission into Western China including Szechuan. He then returned to London to live for some years before returning to China in 1883, settling in Tientsen, and engaging in private business as well as being correspondent for 'The Times' and contributing to Blackwoods' Magazine. He wrote a 'brilliant' study of Sir Rutherford Alcock *An Englishman in China* — one of the most

striking figures in Far East diplomacy: the 'best history which has yet been written of relationships between the Chinese Empire and the outer world'. Michie retired permanently from China in 1895, and paid a short visit to the Far East in 1901 'chiefly with the object of seeing his daughter, who with her husband had been shut up in Peking during the Siege of the Legations'. He had a genial disposition, and his conversational powers secured him friends, 'though his criticisms of men and things were apt to be severe, they were never narrow or personal'.[27]

In China, the *Peking and Tientsin Times'* obituary not only had a more detailed account of his life, but the paper also carried in the same issue a lengthy account of the man in a leader, with a fulsome introduction:

Tientsin and North China generally would be stultified if the passing of a publicist of the ability and personal eminence of the late Alexander Michie were allowed to be dismissed with the commonplaces of an obituary notice.

The writer goes on:

Mr. Michie, though he knew no Chinese, was an adept in reading the Chinese character, and throughout his long and useful life managed to gain the esteem and confidence of the ancient people among whom his lot was cast. They esteemed him not so much as the merchant; indeed this is the phase of his life which least repays study [a view endorsed by both Hart and Addis] but as a disinterested and sagacious counsellor, who looked at affairs Chinese wholly from a sympathetic point of view.[28]

The leader closed with the hope 'that later on some steps will be taken to secure some lasting memorial of so striking and distinguished a man.' No such memorial has been found.

Another warm, more personal tribute is to be found in a letter from Charles Addis, a manager in the Hong Kong Bank who was to become the Senior Manager in London, on hearing of Michie's death:

I feel that I have lost a ripe and sagacious counsellor, a wise mentor and a tried friend. How shrewd and kindly was his wisdom; how trenchant his denunciation of shams; how unswerving his pursuit of truth. ... Ay de me! It is a sore loss.[29]

Their friendship had been close, despite Addis being nearly thirty years younger than Michie. Yet his warm regard didn't prevent Addis being critical of him on occasion. In an earlier letter to another friend he observed that though he liked Michie's little book surveying the missionary question, his sympathetic attitude towards them and their message, but there it all ends; there was no conclusion. Addis uses the occasion to comment on his business ability:

The fact is the pamphlet is like the man, with every quality to recommend it except success. Why should Michie have failed time after time in his commercial undertakings? That he has achieved far more in other ways I know very well, but that is not the point. Why has he failed to hit the mark he was aiming at? . . . [perhaps] . . . he was too synthetical, wanting in the business faculty.[30]

According to the Probate Registry, Michie left over £22,000. After benefits for his son, Alexander, and other legacies, daughter Ann received around £9,000, a very useful sum in those days, worth from around one-half to one million pounds today, depending on the index used; this was in addition to the property in Scotland which had already been disposed to her.

He was buried in Highgate Cemetery in London.[31] The neglected grave lies close to the main path to Karl Marx's tomb, passed unregarded by the frequent parties of Chinese making their pilgrimage to Marx, and almost certainly unaware of his near-contemporary's intimate familiarity with their country. Breaking away the ivy on the obelisk, a simple inscription was gradually uncovered:

Alexander Michie

of China,

Born at Earlsferry, Fife,

on the 1st March 1833,

died in London

on the 7th of August 1902,

Aged 69 years.

Appendix II: The Inner World of Mrs. B-T

Whilst aware that B-T's wife, Ann, had mental problems, how deep and long-lasting they were was not discovered until well into the research.

Letters from B-T to Hart, uncovered after much of the research had been completed, in the Special Collection of Robert Hart at Queens University Belfast, had first revealed that in 1902 following the death of their baby his wife had undergone treatment in a hospital in Northampton. Later, on checking to see whether the G. E. Morrison archive in New South Wales contained any comments on B-T, correspondence between Morrison and B-T was found. Morrison had stayed with B-T in Mukden in July 1916. Wondering whether he had any comments to make on B-T during his stay I read his diary for the period they were together. Over lunch one day, B-T had referred to his wife, whom we knew to be living in Scotland, as being in Morningside Lunatic Asylum, but with no information about its location. Having used the Wellcome Museum for material on Michie's medical half-brothers,

I wondered what information they might have, and was amazed to discover that case records existed for her stays in both Northampton and Morningside. Other incarcerations in Mengtze, China and Bethlem, London were also revealed. The Northampton records, located in the archives of St. Andrews Hospital, were only just available because of the date under the 100-year rule for England; the records for Morningside, located in the Lothian Health Services Archives, Edinburgh University Library, were available under the 75-year rule obtaining then in Scotland; access to the Bethlem material had to await 2005, when England reduced the 100-year rule to 75 years under the new Freedom of Information Act.

I had hoped that the records might also reveal something about the B-Ts' attitudes and relationships with Chinese, but little regarding that was uncovered. The following is a precis of the major information revealed by the case records. For much of the period psychiatric care was very rudimentary. Restraining the patient from harm to self and others was the primary concern, thus detention and drugs were the prevailing forms of treatment. The records form an extraordinary account of Ann's condition and of the B-Ts' marital relationship

St. Andrews Hospital, Northampton

Ann was admitted under a Reception Order, 10 February, 1902, aged 33. Supposed cause was puerperal convulsions following childbirth about two months previously. The baby was born alive in the UK whilst they were on leave but died shortly after birth.[32]

She was suicidal, suffering from melancholia as well as from acute mania, she was restless and unreasonable, and asserted that she has been the cause of many deaths. She suffered from delusions, was distressed, and worried that her husband may be killed. Ann was sent home on trial on 9 June 1902, and discharged 'recovered' 5 August 1902 [two days before her father's unexpected death]. The notes also indicate insanity in a maternal aunt following childbirth.

Hopital Francais de Mong-Tze, Yunnan, China

Ann was in the hospital in November to December 1906, probably being released for Christmas, and again in January to May 1907, the dates are given in the Bethlem records. The hospital was probably a French missionary one with very limited psychiatric resources and it was decided that treatment in the UK was preferred. No records could be found in France, but it is unlikely they would add information substantially different from the other records. Ann also mentions this hospital admission in her April 1915 letter seeking admission to Morningside. What she described as 'head trouble' began after a row with her husband when he displayed jealousy following the discovery of Ann's romantic attachment to a young Englishman, Saker, on the staff of the Customs. She entered hospital when Saker left Mengtze.

Bethlem Royal Hospital, London

Ann entered Bethlem on 5 September 1907. Clearly the Mengtze hospital was not equipped to deal with her and she was returned to Britain accompanied by a nurse, who found the experience a great trial. The nurse records that Ann's condition worsened on the journey: she made herself objectionable by running about among the other passengers, had hallucinations, and threw her luggage into the sea. Ann also claimed to have attempted suicide on board. In hospital she continued to suffer from hallucinations: all the armies and navies of the world were in her room, she was persecuted by Freemasons, abused by English, French and Chinese, and accused of 'gross sexual practices'. She was described as having particularly an aversion to her own sex. She was discharged 'well', 1 April 1908.

Morningside

Ann was admitted into Craig House, at the Royal Edinburgh Asylum, Morningside as a voluntary boarder on 27 April 1915, and she remained there initially for four years. She seems to have initiated the contact, displaying considerable insight into her condition. These files contain the fullest set of letters and medical notes.

I was warned that the Morningside material was 'rather near the bone', and so it proved. What came to light in addition to the medical notes, was a remarkable set of writings by Ann that were almost embarrassingly unrestrained and intimate, and unexpectedly explicit about the marital relationship. They revealed the strong romantic attraction by Ann to a young member of her husband's staff in Mengtze. Whilst she denied that this attachment was fully physically consummated, according to her B-T clearly thought it was. What is certain is her continued infatuation with the young man. Further her revelations showed a strong sexual awareness from an early age and auto-eroticism which enabled her to reach climaxes using what she called 'thought-keys'. The records clearly show her suffering from delusions and hallucinations and a persecutory complex. (Her letters also reveal a capacity to be very forceful; for example chastising her solicitor for writing to her doctors about the undesirability of her travelling.) It is possible, of course, that what she reported was all part of her delusions, but the romance and the auto-activity have a ring of authenticity; and it was certainly the case that the subject of her romance immediately resigned his posting, and on his leaving Ann had a mental breakdown requiring hospitalization.

Her admission was preceded by a long letter requesting help to a Dr. Smith written on 21 December 1914. The letter begins:

> Do you think I have any chance of permanent security from my persecutors? I know they are real. And I know they are most of them in the flesh. They are masons and can perfectly well stop annoying me if they like. Most of my present enemies are the people of the village, I am convinced – and have deliberately changed my love messages from the Customs into indecent and malignant messages of hate.

[The alleged messages are clearly deemed to be telepathic and from Saker.] She then relates her early childhood. After her mother's death in China she spent her first two years in Scotland; she was then looked after by an English aunt who was very strict, and Ann was often punished by her. She claims to have had dreams of a sexual nature at a very young age, at about three or four years old, and engaged in activities from which she derived physical pleasure. She stopped at puberty but began again when engaged to be married and became excited, so much so that her father once had to take her away from B-T. She was able to obtain sexual gratification by using what she called a 'thought-key', which appears to have involved imagining beatings; she used this as her husband 'would not give me all I wanted as often as I wanted it', and intercourse with him 'did not bring pleasure of itself'. She used the 'thought-key' 'all through married intercourse of fourteen years' (presumably the period from her marriage in 1894 to around the time of the incident in Mengtze and admission to hospital there and Bethlem in 1907). She appears to have told the details to her husband, who initially told her to desist in this activity, but much later appears to have accepted the situation, possibly as part of her mental condition, and 'gave me permission to solace myself'.

She describes how the romance in Mengtze had begun some eight years earlier. Her husband became very hard and grumpy. Though she enjoyed the status of being the wife of the Commissioner, she was left alone a good deal, especially when B-T went on trips. When he did so he suggested that the English staff member, Saker, slept in the guest-room as there were bad characters about.

> I began to meet the man in dreams and he was surrounded with a halo of romance to me, and I became fond of him.

This led her to think of her friend instead of the 'thought-key' to achieve arousal. Her husband suspected a romantic relationship between Saker and his wife and they had rows when he showed jealousy. He insulted them both and said to her friend, 'If you had not been ploughing with my heifer you would not have guessed [found out] my riddle'. An unexpectedly crude phrasing from B-T expressing an understandable level of hurt; the riddle presumably refers to his wife's strength of sexual desire and his inability to satisfy her. Ann also alleges that she later informed another Customs friend in the Peking Club that her husband had threatened to kill Saker. She ends the letter with a rationalizing postscript blaming her husband: 'I could not abstain from pleasure because my husband always wished me to have it'.

A later letter dated 16 November 1915 reads:

> My husband does me so very much harm – I could almost condescend to hate
> him – only I think it the old devilish women who have him entirely in thrall,
> unknown to himself. Why does he not get a Japanese mousme [Japanese
> for young girl or daughter, a term often used by 19c expatriates in the East
> to denote a plaything], of the class provided by French engineers for their
> subordinates in the interior of China or at least in Yunnan, I am told they are
> clean and very efficient companions!

Her case is taken over by the most senior doctor in the asylum, Dr. Robertson.[33] The notes refer to Ann's background, and the doctor appears to know the families of both her parents. Her maternal grandfather [Robison] was feared for his terrible temper, another maternal aunt was cataleptic, and another had an uncontrollable temper; her brother had several episodes of insanity. There were various eccentric people on her father's side [Alexander Michie, snr.], several being exceptionally clever, but they were all 'eminently sane and level-headed'. Both Ann's medical paternal uncles had been dead for some years, so one wonders how the doctor knew so much about the family.

These medical notes describe Ann's hallucinations and delusions, which the doctor regards as the result of a breakdown of the normal separation between the earthly and the spiritual world. Ann's spiritual world is ruled, she says, by Freemasonry and arranged in rings or circles, each with a separate password; the one for the highest ring is 'Bum' and the highest authority in the Grand ring is the 'Bum Master'. Old women are in the rings who are jealous of her, and Ann interrupts ordinary conversation to swear at them or answer their questions. She claims that they are jealous of her love for Mr. Saker and cannot bear that she resisted her feelings and remained faithful to her husband. After death she and Mr. Saker will pass into rings and be together. 'Love will be revived in Heaven.' Ann accuses her tormentors of being able to change affectionate thought-messages to and from 'the man I love' into cruder formulations, and force her to have sexual climaxes. In one of her letters to her doctor Ann refers to bringing herself to climax in the Peking Club.

One letter to Dr. Robertson in 1916 reports her receiving a message from her sister-in-law in Southsea who thinks her brother doesn't know how to treat her. Another letter refers to God and to her love for Saker being revived in Heaven. She had to choose between her husband and Saker and she chose the latter. But she is content to wait, and goes on:

> I am quite willing to do all I can for my husband who, however, has no religion, but I think does believe in God now, though he used not to'. [This is one of the rare references to B-T's possible religious views.]

Numerous case notes refer to Ann losing control and using 'the most appalling language'. Some of these outbursts include smashing things and happen after receiving letters from her husband or stepsons. She occasionally strikes another patient. But much of the time she spends playing the piano, reading, and playing tennis.

B-T returned on leave, and on 26 June 1919, having spent over four years in the hospital, Ann was discharged with him, despite there being no improvement in her condition. She was readmitted voluntarily on 6 August 1921 following B-T's retirement from China, and was discharged without improvement on 12 November 1921, still having hallucinations and sexual fantasies. On hearing a violin she feels 'that part of her body corresponding to the strings being twitched'. She is admitted again for a couple of months in 1922, her conduct towards her husband having been more violent than usual. She continued to have outbursts of temper at night in hospital when she batters the door and screams. There is no record of further admission for five years. Her last recorded admission was on 2 May 1927 when she returns voluntarily for admission in a state of hyperexcitability. It is recorded that her stepson [Leonard] is returning from abroad and she doesn't want to meet him. Noisy and obscene language continues until she is discharged, relieved but 'not materially changed' over two years later on 27 July 1929.

Six months after discharge she wrote to Dr. Robertson on 22 January 1930. Apart from a few odd allusions, the tone is very tranquil. Her husband is for the first time referred to by name almost affectionately: 'Charlie has bought a copy of the Encyclopaedia Britannica', and 'we have a dear little home' to which she wishes to invite Dr. Robertson sometime.

> Charlie goes to London, Bournemouth and Portsmouth four times a year to see friends and relatives. They have been disagreeable epoques for me, but last time I was better on [my] own.

No other records have been found, and though family letters reveal that Ann continued to suffer mental problems, there do not appear to have been further episodes of institutionalization after 1929. Perhaps the death in 1932 of her consultant, Dr.

Robertson, whom she had known over many years had also been a discouragement. It has also been said that she could have been certified and placed permanently in an asylum but that B-T didn't wish this, preferring to look after her so long as he was able. He must have reached some kind of accommodation with himself over her earlier indiscretions, perhaps overcoming any jealousy he felt by explaining it as part of her mental condition. It is tempting to suggest that his familiarity with the prevalence of the world of spirits in Chinese culture might have encouraged a tolerance of how real this world can seem, though he seemed too much of a sceptic to have believed in the spirits. He must have found the whole situation distinctly distasteful, especially as he must have felt it reflected on his manhood; there was also the social embarrassment, for at the time mental instability was less understood and accepted.

Whilst by no means attempting any analysis of her condition, one is struck by the different layers of guilt underlying these accounts, from her role in the deaths of her mother and those of her babies (see the St. Andrews note); her auto-sexual experiences, and her romantic episode. All of these compounded by and interwoven with her mental condition. One is also struck by her unabashed detailing of her feelings and experiences, her doctor also noted that she recounts her past history in great detail and without reserve. She writes eloquently and extraordinarily explicitly about her sexual needs at a time when expressing female desire was generally taboo, particularly so in the world she inhabited.

Given the Freudian character of the imagery Ann uses, the question arises whether this derived from her own imagination and her extraordinary capacity for lucid expression or whether she had some familiarity with Freud's work. Two factors are relevant here: a) the timing of her initial letter to Morningside in 1914 and b) its content in terms of the concepts used. The years following 1912 have been located for the beginnings of the popularization of Freud for an educated lay public in Britain (Dean Rapp, *The Early Discovery of Freud by the British General Educated Public, 1912-1919*, The Society for the Social History of Medicine, vol. 3, No. 2, Aug. 1990). The first reference to psycho-analyses in a general interest magazine was found in an article *Is Love a Disease?* in *The Strand* magazine in January 1912, by William Brown, D.Sc. of King's College, University of London. Ann was in China at the time and it is conceivable that she may have picked up a copy of *The Strand* Magazine in one of the expatriate clubs. But she wouldn't have got anything of her imagery from that article which refers to the unconscious but focuses on the technique of talking therapy. Later that year, Freud's disciple Ernest Jones' *Papers on Psycho-Analyses* was published, but book-sellers in China were unlikely to be interested in stocking it, for her social milieu was not likely to have been fertile ground for Freud's radical theories. There has been an attempt to argue that Freud was known in China as early as 1919 but this was criticized by Hilary Chung in *China Quarterly*, Sept. 1994, No. 139 as revealing little 'that cannot be equally interpreted in terms of realism or Chinese tradition'. In any case Ann had left China several years earlier, in April 1913. It is possible that she may have come across Freud in the period between returning home and penning her letter. Possible, but unlikely. Whilst psychoanalytic ideas were known in Britain in the years leading to the First World War (John Forrester, *1919: Psychology and Psychoanalysis, Cambridge and London – Myers, Jones and MacCurdy'* in Psychoanalysis and History, Vol. 10, No. 1 2008, footnote 19, p. 68), they would have been largely confined to a small group of professionals, already divided in their approach. Psychoanalytic practice expanded more after the end of the First World War with the experience of treating shell-shock. The date of Ann's letter in 1914 would have been very early in the period of widening consciousness of Freud's work in Britain, especially when she would have been preoccupied with all the attendant time-consuming activities of expatriate resettlement in her small seaside village. Most telling of all, there is nothing in her letter which reveals any knowledge of Freud's own concepts and terminology. That her imagery was 'Freudian' is clear, but there is much in art and literature in the centuries before Freud which could be so characterized. All this points to the likelihood of the imagery being her own and not derived from Freud's writings.

Clearly her condition was a source of distress, yet there is almost an element of drama in the telling, almost as if she wished to shock the hearer. This is not to deny that her experiences were real to her, and she was sufficiently aware of her problem to seek help. At least in part, her frank detailing may have been deliberate, to shock others and a means of presenting herself more centre-stage.

How far the relationship actually went between Ann and Saker cannot be known. Perhaps the romance wasn't fully physically consummated, despite B-T's obvious belief, according to Ann, that it was; though there is the fact of Saker's immediate resignation.

Her doctor notes that the B-Ts' 'whole married life has been stormy'. We cannot know the full story, but in different ways, each of them suffered.

Appendix III: Examples of B-T's Writings

This Appendix contains two items referred to in the text:

(i) Extract from 'The San Kuo', a lengthy review-article by B-T probably written a few years after he had decided on a full translation of the work. From *China Review*, 1890/1, vol. xix, No. 3, pp. 168–78. The article discusses what the work is about, considers the difficulties in how it might be described given that it combines actual history and elaboration, and presents the gist of the narrative and its characters. This extract focuses on the problem of how to describe the work.

The article begins with introductory comments on the context of the forty year period of the Three Kingdoms, and goes on to discuss the work.

> The work referred to by most people under the name of the *San-Kuo,* or even under the fuller title, is a *Yen-i* or Paraphrase of History according to Mayers, who published a brief account of this and other romances in Notes and Queries for August 1867. The term Paraphrase seems to be more fitting than that of romance, for the *romantic* portion consists almost entirely of legends that have grown up and wreathed themselves round the figures of two or three of the more important characters. These are of the same class as those relating to King Arthur and his Knights of the Round Table; those that the myth-finders tell us belong no more to Arthur than to Joshua, as they are sun and nature myths common to all the world and cropping up in all sorts of places in all sorts of disguises. They have assumed the dress with which the common people of every time and every country have clothed their heroes.
>
> The *San Kuo* cannot be considered a novel in the common sense of the term, not even a historic novel like Scott's. There is historic basis and authority for all the more striking events and the book itself bears witness to this, for the number of characters is far greater than one would be likely to invent and it would be unnecessary and a serious defect for any novelist to burden his pages with such an enormous number of characters. Seven hundred creations would tax the most prolific invention, and to keep these distinct and move them in due and timely order, to account for some and to dismiss the others and not to let them rise again in awkward places would be indeed a gigantic task. But in the *San Kuo* no man once killed appears in a later chapter, though, if he only flees, he is sure to be heard of again. Even with the history as a check, there is no question as to the genius of the romancer, or whatever we may term the author of the *San Kuo* whoever he was , for this is a doubtful point. It required a mind of no mean order to introduce so many men, to let each work out his own part, speak and act consistently; but they and their entrances and exits are all managed with consummate skill.
>
> To my mind the *San Kuo* has more the character of a long historic drama than of a novel or romance, the author having confined his attention to the writing up of parts for the different actors, that their words and recorded deeds may be in keeping with each other. Certainly, if such was his aim, he has admirably succeeded. The characters speak as if on the stage, the battles seem stage battles, the actors almost smell of paint. They talk much compared with what they do, their emotions are described like the instructions to the player, and the book abounds with strong contrasts and dramatic situations. The continuous use also of Oratio Recta, and the entire development by this means, strengthens the idea. If on the other hand we regard the book as a novel, at least in the ordinary sense of the term, we find a lack of some very important particulars.
>
> In the first place there is an absence of plot. The meeting of the three great heroes Liu Pei, Kuan Yun and Chang Fei and their subsequent adventures, and

later the introduction of Chu-ko Liang as a sort of *Deus ex machina,* can hardly be termed a plot. Certainly they all laboured and suffered and fought, always drawing nearer and nearer to the China, when the representative of the Hans, in the person of Liu Pei, sat on the throne as titular Emperor of Shuh. But this as a plot is feebly strung together and is by no means made a leading feature. The author endeavours rather to impress the conventional Liu Pei's character upon us than to interest us in his adventures or show him rising superior to his ill fortune. Then again the whole narrative is too clearly historical, to allow the necessary freedom to the plot of a story, and in this connexion we must remember that the history is that of fifteen centuries ago, when matters were recorded which would be neglected by the modern historian, and omissions made which are now regarded as of great importance. Another objection to the term novel is the very great prominence given to the rival houses of Wu and Wei, although Liu Pei is *the* hero of the book. The final victory lay really with the House of Wei, founded by Ts'ao Ts'ao, and this character, though a mighty and very important one, is clearly subsidiary to Liu Pei as far as the book is concerned. Scarcely any novelist would have been satisfied with the very partial success of Liu Pei in Shuh, which country Wei excelled in power, and Wu in wealth. Nor would he have missed the golden opportunity for ending his story at the point where Liu Pei sat upon the throne of Shuh as Emperor, representative of the Han Dynasty. No novelist would have allowed his hero's son to die degraded, or have removed his important subordinate characters in such ways as they disappear. On the whole I should prefer to call the *San-Kuo* neither a romance nor a novel but rather a history, a historical drama not written for the stage.

The article describes the work's popularity, and its suitability for young people:

There is barely a word in the one hundred and twenty chapters that could not be translated in the primmest of young ladies' schools or read in any drawing room.

There follows an outline of the story, describing the personalities of the central characters and goes on to discuss other aspects of the narrative.

(ii) Extract from 'A Handful of Cash' an interesting note on a random collection of coins that B-T happened to have in his pocket that had been in use over several centuries. From *China Review*, 1888/9, vol. xvii, No. 6, pp. 357–9. The extract reflects his appreciation of Chinese culture:

Chinese farmers always make a fuss about going through their paddy fields, so I always fill a pocket with cash [small coins] and give them a handful if they grumble.' Not very long since I heard these words from a Nimrod visitor who was enquiring about the prospects of snipe in one of the ports. It expresses very well the contempt of the majority of sojourners in Far Cathay for the national coin, and is a fair measure of the carelessness with which they fling about these pieces of money, of small value in exchange, certainly, since ten or more of them go for a cent, but yet deemed worthy of being again practically subdivided in Government accounts. Small also as they may appear to the foreigner who pays them in handfuls, the writer knows of a class of humble workers 'hewers of wood and drawers of water,' who only get ten of them *per diem* for acting as cooks and general attendants upon ten workmen employed more lucratively, each of whom contributes half a cash and the public treasury making up the balance.

But instead of throwing a handful to a discontented peasant, that he may count, and string them up instead of grumbling, suppose we sort them out and gaze at the characters on the faces which give us some idea of the time when they were cast. As a rule the inspection will repay one for the expenditure of time and trouble.

Having taken a handful at random, they were sorted out and placed in order of date. First I found one cast in the reign Chen Tsung in the Sung Dynasty, between the years 1017 and 1022. The age of this one, the doyen of my handful, entitles it to a great deal of respect. Eight hundred and sixty years represent quite a respectable antiquity. When it was cast, Canute, after a fierce struggle, had just wrested the Crown of Britain from Ethelred the Unready, in revenge for the massacre of his countrymen. It seems difficult to fancy oneself, paying a tram-fare or buying a post-card with a coin of Canute's reign. But yet this is equivalent and Canute himself lived long enough ago to invite the investigation of modern sceptical historians into the truth or falsehood of the advancing tide anecdote. Surely a people who use every day coins of such an age have something to be proud of, and is it to be wondered at that they do not throw aside their time-worn and well-tried customs on the advice of any smart diplomatic fledgling? Since this piece of copper became a coin, no less than fifty-nine emperors have ascended the dragon seat and been gathered to their fathers, and what has the world not seen? The coin is much worn, as may well be imagined, but the characters are easily discernible, though the raised rim on the reverse has almost disappeared. The shape is just that of the present coin.

There follows a description of all the coins found in his handful in chronological order, with the next one also from the Sung Dynasty, followed by 'sixteen beautifully made coins' from around 1635 which had originated in Japan and found their way into circulation in Fukien. Others are from the eighteenth and nineteenth centuries.

The note ends:

In conclusion it is fair to add that this does not pretend to be even the beginning of an essay on Chinese coinage. All it aims at showing is, that there may be found something of interest in even a 'handful of cash'.

Notes

Chapter 1

1. Preface by Arthur Waley to the abridged 1929 edition of *Dream of the Red Chamber*, translated by Wang Chi-chen.
2. Dawson, *The Chinese Experience,* pp. 236–7.
3. See Spence, *The Chan's Great Continent,* pp. 20–32.
4. One of the most influential foreign explorers was James Legge (1815–97), who went to China as a missionary, became a major sinologist and later the first professor of Chinese at Oxford University. His eight volumes of the *Chinese Classics* were published between 1861 and 1872, and his six volumes of the *Sacred Books* between 1879 and 1891 (Girardot, *The Victorian Translation of China,* pp. 6–13).
5. Hsia, *The Classic Chinese Novel.* Chinese official attitudes towards these six novels underwent change during the twentieth century. Prior to the Cultural Revolution, they had been proclaimed as national classics but were thereafter dismissed as 'relics of the feudal past totally incompatible with the thought of Mao-Tse-tung.' Though officially repudiated, the earlier status 'still claims the silent allegiance of mainland scholars seriously concerned with the nation's literary heritage' (Hsia, *The Classic Chinese Novel,* preface to the 1996 edition, p. xi). Later, however, the six novels were re-accorded an enhanced prestige, and the 'new designation for traditional novels, "the classic novel", signalizes conclusively a change of national attitude' (Hsia, *The Classic Chinese Novel,* p. 2).
6. The following dates for full translations into English are derived from Nienhauser, *The Indiana Companion to Traditional Chinese Literature,* pp. 668–70, and Davidson, *List of Published Translations from the Chinese into English, French and German,* pp. 12ff: *The Water Margin* (also known as *All Men Are Brothers*), 1933; *The Golden Lotus,* 1939; *Journey to the West* (*Monkey*), 1942; *The Scholars,* 1957; *Dream of the Red Chamber,* 1958.
7. Roberts, *Three Kingdoms,* p. 412, discusses Lo's possible dates.
8. Roberts, *Three Kingdoms,* p. 454. Moss Roberts states that the Mao Chinese text of the mid-1660s was the one used for all translations that have been made of the novel.
9. I am indebted to Dr. Bernard Fuehrer of SOAS for this point.
10. Later, I discovered the reason for the elusiveness of the record: it was not the centre's fault but my ignorance of the quirks of documentation. Registration of birth had to

take place within six weeks; sickness or superstition frequently led to registration being delayed as long as possible. In B-T's case, his birth appeared in the register for January–March 1858, not in the expected register for his birth month, the preceding December.

11. See e.g. Plummer, *Documents of Life*.

12. The word probably derived from one definition of 'budget' as a quantity of written or printed material and seems to have been used in the nineteenth century to mean a domestic report (e.g. see Porter, *From Belfast to Peking*, p. 66).

13. Readers interested in the use of letters for historical purposes might find the following article useful: Charmian Cannon, 'Ladies of Leisure? The Everyday Life of an Edwardian Mother and Her Daughters', *Women's History Magazine* 43 (March 2003).

14. Wright, *Hart and the Chinese Customs*, p. 866. One erudite history of footnotes is found in Grafton, A., *The Footnote: A Curious History* (Faber and Faber, 2003).

15. Anderson, 'A Belated Encounter'.

16. Argument about imperialism in China has been diverse and wide-ranging. Nineteenth-century imperialists cloaked their political or commercial activities with a moral imperative, and the post-Second World War anti-colonial climate tended to produce overly simplistic views; recent writings as we shall see, have been more sophisticated and nuanced.

17. Ferro, *The Use and Abuse of History*, p. 274.

18. Bickers, *Britain in China*, see especially Chap. 2.

Chapter 2

1. Webb, *Coastguard!* p. 13.

2. Webb, *Coastguard!* pp. 32–6.

3. Hobsbawm, *Uncommon People*, p. 24.

4. Webb, *Coastguard!* p. 50.

5. WSG, 22 October 1868.

6. Burnett, *Plenty and Want*, p. 94.

7. Cole and Postgate, *The Common People, 1746–1946*, p. 354; see also Jay, *Sterling: Its Use and Misuse*, for a valuable analysis of the incidence and problems of measuring changes in the value of money over the period from 1451 to 1983.

8. According to the curator of the Littlehampton Museum, there were forty-one private schools in the area, for there was no state school until after the 1870 Education Act.

Chapter 3

1. The 1881 Census showed Herbert working as a 'boy writer', i.e. a clerk, in the Chatham Naval Dockyard. He thus continued a familial maritime connection, possibly as a budding civil servant. He resided near his work, in 13 Mills Terrace, Chatham, living there with his mother and sister Edith Elizabeth, who was learning needlework in the School of Art. They were no longer at that address in 1891, and I could not ascertain whether the mother had died by then.

2. *Royal Hospital School Prospectus*, p. 2. The objects of the charter were

> to erect and found an Hospital within Our Mannor of East Greenwich in Our County of Kent for the reliefe and support of Seamen serving on board the Shipps or Vessels belonging to the Navy Royall . . . And for the Sustentation of the Widows and the Maintenance and Education of the Children of Seamen happening to be slain or disabled . . . Also for the further reliefe and Encouragement of Seamen and Improvement of Navigation.

The bricks for the building were supplied by a Mr. Foe, a general merchant who owned a brickyard in Essex, he became better known as Daniel Defoe, the author of *Robinson Crusoe*. From 1821 to 1841 the school was co-educational, but it reverted to being boys only afterwards, on the grounds of 'evil communication'! There was also the problem of cheating — girls finding ways of hiding in their hair answers to examination questions. For a history of the School see Macleod, *History of the Royal Hospital School*, pp. 182–202.

3. University of Cambridge, Department of Manuscripts, MSS.RGO7, item 8.

4. The property used by the Royal Naval School was sold to the Worshipful Company of Goldsmiths, and the buildings were reopened in 1891 as the Goldsmith's Company's Technical and Recreative Institution, the precursor of Goldsmiths' College, now part of the University of London (Firth, *Goldsmiths' College*, pp. 13, 25).

5. PRO Admiralty ADM12, 967, 71–22a. See also MacLeod, 'History of the Royal Hospital School', pp. 193, 196. It is conceivable that the reference is to a different Taylor, but the name and age suggest our man.

6. With the help of the Archivist of the HSBC where B-T banked an effort was made to see whether there was any evidence of monetary transmissions to his family, but none of the statements found revealed anything.

7. Wright, *Hart and the Chinese Customs*, p. 866.

Chapter 4

1. Slack, *Opium, State and Society*, pp. 1–3.

2. Throughout the nineteenth century, opium was widely used despite many edicts against it. One traveller in China in 1894, later to become resident China correspondent of *The Times* (of London), was highly sceptical of the edicts:

> They are drawn up by Chinese philanthropists over a quiet pipe of opium, signed by opium-smoking officials, whose revenues are derived from the poppy, and posted near fields of poppy by the opium-smoking magistrates who own them. (Morrison, *An Australian in China*, p. 48)

3. Lin sent a courteous but firm appeal to Queen Victoria asking that the British desist from selling opium to China and complaining that China sends useful things such as tea, rhubarb, ginger, silk and textiles while foreigners send to China toys and opium — an evil that is not allowed in Britain, so why sell it in China ? ('Lin Tse-hsu's Moral Advice to Queen Victoria'; see Teng and Fairbank, *China's Response to the West*, p. 24)

4. Morse, *The International Relations of the Chinese Empire*, Vol. 3, p. 445.

5. The treaty system has also been seen to have value from China's perspective, as it 'supplemented the tribute system as a device for incorporating the foreigner' (Fairbank, *Trade and Diplomacy on the China Coast*, p. 464).
6. *The Times*, 18 July 1842.
7. ILN, 4 June 1842. Opposition in Britain to the opium trade became more prominent after the 1860 Second Anglo-Chinese War (also known as the Second Opium War): missionaries felt their attempts at conversion were being frustrated by perceptions that the trade demonstrated the immorality of Christians; further, prohibition was backed by the temperance movement; see Brook and Wakabayashi, *Opium Regimes*, pp. 37–45; Slack, *Opium, State and Society*, p. 4.
8. Solly, *These Eighty Years*, Vol. 1, p. 434. Solly fathered a minister son, Henry Shaen Solly, who, as will be seen later, married into the family which became very significant in B-T's personal life.
9. Spence, *The Search for Modern China*, p. 141.
10. Wood, *No Dogs and Not Many Chinese*, p. 2. Extraterritoriality was abolished in a Sino-British treaty signed in Chungking, China's wartime capital, in 1943, Wood, p. 296.
11. PRO, FO671/282, January 1904.
12. PRO, FO 671/275, August 1903.
13. Bickers, *Britain in China*, pp. 122–37.
14. See, for example, Wood, *No Dogs and Not Many Chinese;* Bickers, *Britain in China*; Maugham, *On a Chinese Screen*.
15. Morse, *The International Relations of the Chinese Empire*, Vol. 2.
16. Morse, *The International Relations of the Chinese Empire*, Vol. 3, pp. 55–6; Wright, *The Chinese Steam Navy, 1862–1945*, p. 111. The United States was more preoccupied with establishing itself in the Pacific through its war with Spain and the annexation of the Philippines.
17. Morse, *The International Relations of the Chinese Empire*, Vol. 3, Chap. 5.
18. Hsu, *The Rise of Modern China*, p. 383.
19. Morse, *The International Relations of the Chinese Empire*, Vol. 3, pp. 128–55.
20. China then became mostly free of foreigners until the decade of the 1950s, when Russian aid brought technocrats and other advisers (Spence, *To Change China*, pp. 282–5). For changes in the British experience, see Bickers, *Britain in China*, especially Chaps. 5, 6.
21. Cohen, *History in Three Keys*, p. 14.
22. For a general account of the Taiping, see Spence, *God's Chinese Son*. A summary can also be found in Hsu, *The Rise of Modern China*, pp. 233–6.
23. Girardot, *The Victorian Translation of China*, p. 49. Links between the Taiping and some missionaries is explored in Smith, 'Notes on Friends and Relatives of Taiping Leaders', pp. 117ff.
24. MacNair, *Modern Chinese History*, pp. 348–50. Hung's early Christian mentor, Rev. I. J. Roberts, was disgusted with what he saw during his long sojourn in Nanking and considered Hung not to be 'soundly rational about anything'.
25. Eventually, Captain C. G. Gordon ('Chinese Gordon', who later secured fame as 'Gordon of Khartoum') of the British Royal Engineers was appointed to head what had become

known as the 'Ever-Victorious Army'. It became the model for the less-publicized Franco-Chinese Ever-Triumphant Army, under Prosper Giquel, which participated in the final campaigns ending the civil war. See Leibo, *A Journal of the Chinese Civil War 1864 by Prosper Giquel* and *Transferring Technology to China*, pp. 26, 59; Giquel, *The Foochow Arsenal and Its Results*, p. 3.

26. Morse, *The International Relations of the Chinese Empire*, Vol. 2, p. 113; Spence, *The Search for Modern China*, pp. 183–8; CHC, Vol. 10, Part 1, pp. 456–77.
27. Horowitz, 'Power, Politics and the Chinese Maritime Customs', p. 552.
28. McAleavy, *The Modern History of China*, p. 100. A few years later, in 1869, Kung was to declare to Alcock, the British minister in Peking, 'Take away your opium and your missionaries, and you will be welcome' (Morse, *The International Relations of the Chinese Empire*, Vol. 1, p. 220).
29. Wright, *The Last Stand of Chinese Conservatism*, p. 14.
30. Li was to express the view in 1872 that under ideal conditions it would take a century before China could challenge the West militarily; see David Pong's article in Chu and Liu, *Li Hung-chang and China's Early Modernization*, p. 87. Li had been one of the small band of reformers who helped the dynasty reassert itself in the period known as the 'T'ung-chih Restoration' (CHC, Vol. 10, Part 1, p. 477).
31. McAleavy, *The Modern History of China*, p. 116.
32. Morse, *The International Relations of the Chinese Empire*, Vol. 2, p. 209. Kung's earlier critical view of 'the foreigner' did undergo change.
33. Chu and Liu, *Li Hung-chang and China's Early Modernization*, p. 7.
34. The term *tzu-ch'iang*, or 'make ourselves strong', was probably first used by Feng Kuei-fen (see Teng and Fairbank, *China's Response to the West*, p. 50; Leibo, *Transferring Technology to China: Prosper Giquel and the Self-Strengthening Movement*, p. 60).
35. Hsu, *The Rise of Modern China*, pp. 282ff. Some historians regard these stages as too neat to be convincing. It is also worth noting that there were different views of the effectiveness of innovation. Yen Fu, in his reformist period, said of the earlier Self-Strengthening innovations that they

> were like a good orange tree . . . which . . . after it was transplanted produced thick-skinned oranges. The tree looks as if mid-way between life and death and we do not get the fruit we sought. (Teng and Fairbank, *China's Response to the West*, p. 150)

But there were also positive assessments; 'the remarkable progress' made in military reform is recognized as an example (Wright, *The Last Stand of Chinese Conservatism*, pp. 196–220).
36. Van de Ven, 'The Onrush of Modern Globalization in China', especially pp. 167–76. However, industrialization remained a relatively small part of the economy: by 1911, manufacturing, mining and railways together represented only six to seven per cent of capital invested in agriculture (CHC, Vol. 11, Part 2, pp. 416–7).
37. Bickers, *Empire Made Me*, p. 11. This detailed study of a policeman in Shanghai is a rare example of the story of a less successful 'servant of empire' whose history, racism and violent personality contrast vividly with that of the gentle, scholarly B-T.

Chapter 5

1. Governors overlooked one province; originally, governors-general, or viceroys, overlooked a larger area.
2. Biggerstaff, *The Earliest Modern Government Schools in China*, pp. 202–3.
3. Giquel, *The Foochow Arsenal and Its Results*, p. 10.
4. Roche and Cowen, *The French at Foochow*, p. 7. A description of the dockyard is also given in this book.
5. Giquel, *The Foochow Arsenal and Its Results*, p. 36.
6. Leibo, *Transferring Technology to China*, p. 85, suggests Hart was suspicious of French control.
7. Leibo, *Transferring Technology to China*, pp. 17, 26, 90.
8. Wright, *The Chinese Steam Navy, 1862–1945*, pp. 30–31.
9. The Royal Naval College had originally been established as the Royal Naval Academy in Portsmouth; it transferred to Greenwich in 1873, occupying premises of the Royal Greenwich Hospital. The transfer was not finally settled until 1876, and for a time the college was still known, confusingly, as the Portsmouth College.
10. Leibo, p. 116; Biggerstaff, *The Earliest Modern Government Schools in China*, p. 223.
11. Wright, *The Chinese Steam Navy, 1862–1945*, pp. 22, 30.
12. Biggerstaff, *The Earliest Modern Government Schools in China*, p. 252.
13. An account of Yen Fu can be found in Schwartz, *In Search of Wealth and Power*. For a history of translation in China, see Hung and Pollard, 'Chinese Tradition'.
14. Wang, *Chinese Intellectuals and the West, 1872–1949*, p. 194.
15. Teng and Fairbank, *China's Response to the West*, pp. 149–50.
16. Wild animals continued to be reported there even as late as 1917, according to that year's *Directory and Chronicle* .
17. NCH, 20 June 1890.
18. Coates, *The China Consuls*, p. 210.
19. In Shanghai, 'the bulk of people in the treaty port service trades were working-class, or lower middle-class' (Bickers, *Britain in China*, p. 70). See also Maugham, *On a Chinese Screen*, p. 207.
20. Bickers, *Britain in China*, p. 78.
21. Coates, *The China Consuls*, p. 160.
22. Coates, *The China Consuls*, p. 35.
23. See, for example, Power, *The Ford of Heaven*.
24. Wood, *No Dogs and Not Many Chinese*, pp. 134–5.
25. The six might have included stillbirths or known miscarriages.
26. Wright, *The Chinese Steam Navy, 1862–1945*, p. 61.
27. Fairbank, Bruner and Matheson, *The I.G. in Peking*, Letter 490, n. 3.
28. ILN, 30 August 1884.
29. Eastman, *Throne and Mandarins*, p. 152.
30. Leibo, *Transferring Technology to China*, pp. 142–9.
31. Wright, *The Chinese Steam Navy, 1862–1945*, p. 24.
32. Royal Astronomical Society, *Monthly Notices*, 1938.
33. CRcdr., 1890, pp. 96, 242.

34. Conditions of service in the dockyard were attractive. Financial rewards were good, especially for those serving full five-year contracts; free, commodious accommodation was provided, and to boost morale and help retain staff, brevet rankings were given (Pong, 'Li Hung-chang and Shen Pao-chen', p. 191).

35. *Sien-shang* (*xiansheng* in pinyin), literally meaning 'first-born', is also used for a respected elder, sir or teacher.

36. Porter, *From Belfast to Peking,* p. 58. Porter was examined in Chinese for three days in the most august presence of Robert Hart, head of the Chinese Customs, a Chinese scholar who had taught Wade (who at that time was the Chinese secretary and chief secretary of the Legation), and Sir Rutherford Alcock, the British Minister in Peking (Porter, *From Belfast to Peking,* pp. 11–12). Another account of learning Chinese by a student-interpreter can be found in Cranmer-Byng, *The Old British Legation at Peking, 1860–1959,* p. 76.

37. Poole, *A Diary in Peking,* 22 May 1900.

38. Yule and Burnell, *Hobson-Jobson,* p. 581.

39. Giles, H. A., 'Two Romances', in *The Chinese Student,* Giles speaks of B-T as earning himself an important niche among those Chinese scholars of the age who will be remembered.

40. This was the view of Sir Robert Scott of the Consular Service (Giles, *The Siege of the Peking Legations,* p. xix).

41. Wood, *No Dogs and Not Many Chinese,* p. xiii. As will be seen in the next chapter, Wade was also involved in the Customs Service.

42. Aylmer, 'The Memoirs of H. A. Giles,' p. 79.

43. Aylmer, 'The Memoirs of H. A. Giles,' p. 70.

44. Aylmer, 'The Memoirs of H. A. Giles,' p. 22.

45. Bickers, *Britain in China,* p. 83.

46. Bickers, *Britain in China,* p. 83, and n. 45 on p. 110.

47. B-T's second wife was to make reference to Masons in her fantasies (see Appendix II).

48. Giles, *The Siege of the Peking Legations,* p. xx.

49. Aylmer, 'The Memoirs of H. A. Giles,' p. 27.

50. The Journal of the North China Branch of the Royal Asiatic Society gave regular lists of members. The London RAS was established in 1823, and a Hong Kong Branch was set up very early in the life of the colony, in 1847. It closed in 1859 when the North China Branch of the RAS took over its role in that part of the world. The RAS in China ceased to function in 1949 with the founding of the PRC. The Hong Kong Branch was re-established in 1959; it is still active and publishes a journal. (See the introduction to the *Catalogue of Books on China and Hong Kong* in the RAS [Hong Kong Branch] Collection, November 1987.)

51. JNCBRAS (1885):pp. 81–86.

52. Maugham, *On a Chinese Screen,* p. 22.

53. Elder, *China's Treaty Ports,* p. 48.

54. Trevor-Roper, *The Hermit of Peking,* p. 266.

55. Lin, *Flowers in the Mirror.*

56. Humnel, *Eminent Chinese of the Ch'ing Period,* p. 473.

57. JNCBRAS (1885): 200. This is where B-T uses the hyphen for the first time.

58. JNCBRAS (1885): 286.
59. NCH, 26 May 1886.
60. E.g. 'Deposing an Emperor — A Chinese Cromwell', CR, 1888–89, Vol. 17, No. 6, pp. 359–60, plus several brief notes in the same issue.
61. See Appendix III; CR, 1888–89, Vol. 17, No. 6, pp. 357–9. There are also a few short notes on page 359 of the same issue, recorded in Cordier, *Bibliotheca Sinica,* pp. 1853, 1854, 1873.
62. CR, 1889–90, Vol. 18, No. 3, pp. 147–51.
63. CR, 1890–91, Vol. 19, No. 2, pp. 126–8.
64. See Appendix III; also, CR, 1890–91, Vol. 19, No. 3, pp. 168–78.
65. CR, 1892–93, Vol. 20, No. 1, pp. 33–5.
66. This suggestion was made tentatively to the author by a sinologist who doesn't wish to be named.
67. Aylmer, 'The Memoirs of H. A. Giles', p. 33. The dictionary was published in 1892. It would be surprising if B-T, having written a lengthy review, would not have tried publishing elsewhere, but no such publication yet been found. Giles, in his preface to *A Chinese Biographical Dictionary* (Quaritch and Kelly and Walsh, 1898), thanks B-T for several notes on the warriors of the Three Kingdoms.

Chapter 6

1. Hong Kong Museum of Art, *Gateways to China,* pp. 52, 99, 101; Wood, *No Dogs and Not Many Chinese,* p. 67.
2. Cranmer-Byng, *The Old British Legation at Peking,* p. 47, quoting the 1861 Kung memorandum arguing for the establishment of the Tsungli Yamen, an office for managing relationships with foreign countries. The supporting argument drew parallels with an episode from the *Three Kingdoms* — another example of the significance of the *Three Kingdoms* in Chinese culture.
3. Wright, *Origin and Development,* pp. 7–12. There were multiple incentives for the Customs officials to undercollect: the prospect of receiving 'squeeze', the inconvenience of official collection (recording and storing the payment) and the desirability of not raising government expectations for future levels of Customs income. One view concluded:

   > The natural desire of the smuggler to pay as little as possible was matched by the desire of the collector to receive as little as possible. (Hutcheon, *Shanghai Customs,* pp. 87–8)

4. Morse, *The International Relations of the Chinese Empire,* Vol. 2, Chap. 1; also Van de Ven, 'The Onrush of Modern Globalization in China', p. 177. An interesting and detailed account of the sequence of events is to be found in Michie, *An Englishman in China,* pp. 143–54.
5. Wright, *Origin and Development,* p. 14. A useful concise account of the history of the Service is in Foster-Hall, *The Chinese Maritime Customs.*
6. Wade later became the first professor of Chinese at Cambridge from 1888 to 1895. Wood, *No Dogs and Not Many Chinese,* p. 68.

7. Following the 1860 Convention of Peking, the Tsungli Yamen, an office dealing with foreigners, in effect an embryonic foreign ministry, was established in 1861. Until this point, China had resisted setting up such an office, disdaining the formal recognition of equality which negotiating with foreign governments would have implied. The Tsungli Yamen became the arm of government responsible for a geographically widened Customs Service, which was now established as the Imperial Chinese Maritime Customs.

8. Horowitz, *Mandarins and Customs Inspectors,* pp. 43–7. Lay did, however, appear to have a broader vision for the Service than just dealing with revenues. He believed that China needed the assistance of foreigners and encouraged his inspectors (later called commissioners) to find ways of making themselves appreciated, acquiring influence that could later be used for China's modernization (Leibo, *Transferring Technology to China,* p. 17).

9. Wright, *The Chinese Steam Navy, 1862–1945,* p. 190.

10. Drage, *Servants of the Dragon Throne,* p. 258.

11. Wright, *Origin and Development of the Chinese Customs Service, 1843–1911,* pp. 1–6.

12. Fairbank, Bruner and Matheson, *The I.G. in Peking,* p. 22.

13. Morse, *The International Relations of the Chinese Empire,* Vol. 3, p. 36.

14. Wright, *Hart and the Chinese Customs,* pp. 2–3, 330–2.

15. Cheng, *Postal Communication in China and Its Modernization,1860–1896;* see Fairbank's introduction to *Trade and Diplomacy on the China Coast.*

16. Although foreign loan repayments were guaranteed by the Service, they were usually repaid from other sources (Horowitz, *Mandarins and Customs Inspectors,* p. 52).

17. Van de Ven, 'Robert Hart and Gustav Detring during the Boxer Rebellion', p. 546.

18. Van de Ven, 'The Onrush of Modern Globalization in China', p. 180.

19. CHC, Vol. 12, p. 178.

20. Circular 8, 21 June 1864, in Chinese Maritime Customs, *Documents Illustrative of the Origin, Development, and Activities of the Chinese Customs Service,* Vol. 1, pp. 36–47; also reproduced in Morse, *The International Relations of the Chinese Empire,* Vol. 3, Appendix D, p. 453, and MacNair, *Modern Chinese History,* pp. 384ff.

21. Chinese Maritime Customs, *Documents Illustrative of the Origin, Development, and Activities of the Chinese Customs Service,* Vol. 1, p. 37.

22. Horowitz, 'Power, Politics and the Chinese Maritime Customs', pp. 565ff, discusses the political context of Circular 8.

23. SOAS Archives, Aglen Letters, 28 March 1910. Much later, in criticizing Aglen's policy in a letter to Paul King, Maze, who replaced Aglen as I-G cites Hart:

> The Principles which Hart's unparalleled knowledge of Chinese psychology induced him to lay down in the early days, that the Customs must act with and assist and not ignore or displace Chinese authority, are as true today as when he first circularized them . . . Attempts to develop the service into a sort of imperium in imperio, apart from the stupidity of such a policy, can only have one culmination — humiliation and defeat. (SOAS, Maze PPMS 2, Vol. V, p. 399, 18 April 1931.)

Aglen, a Hart protégé, was unwise to neglect his master's advice and was dismissed from his post.

24. SOAS, Aglen, PPMS 211355, letters, 14 September 1911.
25. Coates, *The China Consuls,* Appendix II. See also Porter, *From Belfast to Peking.*
26. Horowitz, 'Power, Politics and the Chinese Maritime Customs', pp. 551–81, gives a more nuanced account of the relationship among the Tsungli Yamen, Hart and the West; and Bickers, 'Purloined Letters: History and the Chinese Maritime Customs Service', pp. 691–720, considers 'the Hart project' an historiographical attempt to ensure a positive perception of Hart's role for China. See also Horowitz, *Mandarins and Customs Inspectors,* pp. 41–57.
27. Wright, *Hart and the Chinese Customs,* p. iii.
28. Preston, *Besieged in Peking,* p. 42.
29. Wright, *Hart and the Chinese Customs,* p. 829.
30. Fairbank, Bruner and Matheson, *The I.G. in Peking,* 342. It has been suggested that Hart was not above lying, even to Campbell. This may not have been consciously deliberate: Hart had the kind of subtlety which caused his statements and activities to be variously interpreted — perhaps even by himself.
31. Chen and Han, *Archives of China's Imperial Maritime Customs,* p. xiv.
32. Morse, *The International Relations of the Chinese Empire,* Vol. 2, Chap. 18, pp. 369–72. Hart had wanted his brother James to succeed him as inspector general as he thought he would be able to influence James; when it became clear that Detring, a very strong, independently minded Customs commissioner, was being backed by the powerful Li Huang-chang, Hart changed his mind and decided to resign the appointment.
33. PRO, FO671/275, provides an example of this when, because of long delays, the British Minister requested on 15 October 1903 that the imperial highness transfer the authority for issuing certificates from a Chinese body, the Taotai, to the ICMC . The request was granted.
34. Lam, *Memoirs of 35-Year Service in the Chinese Maritime Customs,* p. 75. Lam's *Memoirs* also contains a picture of the kinds of activities undertaken in a Customs office.
35. Fairbank, Bruner and Matheson, *The I.G. in Peking,* 53.
36. Elder, *China's Treaty Ports,* 'A Career in the Customs', p. 46.
37. Aitcheson, *The Chinese Maritime Service in the Transition from the Ch'ing to the Nationalist Era,* p. 176.
38. Porter, *From Belfast to Peking,* pp. 67–70.
39. Smith, Fairbank and Bruner, *Robert Hart and China's Early Modernization,* p. 128. The Belfast archive of Hart's papers contains many letters from young girls and women, some of whom sent him little presents or requested photographs of him. One Customs recruit, Alexander Michie, Jr., future brother-in-law to B-T, testifies to Hart's sensuality: a few months into his first posting, Michie is recalled to Peking and is surprised by Hart's initial greeting: 'Your lips are redder, I think, than they were! Have you been kissing many pretty girls down South?' 'Not too many, sir' came the speedy reply, as Michie was wondering what was to come next. Hart then informs him that he is to be promoted to being Hart's private secretary (Michie, 'Sir Robert Hart', p. 627).
40. Coates, *The China Consuls,* p. 100.
41. Coates, *The China Consuls,* p. 60.
42. Chen and Han, *Archives of China's Imperial Maritime Customs,* Vol. 4, Chronology, 1858–1865.

43. Smith, Fairbank and Bruner, *Robert Hart and China's Early Modernization,* p. 363.
44. Lan and Wildy, 'Declaration Made by Robert Hart on His Domestic Life.' See also Chen and Han, *Archives of China's Imperial Maritime Customs,* Vol. 4, Chronology, 1866–1879.
45. Smith, Fairbank and Bruner, *Robert Hart and China's Early Modernization,* p. 522.
46. While on leave he also undertook to give guidance to a Chinese informal mission to Europe to learn about Western practices. But the observations of the group were, disappointingly, mainly confined to what particularly intrigued them, such as tall buildings, gaslight, elevators, etc. (see CHC, Vol. 2, p. 73).
47. Chen and Han, *Archives of China's Imperial Maritime Customs,* Vol. 4, Chronology, 1866–1879.
48. Smith, Fairbank and Bruner, *Robert Hart and China's Early Modernization,* p. 363; also Chen and Han, *Archives of China's Imperial Maritime Customs,* Vol. 4, p. 552. But see Fairbank, Bruner and Matheson, *The I.G. in Peking,* p. 23, where Little's introduction suggests that his wife did return for rare, brief visits and that the longest time during which they did not see each other may have been seventeen years.
49. University of Hong Kong, Special Collection of Robert Hart material, Letter dated 11 June 1905.
50. SOAS, Aglen, PPMS 211355, letters, April 1896.
51. Fairbank, Bruner and Matheson, *The I.G. in Peking,* p. 13. This understanding was not one that Hart approved, holding the view that this position gave the post a political character that 'I had always divested it of'. Similarly, he disapproved of the demands of the China Association and the Shanghai Chamber of Commerce that the commissioner there be British (Fairbank, Bruner and Matheson, *The I.G. in Peking,* 1279, 1281).
52. SOAS Archives, Aglen Letters, 7 November 1905.
53. PRO, FO 676/196.
54. Aitcheson, *The Chinese Maritime Service in the Transition from the Ch'ing to the Nationalist Era,* p. 225.
55. King, *In the Chinese Customs Service,* pp. 48–9.
56. SOAS, Aglen, PPMS 211355, letters, 13 October 1910.
57. SOAS Archives, Aglen Letters, 7 April 1911.
58. King, *In the Chinese Customs Service,* p. 227.
59. PRO, FO371/1089. G. E. Morrison writes in a similar vein to another journalist about the prospect of a return by Hart; see Lo Hui-min, *The Correspondence of G. E. Morrison,* p. 593.
60. SOAS, Aglen, PPMS 211355, letters, 14 September 1911. Hart died a wealthy man, his estate being valued at over £140,000, worth at the very least sixty times that at today's values.
61. NCH, Special Supplement, 11 May 1906, p. 233.
62. PRO, FO 631/4705; see also 15707 and 21503. By this time, the Foreign Office clearly sees Hart as a 'very slippery customer' and believes he is privately playing for Bredon's appointment by delaying his return to China. Bredon wrote a long memorandum, pleading to be appointed Inspector General and threatening to make a fuss if he is not. While Hart probably was fairly slippery, ambiguity doubtless an aid to survival, this view of Hart's motivation is somewhat contrary to the tenor of his letters to Aglen though he could conceivably have been riding two horses.

63. Foster-Hall, *The Chinese Maritime Customs*, p. iii.

64. Morrison, *An Australian in China*, pp. 36–7. He became the first permanent correspondent of *The Times* in March 1897, and Peking was his base for over twenty years. Journeying long distances across difficult terrain, often by foot, was one of his joys, and he travelled extensively in Australia and the Far East, especially China.

65. Wright, *Hart and the Chinese Customs,* p. 897. The first Chinese to be appointed acting commissioner was in 1925, and Chinese full commissioners were appointed for the first time in 1929, when two Chinese staff members became heads at Hangchow and Soochow (CY, 1935–36, p. 1264). If a claim made by Maze is correct he must have made the promotions as soon as he became Inspector General in 1929. For in a letter to Hippesley (another commissioner), he claimed to have introduced equality of opportunity for qualified Chinese staff. Maze said that Merrill (another commissioner) suggested to Aglen in 1912, when Aglen was I-G

> that Chinese ought to be made eligible for positions of greater responsibility in the Service, but unfortunately his sagacious advice fell upon deaf ears, and it was left to me at the eleventh hour to institute this highly essential reform.

At the time Maze wrote this, he was bitter in his criticisms of Aglen, whom he replaced as substantive I-G after a short interregnum by an acting appointment (SOAS, Maze, PPMS 2, Vol. VII, 1 April 1932). See also Lam (*Memoirs of 35-Year Service in the Chinese Maritime Customs*, pp. 128–9), who confirms that Maze had an important role in the sinofication of the Service. According to an informant in the Second Republican Historical Archives, the first Chinese deputy inspector general was Ting Kweitung, who was appointed in 1942; Ting was one of the second batch of graduates of the Customs College in 1913 and therefore a student when B-T was co-director of the College.

66. CHC, Vol. 12, p. 183. The first Chinese appointed to the various rungs of assistant commissioner were indeed non-Manchu.

67. Aitcheson, *The Chinese Maritime Service in the Transition from the Ch'ing to the Nationalist Era*, p. 235.

68. Fairbank, Bruner and Matheson, *The I.G. in Peking*, 906 and n. 2 which states that Michie's appointment does not appear in the Service Lists and may have been only for a few months.

69. See Michie, 'Sir Robert Hart', pp. 625–39. As will be seen later, it would appear that Michie, Jr., had been an alcoholic and also experienced mental health problems; the kindnesses may have related to Hart's tolerance and support.

70. SOAS, Maze, PPMS, Vol. XX, 26 July 1925.

71. King, *The History of the Hongkong and Shanghai Banking Corporation*, p. 28.

72. SOAS, Addis, PPMS 14/67, item 184, 28 December 1900.

73. SOAS, Addis, PPMS 14/67, item 74, 6 January 1901.

74. See Bickers, 'Purloined Letters'; Horowitz, 'Power, Politics and the Chinese Maritime Customs'; Van de Ven, 'Robert Hart and Gustav Detring during the Boxer Rebellion.'

75. Smith, Fairbank and Bruner, *Robert Hart and China's Early Modernization;* see especially pp. 5–22.

76. Morse, *The International Relations of the Chinese Empire*, Vol. 3, pp. 401–2.

77. Foster-Hall, *The Chinese Maritime Customs*, p. 35.
78. Bickers, *Britain in China*, p. 121.
79. SOAS, Maze, Vol. V, p. 399, 18 April 1931.
80. Atkins, *Informal Empire in Crisis*, p. 106.
81. See Foster-Hall, *The Chinese Maritime Customs*.
82. PRO, FO671/276.
83. Until 1929, the proportion of Maritime and Native Customs' net revenue paid towards foreign loans and indemnities remained high especially in the period following the Boxer episode, e.g. 80 per cent in 1912, but it fell to 42 per cent in 1929, and to 28 per cent in 1934 (CY, 1935–36, p. 1284).
84. Kwong, 'The Chinese Maritime Customs Remembered', p. 23.
85. Lam, *Memoirs of 35-Year Service in the Chinese Maritime Customs*, pp. 139–40.
86. Teng and Fairbank, *China's Response to the West*, p. 199.

Chapter 7

1. Brunero, *Britain's Imperial Cornerstone in China*, p. 53.
2. CHC, Vol. 12, pp. 182–3. A list of official ranks is to be found in Chen and Han, *Archives of China's Imperial Maritime Customs*, Vol. 4, p. 555. Another listing is in Fairbank, Bruner and Matheson, *The I.G. in Peking*, pp. xxiv–xxvi.
3. Aitcheson, *The Chinese Maritime Service in the Transition from the Ch'ing to the Nationalist Era*, p. 101. The Marine Branch was part of the Outdoor Staff, who were more likely to be working class in background.
4. Wood, *No Dogs and Not Many Chinese*, p. 99.
5. Bickers, *Britain in China*, p. 137.
6. Fairbank, Bruner and Matheson, *The I.G. in Peking*, 1052. Though, it should be said that Michie speaks of Hart's 'rigorous self-sustained intellect that has moulded and still controls [the Customs]' (Michie *An Englishman in China during the Victorian Era*, Vol. 2, p. 156.
7. Fairbank, Bruner and Matheson, *The I.G. in Peking*, 906.
8. For examples of works by Michie, Jnr., see citations in Bibliography.
9. I was informed by Sun Xifu, formerly of the Second Republican Historical Archive, that the Service List in the archive indicates that Michie's top rank was First Assistant A, his last posting being assistant-in-charge of Szemao (Simao) Customs House in southern Yunnan, for about twenty months starting 12 August 1913. Addis once recorded in his diary, 'Young Michie has finished his drinking bout. It was time for he was "seeing things" and could not sleep' (SOAS, Addis, PPMS 14/10, Diary for 1898, 22 August). Michie retired early from the Customs and in 1925 wrote to Maze, then still a commissioner and an old buddy, that he had given up a clerkship in London and had been in a low state of mental health (SOAS, Maze, PPMS 2, Vol. XX, p. 45, 26 July 1925). Though Michie appears to have given up drinking, he still suffered from mental problems and was likely to have been manic-depressive for thirty years, according to the records of the Royal Bethlem Hospital where he was a voluntary boarder from 26 December 1926 to 15 June 1927 (overlapping a period when his sister was also in a mental hospital, see

Appendix II). Like his sister, Michie too had sexual difficulties: he has been recorded as having suffered from syphilis before marriage and had been known to 'offend women'; he and his sister probably also shared a rather loveless childhood, motherless, separated and with an absent, often far-off, father (see Appendix I). Against the pleas of Michie's wife and their general practioner, who feared that having entered Bethlem in deep depression, Michie was about to enter a manic phase, the hospital curtly stated that as a voluntary patient recovered from his depression they could not detain him and so he left the hospital. The records describe his mother's side of the family as being artistic and 'highly strung'; he was certainly talented, a competent linguist (while in China he had also acted as Chinese interpreter to the Italian legation), and painted and sketched while in hospital.

10. Registers of Scotland, Registers of Sasines, December 1889.
11. SOAS, *Catalogue of the Papers of Sir Charles Addis,* p. ix. Cain and Hopkins, *British Imperialism, 1868–2000,* pp. 598–9, also gives something of Adiss' important activities.
12. SOAS, Addis, PPMS 14/67, item 47, 8 April 1893.
13. Various indexed letters about Michie in the 1890s appear in Chen and Han, *Archives of China's Imperial Maritime Customs.*
14. NCH, 6 April 1894.
15. SOAS, Addis, PPMS 14/137, 3 March 1895.
16. CT, 28 January 1888, 23 February 1889, 31 May 1890.
17. PTT, 16 June 1894. Ann was known by intimates as 'Birdie', probably because of her singing (SOAS, Addis, PPMS 14/10– item 21, 20 June 1898).
18. King, *In the Chinese Customs Service,* pp. 28–9. Today, we would wonder why the expatriates did not eat more Chinese food rather than rely on tinned European foods.
19. PTT, May 1896.
20. *Celebrations of the Seventieth Birthday of Li Hung-chang at Tientsin, Feb. 1892.*
21. Detring vied with Hart in wanting to be confidential guide to the Chinese government, and with Li Huang-chang's backing he might well have replaced Hart as inspector general in 1885 when Hart was offered the post of British Minister. For Hart's many comments on Detring, see the index to Fairbank, Bruner and Matheson, *The I.G. in Peking*; 3, n. 2, gives an outline of Detring's career. See also Van de Ven, 'Robert Hart and Gustav Detring during the Boxer Rebellion.'
22. Wang, *Chinese Intellectuals and the West, 1872–1949,* p. 194.
23. CHC, Vol. 13, p. 796.
24. Fairbank, Coolidge and Smith, *H. B. Morse,* p. 224.
25. SOAS, Aglen, April 1896.
26. Addis notes in his diary for that day:
    Birdie Michie now Mrs. Brewitt Taylor and her husband at dinner . . . It was like old times. Birdie seems to have recovered a good deal of her lost health, and was in excellent spirits. They are on their way to Peking where Taylor is to act as assistant Chinese Secretary. (SOAS, Addis, PPMS 14/10 item 21)
27. Wood, *No Dogs and Not Many Chinese,* p. 217.

28. The UCS was linked with the secular University College London, the 'godless institution of Gower Street' (Usher, Black-Hawkins and Carrick, *An Angel without Wings*, p. 7).
29. For one fictionalized account of this, see *Old Filth* by Jane Gardham (Abacus, 2004).
30. See Appendix II.

Chapter 8

1. Brewitt-Taylor, *Economic Policy*. The booklet was found in the British Library and my thanks are due to Dr. Frances Wood for the translation.
2. Fairbank, Coolidge and Smith, *H. B. Morse*, p. 19.
3. Fairbank, Coolidge and Smith, *H. B. Morse,* p. 98. See also Brunero, who also states that commissioner appointments generally came after around twenty years of service, *Britain's Imperial Cornerstone in China*, p. 23.
4. King, *In the Chinese Customs Service*, p. 190.
5. Smith, Fairbank and Bruner, *Robert Hart and China's Early Modernization*, p. 118.
6. Fairbank, Bruner and Matheson, *The I.G. in Peking,* 1056, 1217.
7. Preston, *Besieged in Peking*, p. 100, gives this date, while the Roll of Honour for the civilian volunteers gives the starting date as 20 June (PRO, FO17/1720). Both sources agree with 14 August as the date the siege was lifted.
8. Wright, *Origin and Development of the Chinese Customs Service*, p. 101.
9. Morse, *The International Relations of the Chinese Empire,* Vol. 2, Chap. 11, discusses the reasons for hostility toward missionaries, including their potential for dividing families by undermining traditional belief systems; see especially pp. 220–2.
10. CHC, Vol. 10, Part 1, p. 573; see especially Paul Cohen's Chap. 11 on Christian missionaries and their impact to 1900; also see his account of the Boxers, *History in Three Keys*.
11. NCH, 14 February 1900.
12. NCH, 30 May 1900.
13. MacDonald, *The Siege of the Peking Embassy,* p. 109; Morse, *The International Relations of the Chinese Empire,* Vol. 3, pp. 227–32.
14. See the memorial of Hsu Ching-cheng and Yuan Ch'ang, who pleaded during the siege that certain named officials supporting the Boxers be killed:

    > Then your Majesty can kill us to redress the imbalance in the deaths . . . [of several ministers] . . . We cannot help shedding tears in preparing this memorial and we cannot overcome our extreme grief and anxiety.

    They were executed shortly after presenting their memorial (Teng and Fairbank, *China's Response to the West,* pp. 190–3).
15. University of Hong Kong, Special Collection of Robert Hart, 3 June 1900.
16. Fairbank, Bruner and Matheson, *The I.G. in Peking,* 1141.
17. Fairbank Bruner and Matheson, *The I.G. in Peking,* 1142.
18. University of Hong Kong, Special Collection of Robert Hart, 10 June 1900. Most of the Customs personnel were allocated a small, inferior house, which some noted as 'another example of Legation jealousy of Customs power' (Fairbank, Bruner and Matheson, *The I.G. in Peking,* note to 1173, the last of Hart's letters to Campbell before the siege).

19. British Library, Morrison G. E. Diaries, BL Mic., A19829, 26 July 1900.
20. Hoe, *Women at the Siege*, pp. 190–2.
21. Cranmer-Byng, *The Old British Legation at Peking*, p. 78.
22. Preston, *Besieged in Peking*, pp. 100–1.
23. Mateer, *Siege Days*, pp. 228–9.
24. Preston, *Besieged in Peking*, pp. 62–3, 188. See also Fairbank, Bruner and Matheson, *The I.G. in Peking*, 1173, n. 3.
25. Hoe, *Women at the Siege*, p. 237.
26. Preston, *Besieged in Peking*, p. 153.
27. Wright, *Origin and Development*, pp. 105–6.
28. Poole, *A Diary in Peking*, 1 August 1900. National character as seen from the behaviour of those wounded in the siege parallels this perception of the Japanese; see Ransome, *The Story of the Siege Hospital in Peking*, p. 20.
29. University of Hong Kong, Special Collection of Robert Hart, 4 August 1900.
30. Preston, *Besieged in Peking*, p. 248.
31. NCH, 9 January 1901.
32. Giles,*The Siege of the Peking Legations*, p. 112. Customs staff often lived inside or close to the legations quarter, usually in the Customs compound (see Moser and Moser, *Foreigners within the Gates*, p. 122).
33. Allen, *The Siege of the Peking Legations, Beijing*, pp. 81–2. The fact that B-T's 'Boy', who might have been an adult, made the precarious way into the compound could reflect a strong sense of loyalty — or merely hope of reward, though this seems less likely given the danger involved.
34. Wright, *Hart and the Chinese Customs*, p. 866, n. 8. Also see B-T's obituary in the *Monthly Notices* of the Royal Astronomical Society, which states that the translation of the long novel had to be rewritten, and H. A. Giles noted the destruction of the work in *Two Romances* in The Chinese Student.
35. Cohen, *History in Three Keys*, p. 106.
36. Fairbank, Bruner and Matheson, *The I.G. in Peking*, 1173, Note. (There is no number for this special Note)
37. *The Times*, 17 July 1900, p. 4. Morrison was able later to cite the eulogistic obituary to claim a higher salary!
38. SOAS, Addis, PPMS14/144, obituary. Addis also said that Michie had been engaged on writing his book on Alcock at the time of the Seige, and this had been a boon to him as he was heart-broken at the supposed loss of his daughter, SOAS, Addis, PPMS 14/232, 27 May, 1901.
39. MacDonald, *The Siege of the Peking Embassy,* see also *The Times,* 11 December 1900, p. 10:

    > Of the volunteers belonging to the Imperial Maritime Customs, Messrs Brazier and Brewitt-Taylor came under my eye as doing special good work.

40. PRO, FO17/1721.
41. NCH, 21 January 1903.
42. Hevia, *English Lessons*, pp. 90ff.
43. Preston, *Besieged in Peking*, p. 219.

44. Trevor-Roper, *The Hermit of Peking,* p. 52.

45. Giles, *The Siege of the Peking Legations,* p. 178.

46. SOAS, Hart, Letters to Aglen, November 1900.

47. Preston, *Besieged in Peking,* p. 221. Addis alleged that Chinese converts were allowed two days looting by the Bishop and asks 'How do the missionaries reconcile this with the gospel?' SOAS, Addis, PPMS 14, leaves from a diary, 21 December, 1900.

48. Needham, *Paper and Printing,* p. 174.

49. There is uncertainty over whether one or two copies were made in addition to the original: Couling, *Encyclopaedia Sinica,* suggests one, but Needham states two. It has been suggested that the original may have been destroyed by a succeeding dynastic emperor or been buried with the last Ming emperor. The interesting point has also been made that no two copies of the same *chüan* have yet been found. Trevor-Roper, *The Hermit of Peking,* p. 378, holds the view that the original and a copy were destroyed by fire in the eighteenth century but offers no source for the statement; he also suggests that 'the greater part of it had already escaped into private hands' even before the fire. The Hanlin was regarded as the highest seat of learning in China, a national academy. The locations of all known *chüan* in Britain are listed in Helliwell, 'Holdings of *Yongle dadian* in United Kingdom Libraries'.

50. Allen, *The Siege of the Peking Legations, Beijing,* pp. 125–8.

51. Poole, *A Diary in Peking,* pp. 23–6.

52. Preston, *Besieged in Peking,* pp. 232–3.

53. CSPSR, 1927. One example resulting from this was the setting up of the UK Universities China Committee, which was founded in 1926 and endowed by the British government in 1931 with £200,000 from the Boxer indemnity (Aylmer, 'The Memoirs of H. A. Giles', p. 71).

54. King, 'The Boxer Indemnity — "Nothing But Bad"', pp. 663–89.

Chapter 9

1. Wood, *No Dogs and Not Many Chinese,* pp. 96, 127.

2. Johnston and Erh, *The Last Colonies,* p. 86.

3. Bickers, *Britain in China,* p. 91.

4. Queens University, Belfast, Robert Hart Special Collections, MS 15/2, 7 April 1908.

5. Aitcheson, *The Chinese Maritime Service in the Transition from the Ch'ing to the Nationalist Era,* p. 142.

6. Johnston and Erh, *The Last Colonies,* p. 95.

7. B-T's comments are from the SHAC Maritime Customs Service 679(1), 32363, 'Swatow Semi-Official Correspondence, 1900–03'. The letters quoted date from 21 September 1900 to 23 April 1901; in addition to the SHAC archives in China they can be found at University of Bristol, Maritime Customs Service Archive, Unit 3, Reel 135.

8. SOAS, Addis, PPMS 14/137, 24 March 1901.

9. Brewitt-Taylor, preface to *Chats in Chinese.*

10. B-T, Letter to his son Leonard's widow, Elizabeth, 23 January 1934.

11. SOAS Addis, PPMS 14/137, 17 January 1902. The three critical periods would have been the two difficult pregnancies and the Peking siege. Thus, of B-T's six children

224 Notes to pp. 93–95

known to have been born alive, four of them died as babies, with only two surviving into adulthood. Both of Ann's dead babies were girls; all of Alice's four births were boys.

12. Queens University, Belfast, Robert Hart Special Collections, MS15/2, 20 February 1901. I was initially thrown by the date of the letter, as this would have placed the episode while the Brewitt-Taylors were still in Swatow and would make the cheerful tone of Michie's letter to Addis around then surprising. Probably the newness of the year caused the error of writing the year as 1901 rather than the correct 1902; this would also be more consistent with the letters from Michie to Addis and B-T to Hart. The 1896 reference was to the loss of the baby who was born alive in Tientsin but died shortly after birth. Kathleen, the author of the letter, has been described as a 'nice, pretty girl', probably the kind of girl Hart found attractive.

13. Queens University, Belfast, Robert Hart Special Collections, MS.15.2, 7 March 1902. B-T was then staying at 63 Harley Street, which was the home of his wife's uncle, Dr. George Thin, his wife, a cousin, and three live-in servants (according to the 1901 Census). On receipt of B-T's letter, Hart wrote to Ann via the London Office on 24 March 1902, probably regarding her health (Fairbank, Bruner, and Matheson, *The I.G. in Peking*, 1235).

14. See Appendix II.

15. The Register of Sassines for 1889, Fife public records p. 5934, refers to the disposition

> of a tenement of land, with Yard thereof, bounded on the south by the common Street and on the north by the Links, in Burgh of Earlsferry, and Piece of Garden ground at the north end adjoining the Links, with access to Well.

It would appear that the 'common Street' was the High Street, where Michie's mother and stepfather lived, bequeathing the house to their sons when they died in the early 1880s. The house they lived in with its long piece of ground to the Links is called West Court, and 'Cathay' was built by Ann at the end of the garden in what is now 6 Links Road. Ann appears to have owned both houses.

16. There is a hint of a weakness, unspecified, in a letter from Michie to his friend Addis, in which he refers to her health, adding: 'My daughter has never been very bright' (SOAS, Addis, PPMS 14/137, 2 February 1898).

17. Plans for the substantial villa were shown to me by David Thomson, chairman of the Elie and Earlsferry History Society, Fife. The plans were submitted in November 1902 and were approved early in 1903, though the house does not appear to have been built until around 1907 or 1908, as it is not listed in the Valuation Rolls until 1908–09. Ann may well have used part of the legacy she was left by her father to finance the villa.

18. Queens University, Belfast, Robert Hart Special Collections, MS.15.2, 12 August 1902. The Brewitt-Taylors were staying in Hazeldene, Ashley Road, in north London.

19. Queens University, Belfast, Robert Hart Special Collections, MS.15.2, 30 January 1903.

20. Peg, 31 December 1902.

21. CHC, Vol. 12, p. 188.

22. Cheng, *Postal Communication in China and Its Modernization, 1860–1896,* p. 104.

23. NCH, 18 August 1905, p. 363.

24. NCH, 18 August 1905, p. 397.
25. SHAC, 137.1802–8, private letter from B-T to Piry, 9 April 1903. For these references to postal correspondence, I am indebted to Lane J. Harris, a doctoral student at the University of Illinois working on the Chinese Postal Service. Lane kindly sent me some impressions he formed of B-T:

   > I find Brewitt-Taylor to have been a fairly conscientious postmaster despite his complaints about social rank and position vis-à-vis Commissioner Hobson [The Shanghai Customs Commissioner] . . . He seems to have taken his job very seriously. He engaged with the Postal Secretary on a wide variety of postal questions making useful, if not always innovative, suggestions . . . Brewitt-Taylor's success as Postmaster is to be expected as being appointed to Shanghai, the Imperial Post Office's busiest district, already implies the value Piry saw in Brewitt-Taylor. Additionally . . . Piry was using Brewitt-Taylor to create administrative space between the Posts and Customs — not an enviable task for anyone. His Semi-Officials run on for pages, 3–5 pages for a single letter are not uncommon, while most other Postmasters wrote a page or two.

   These impressions confirm the view of B-T as sensible rather than exciting — a safe pair of hands.
26. Responding to Piry's appeal to create space with the Customs should not be read as disloyalty by B-T to his main Service. First, Customs staff were themselves ambivalent about being bedfellows with the Post; second, Hart himself recognized that the Post would become independent, for at about the time B-T was seconded, Hart wrote that 'Our Postal work extends rapidly . . . The Postal will be a far bigger Service than the Customs . . . [once it] . . . spreads its wings and takes flight on its own account' (Fairbank, Bruner and Matheson, *The I.G. in Peking,* 1276); and third, B-T would always tend to see himself working in the best interest of the job in hand, and he was likely to follow the lead of his immediate boss.
27. SHAC, 137.1802–8, private letters from B-T to Piry, 18 April 1903, and an undated one apparently just before this date.
28. SHAC, 137.1813–2, Canton Incoming, 1897–1905, Semi-Official from Mayers to Piry, 20 March 1905.
29. SHAC, 137.1762, Special File 36, Memorandum, 19 August 1905.
30. PRO, FO671/282.
31. Bickers, *Britain in China,* pp. 124–5.
32. PRO, FO 671/275, 276 . This is another clear example of the pedagogy of imperialism; see Hevia, *English Lessons.*
33. Murphey, *Shanghai: Key to Modern China,* pp. 7, 22.

Chapter 10

1. NCH, 11 May 1906, p. 233.
2. *Directory and Chronicle for China,* 1917, p. 1010. See also Smith, *European Settlements in the Far East,* p. 171. The Customs house is now a museum and displays a plaque

with the names of the Customs commissioners who held posts there; B-T's name is included.

3. Biggs, *'Chinese' Wilson*, pp. 15–8. Wilson then had to journey another seventeen days to reach Henry, and all the latter possessed about the location of the tree was a scrap of paper on which a map had been drawn of an area straddling Hubei and Sichuan Provinces covering twenty thousand square miles. So, he had to return to Hong Kong by the same route, whence he sent off numerous specimens of interesting plants, and start his journey again. His persistence was justified: he eventually found the tree.

4. B-T mentions this in a letter to Hart, written on his way to Mengtze, referring to a meeting in the border town of Laokai regarding a proposal for a joint customs house with the French, about which he expressed misgivings.

5. NCH, 30 March 1906, p. 706.

6. Snow, *Journey South of the Clouds*, pp. 142–4.

7. Anderson, 'A Belated Encounter', 30 July 1998, p. 8.

8. Stella Benson, Diaries 1902–1933, reel 7, Oct. 1921–Oct. 1925, British Library, Mic.A 20024, October 23, 1922.

9. Grant, *Stella Benson,* p. 196.

10. Stella Benson, Diaries, October 24, 1922.

11. Wood, *No Dogs and Not Many Chinese,* p. 225.

12. NCH, 30 June 1906.

13. SHAC, Customs Service Archive 679(1), Mengtze 32596, 6 April 1906.

14. PRO, FO372/47, 24847, 1907. As was customary, Mrs. Brewitt-Taylor applied to the British Crown for permission to wear the decoration on formal occasions. She requests the King's permission, via the Lord Chamberlain's Office in Buckingham Palace, to 'accept and wear' the decoration, 'Brevett de Kim Bai,' awarded by the Empress of Annam, a French protectorate. But as it was not a 'recognized order of International Chivalry', the request could not be granted. There is a note stating that she did not need permission, but she does not appear to have been informed of this; 'send usual answer' was the only instruction. There is also a note that the native ruler of Annam was declared insane the previous October, which suggests this may also have affected the status of the Empress! Ann probably did wear the decoration — the more one could display on the breast on formal occasions, the better.

15. See Appendix II and the Edinburgh University Library, Special Collections, Lothian Health Services Archive, Letter of 21 December 1914.

16. SHAC, 2 June 1906. (It is possible that it was Sir Robert Bredon that he was addressing if Bredon, as Deputy I.-G. had been delegated to receive reports then.)

17. Fairbank, Bruner and Matheson, *The I.G. in Peking* 1049, n. 2.

18. Fairbank and Teng, 'On the Types and Uses of Ch'ing Documents', p. 38; the others were by T. F. Wade and Hirth (the first edition of the textbook).

19. Brewitt-Taylor, *Textbook of Modern Documentary Chinese for the Special Use of the Chinese Customs Service,* Vol. 1. The fact that B-T volunteered to undertake the task, and the accolade so accorded, clearly was not quite sufficient reward in itself. For, a few years later, after giving the matter some thought and with some diffidence, B-T wrote to Aglen, the new inspector General, requesting some form of recognition for the task of editing the volumes. He points out:

> The work on the new edition was not done in office hours but leisure was found by rising early in the morning . . . I venture to think that a special piece of work of this kind undertaken at the desire of the I.G. . . . might be recognized in some special form. . . . I have heard that Dr. Hirth, who prepared the first edition, was given special facilities for the work by being appointed to the Statistical Department and received a special grant in addition. (SHAC file 679, 22 April 1913)

Clearly, some hope for reward had been on his mind for some time, but he was unwilling to ask for it while Hart was alive. (The reference to the Statistical Department post is odd given that B-T had expressed his reluctance to take such a post.)

20. Even until recently, there was a French coffee shop in Kunming which my wife and I visited, selling a range of patisserie-derived pastries and a kind of croissant; this was a survival from the earlier era of French influence in this part of southern China.

21. SHAC, 19 April 1906. There had been attempts at stricter controls following the Sino-Japanese War, when Confucian scholars attacked opium for contributing to moral decay, but raising revenue became especially important when indemnities were imposed after the Boxer episode (Dikother, Lamaan and Zhou, *Narcotic Culture*, pp. 107–8).

22. SHAC, 2 August 1906. See also Slack, *Opium, State and Society*, pp. 2–4. The years 1905 and 1906 had witnessed the height of domestic cultivation of opium, when China is estimated to have produced seven-eighths of total world output; the new rules B-T refers to would probably have been the plan to reduce the acreage under poppy cultivation. Other observers have stressed that poppy production in poorer areas created a golden opportunity for peasant farmers. Poppy production and distribution facilitated capital accumulation and helped to knit internal trade networks, as well as redistributing wealth away from the coast (Brook and Wakabayashi, *Opium Regimes*, p. 9). Opium had different meanings for different people — recreational, medicinal and, importantly, economic — which was why it eluded control, Brook and Wakabayashi, *Opium Regimes*, p. 25.

23. SHAC, 28 August 1907.
24. NCH, 30 March 1906.
25. SHAC, 5 June 1906.
26. SHAC, 14 May 1906.
27. Symonds and Grant, Introduction to *The Confessions of Aleister Crowley*, p. 19.
28. Symonds and Grant, *The Confessions of Aleister Crowley*, p. 504. The *Chambers Biographical Dictionary*, 1990 ed., p. 368, states that Crowley was English. He was born in Leamington, but he claimed that his family had settled in England, having moved from Ireland, during the time of the Tudors (Symonds and Grant, *The Confessions of Aleister Crowley*, p. 35).
29. Symonds and Grant, *The Confessions of Aleister Crowley*, p. 496.
30. SHAC, May 1907.
31. Wood, *No Dogs and Not Many Chinese*, p. 225.
32. SHAC, 9 July 1906.
33. Smith, *European Settlements in the Far East*, pp. 79–81.
34. PTT, 21 March 1896.

35. PTT, 13 October 1900.
36. PRO, FO678/1144/5.
37. SHAC, 8 December 1905.
38. SHAC, 2 August 1906.
39. Queens University, Belfast, Robert Hart Special Collections, 7 August 1906. The letter also suggests that she, or perhaps she and her father or husband, had owned a property in Peitaiho, some time before B-T made his purchases of land there in January:

> I wonder how Peitaiho is looking this year! I thought that I could never again be happy in being absent a summer from my dear little home on the hill by the sea — but a Kind Providence rules these things always for the best even if we cannot see it at the moment, and certainly we neither of us can complain of our lot here.

40. SHAC, 29 December 1906.
41. For example, Wood, *No Dogs and Not Many Chinese,* p. 137.
42. Fairbank, Coolidge and Smith, *H. B. Morse,* pp. 183–232.
43. See Appendix II. Saker had relatively recently joined the Customs. He was one of a batch of six new recruits who had arrived in Shanghai in November 1903. Hart commented on their general calibre: 'I cannot say I consider their personal statements very promising'; Saker had come fifth in the examination results of the six (Chen and Han, *Archives of China's Imperial Maritime Customs,* Letter 3206; Fairbank, Bruner and Matheson, *The I.G. in Peking,* 1303).
44. Information provided via email by Professor Robert Bickers, Bristol University, from the SHAC records.
45. Perhaps Saker had read the ironically humorous 'Open Letter to a Fourth Assistant B', which had appeared in 1896, and had heeded its advice overenthusiastically:

> First of all you must bow your knee to your Commissioner's wife, for in her goodwill are comfort and furlough and good sport. (Elder, *China's Treaty Ports,* p. 50)

46. Appendix II contains excerpts from her and others' accounts, as well as a record of Ann's all known mental hospitalizations.
47. SHAC, 30 December 1907.

Chapter 11

1. See Blyth, *Life of William Ellis,* which contains the following splendid dedication:

> To the pupils of William Ellis, from those of imperial and royal rank to humble toilers for their daily bread, who have received from him or through his life-long labours guidance as to their conduct in daily life: To the fortunate possessors of wealth who have derived from his teaching the knowledge of their moral duty in its use: And to all who have learned from him how best to improve the condition of their less fortunate fellow-citizens, and to help to diminish destitution, vice, and crime, by removing their chief cause: I dedicate this record of his life-history.

Ellis founded a number of schools in London and elsewhere, and he tutored the royal children in social science, itself a novel area at the time (whether this was paid for or not is not known, but in recognition of his work Queen Victoria gave him a book on the Prince Consort autographed by her). One of the schools he founded still flourishes as the William Ellis School, in Parliament Hill Fields, Highgate, London. Ellis was also interested in a wide range of social issues and was active in the movement for the abolition of slavery. Several leading reformers of the day, such as John Stuart Mill and Jeremy Bentham, were numbered among his friends; Ellis describes walking from his home in Croydon to the city, a distance of some nine to ten miles, to have regular discussion breakfasts with them before starting the day's work.

2. Stewart and McCann, *The Educational Innovators,* p. 297. This work also contains assessments of the eduational contributions of both Ellis and Morley, see Vol. 1, sections 16 and 20.
3. Peg, October 1902.
4. Peg, March 1903.
5. *The Gower,* July 1906. The title derived from Gower Street, London, where the school was originally located.
6. PRO, FO 69/268.
7. Daisy's diary, 21 November 1904.
8. Peg, November 1905.

Chapter 12

1. See Appendix II.
2. The other co-director, a customary parallel Chinese government appointment, was Chan Lun, an official; see Chinese Maritime Customs, *Documents Illustrative of the Origin, Development, and Activities of the Chinese Customs Service,* Vol. 2, Circular 1501, p. 615.
3. CHC, Vol. 12, p. 183.
4. Chinese Maritime Customs, *Documents Illustrative of the Origin, Development, and Activities of the Chinese Customs Service,* Vol. 3, Circular 2001, p. 93.
5. SOAS, Bowra, PPMS 69, Vol. 2, p. 248.
6. Chinese Maritime Customs, *Documents Illustrative of the Origin, Development, and Activities of the Chinese Customs Service,* Vol. 2, pp. 61–6.
7. Wright, *Hart and the Chinese Customs,* p. 841.
8. Queens University, Belfast, Robert Hart Special Collections, Box 10, 18 July 1909.
9. CHC, Vol. 11, Part 2, pp. 437–8.
10. The subtitle of Hevia's *English Lessons.*
11. Johnston and Erh, *Near to Heaven.*
12. Raymond Brewitt-Taylor, Letter to Evelyn, 9 August 1908 (hereafter cited simply 'Ray' followed by the date).
13. Ray, 13 September 1908.
14. Ray, 13 September 1908.
15. SOAS, Bowra, PPMS 69, Vol. 2, p. 227.
16. SOAS, Bowra, PPMS 69, Vol. 2, Item 19, pp. 272, 303.

17. Hsu, *The Rise of Modern China*, p. 475.
18. Wood, *No Dogs and Not Many Chinese*, p. 173. One important result of the revolution for the Customs was that the Service took over the actual collection as well as the assessment of duties.
19. Chinese Maritime Customs, *Documents Illustrative of the Origin, Development, and Activities of the Chinese Customs Service*, Vol. 7, p. 235. The official title of the Service changed from Imperial Maritime Customs Service to Chinese Maritime Customs Service.
20. Snow, *Journey South of the Clouds*, p. 113, quoting Sun Yat-sen's will.
21. Chinese Maritime Customs, *Documents Illustrative of the Origin, Development, and Activities of the Chinese Customs Service*, Vol. 3, p. 91.
22. SOAS, Bowra, Vol. 2, p. 248.
23. Ray, 16 January 1913.
24. Peg, 1 June 1913.
25. Ray, 22 July 1913.
26. Ray, 24 July 1913.
27. Peg, September 1913. The sight of three young ladies dressed in splendid Chinese robes was not as outrageous as it might seem, eighteenth-century chinoiserie had left its mark, to be resuscitated in the British Empire Wembley Exhibition of 1924–25 (Bickers, *Britain in China*, p. 50).
28. Peg, December 1913.
29. Peg, January 1914.
30. Peg, March 1914.
31. No comment is made on B-T's having met with the father of the family, Henry Ellis, and if so how they got on together. They must have met, as Henry, then spending part of his time in Lyme Regis and part at Inglefield, Potter's Bar, is recorded in Evelyn's diaries as 'coming home from Lyme' on 20 March, the day before B-T's visit. They shared a strong common interest in astronomy, both being members of the Royal Astronomical Society.
32. Evelyn's diary, 28 May 1914.
33. Evelyn's diary, 7 August 1914.
34. Appendix II.

Chapter 13

1. University of Bristol, Maritime Customs Services Archive, 679(1) 33229, Foochow, 19 March 1915.
2. Johnston, *Twilight in the Forbidden City*, p. 128.
3. CHC, Vol. 12 (Ernest Young's 'Era of Yuan Shih-k'ai, 1912–16'), refers to the 'revival of mandarin airs' around 1914, with the introduction of traditional political ceremonies and symbols (pp. 240–8).
4. Coates, *The China Consuls*, p. 410.
5. King, *In the Chinese Customs Service*, p. 283.
6. SOAS, Bowra, PPMS 69, Vol. 1, p. 178.
7. Spence, *The Search for Modern China*, p. 222

8. CHC, Vol. 12, p. 164.

9. Wood, *No Dogs and Not Many Chinese*, p. 171.

10. SOAS, Bowra, PPMS 69, Vol. 1, p. 180. Mukden was also the location for the famous Mukden Incident of 1931, when a Japanese bomb was said to have helped set the scene for the war in Asia.

11. SOAS, Bowra, PPMS 69, Vol. 1, p.181. I understand that the Customs building was destroyed in recent years.

12. SOAS, Bowra, PPMS 69, Vol. 2, p. 182.

13. State Reference Library of New South Wales, G. E. Morrison Archive, MSS.312/35– 108, Vol. 88, 10 July 1916. Morrison, a very long-distance hiker, was unlikely to have been particularly concerned with limited comfort. Until that year, he had been appointed by President Yuan (who died in the previous month, June 1916) as government advisor, a well-paid post which he had accepted in 1912. He was later to help China's submission to the 1919 Peace Treaty, in Versailles. Becoming very ill about that time, Morrison left for England and died in May 1920 at Sidmouth, Devon (*Australian Dictionary of Biography*, 1891–1939).

14. British Library, Morrison G. E. Diaries, reel 16. See Appendix II.

15. SHAC, Customs Service Archive 679(1), Mukden 31910, 14 September 1916.

16. SHAC, 9 November 1916.

17. SHAC, 14 November 1916.

18. SHAC, April 1916.

19. SHAC, 14 September 1916.

20. CHC, Vol. 12, p. 186.

21. It is not certain who the 'Redbeards' were, but Professor Elizabeth Sinn of the University of Hong Kong suggests that it is a likely ascription for the Russians. There had been bandits known as 'Redbeards', part of the Nien movement (the name derived partly from that of unemployed former Ch'ing mercenaries), but these were said to have been crushed in northern China by the late 1860s (CHC, Vol. 10, Part 1, pp. 310, 315–6, 476).

22. SHAC, 7 January 1917.

23. SHAC, 31 March 1917. The report encloses the resignation letter from the teacher, Dr. Fulton.

24. SHAC, 19 April 1917.

25. SHAC, 27 July 1917.

26. SHAC, 7 September 1917.

27. SHAC, 28 March 1918.

28. SHAC, 20 November 1918.

Chapter 14

1. *Directory and Chronicle for China and the Far East*, 1915.

2. Joan Leaf (daughter of Leonard and therefore B-T's granddaughter), Letter to author, March 2000. Joan possesses a photograph of Leonard in uniform, which neither the Imperial War Museum nor the National Army Museum was able to identify; it might have indicated some kind of volunteer cadetship.

3. Evelyn's diary, 15 August 1914; Peg's budge for that month.
4. The only part of B-T's family of origin invited to Ray's wedding was B-T's brother in Walllington, Surrey, but illness prevented him from attending. Evelyn had already been taken by Ray to meet the family at the end of 1915, but he disliked his boy cousins and was relieved to return home (according to Peg's budges).
5. B-T letter to Evelyn, 1 July 1917.
6. Peg, 27 December 1917.
7. Correspondence between Evelyn and Ray. Daisy had married Roy Suttill late in 1915. B-T, who was fond of Daisy, sent a rather special silver tea service for their wedding.
8. Details on all three deaths are from the obituaries in the University College School's Roll of Honour.
9. B-T to Ray, 4 August, probably 1915.
10. State Reference Library of New South Wales, G. E. Morrison Letters, MSS.312/35-108, Vol. 100, pp. 451–2, 21 September 1918.
11. B-T to Evelyn, 5 December 1918.
12. Burnett, *A History of the Cost of Living*, pp. 298–300.
13. Cannon, 'The Social Situation of the Skilled Worker', pp. 103, 128.
14. Burnett, *A Social History of Housing, 1815–1970*, pp. 246–8.
15. Notice in *The Times* (of London) 4 February 1919.
16. Joan Leaf, Letter to author, 18 June 1999. For an account of American 'low life' activity in Shanghai (gambling casinos, prostitution and drinking bars), see Scully, 'The Low Road to Sino-American Relations', pp. 62–85. Of the estimated forty thousand female sex workers in the city in 1900, two thousand were foreign. Later, apparently, 'Californian' or 'American' girls dominated the demand for foreign prostitutes. Though relatively small in number, they were an obvious group, especially as the successful brothel madams prominently flaunted their success.
17. Peg, 1 February 1919.

Chapter 15

1. This was a body that had been set up both for amateurs and for women astronomers, who were excluded from becoming 'fellows' of the RAS.
2. Evelyn Brewitt-Taylor, Letter to her mother and Win, 6 September 1919. It is not entirely surprising of the man that he should withdraw even during his daughter-in-law and grandson's visit; either he was engaged on urgent business or he wished to avoid confrontation with his wife.
3. Peg, October 1919.
4. The letter was marked in a register as Despatch 3115, and it should have been in SHAC, File 679 (3) 851, Chungking Despatches, Nos. 3110–3326, 1920–22, but despite efforts by Professor Bickers and his team, it could not be found.
5. CMC, Circular 3001, 26 February 1920, in Vol. 3, p. 546.
6. King, *In the Chinese Customs Service*, p. 296.
7. Wood, *No Dogs and Not Many Chinese*, p. 220.
8. Coates, *The China Consuls*, p. 307.
9. Aitcheson, *The Chinese Maritime Service in the Transition from the Ch'ing to the Nationalist Era*, p. 280.

10. SHAC, Customs Service Archive 679(1), Chungking 32045, 6 August 1920.
11. SHAC, 20 August 1920.
12. SHAC, 4 September 1920. The warlords needed the money to finance their military activities, and in the years following the death of President Yuan, opium activity considerably increased (Brook and Wakabayashi, *Opium Regimes,* p. 293).
13. SHAC, 4 October 1920.
14. King, *In the Chinese Customs Service,* p. 252.
15. SHAC, 14 October 1920.
16. SHAC, 27 October 1920.
17. *Women, Writing and Travel, Diaries of Stella Benson 1902–1933* from Cambridge University Library, Mic. A, reel 6, 2 October, 1920. Also available in the BL.
18. SHAC, 15 November 1920.

Chapter 16

1. The villages of Earlsferry and Elie merge into each other; whichever name is used here follows that used in the reference.
2. Ann refers to his trips: 'They have been disagreeable epoques for me, but last time I was better on [my] own.' See Appendix II.
3. Peg, July 1921.
4. Peg, letter to Winnie Ellis, 9 September 1921.
5. Peg, February 1922.
6. The Kingsley Hotel in Bloomsbury Square was a temperance hotel frequented by expatriates, not only non-drinkers. It advertised in the *Directory for China and the Far East.*
7. Peg, 1 June 1922.
8. Peg, December 1922.
9. Peg, 1 January 1925.
10. Peg, 31 December 1923. As B-T is the only grandfather referred to as 'Grandpa' this must have referred to Herbert William with whom we know there was contact. B-T's visits to Portsmouth mentioned by his wife would have been to his sister. This is further evidence of maintained contact with his birth family.
11. Peg, 31 January 1924.
12. Peg, 31 May 1924.
13. Peg, 30 June 1925.
14. Meales, *Highways of the Air,* p. 37. Also see Higham, *Britain's Imperial Air Routes,* pp. 226–7. Not until late 1928 or early 1929 did a Royal Air Force flying boat land in Hong Kong, but no regular British air service followed. In 1931 Deutsche Lufthansa signed an agreement with the Chinese government to operate a route from Berlin to Nanking and Shanghai; in the following year, French Air Orient began an extension of its Saigon service to Hong Kong and Canton. Not until 1936 did a British spur from Penang to Hong Kong place the latter within ten days of London, and in the same year Pan American landed its first clipper in Hong Kong.
15. Peg, 2 June 1926.
16. Peg, 31 October 1926.

17. Publisher's note to the cheap edition, published by Kelly and Walsh in 1929. Kelly and Walsh was a Shanghai-based firm which still survives in that name, no longer as a publisher but as a well-known bookseller in Hong Kong. See also CHC, Vol. 12, Section 8: Benjamin I. Schwartz, 'Themes in Intellectual History: May Fourth and After', p. 435ff.

18. Mair, *The Columbia Anthology of Traditional Chinese Literature,* p. 946.

19. Alexander Wylie was a sinologist, 'one of the oldest and most distinguished of the hyphenated missionary-scholars' (Girardot, *The Victorian Translation of China,* p. 234 and several other citations). He had an extensive private library, of which over seven hundred volumes on Chinese culture and geography formed the basis for the library of the North China Branch of the Royal Asiatic Society (Danielson, 'Shanghai's Lost Libraries Rediscovered', p. 85).

20. Brewitt-Taylor, Preface to *San Kuo, or Romance of the Three Kingdoms.*

21. Edition published by Graham Brash, Singapore, 1985.

22. Edition published by Charles E. Tuttle, 1959.

23. Nienhauser, *The Indiana Companion to Traditional Chinese Literature,* pp. 668–70.

24. Liu, *Startling Moon,* p. 99. The *Dream of the Red Chamber* is another major Chinese traditional novel, written in the eighteenth century.

25. CJSA, July 1926, p. 18.

26. JNCBRAS 57 (1926): 205–7.

27. Edwards, *The Dragon Book,* The 'Small-Footed Maid' is on pp. 126ff. B-T's quotations from the *San Kuo* are to be found on pp. 47, 155–6, 192–3, 216–8, 256–7, 272–3, 278–9.

28. Goodrich and Fang, *Dictionary of Ming Biography,* Vol. 1, p. 980.

29. Brewitt-Taylor, Preface to *San Kuo, or Romance of the Three Kingdoms.*

30. Roberts, *Three Kingdoms,* 1999 ed., p. 413.

31. Mair, *The Columbia Anthology of Traditional Chinese Literature,* p. 946.

32. CR 19.3 (1890–91): 168–78.

33. B-T does state in his preface that, despite being widely read and though 'not written for the stage', the *San Kuo* is perhaps better known through stage performances than actual reading.

34. 'Saga' would be another possible rendering, especially given the book's essentially oral tradition: something said, a prose narrative, encompassing actual history, biography and legend, akin to the Icelandic and Norwegian sagas.

35. CLEAR 17 (December 1995): 157–8.

36. Internet discussion on China the Beautiful website, available at http://www.chinapage.com/china.html (accessed January 2000).

Chapter 17

1. SOAS, Maze, Vol. VI, PPMS 2, p. 442, 15 May 1931. MacDonald's response to Maze was to thank him for letting him see the material, praising his great service to China and to the Service. Demonstrating that fellow expatriates did not always share the same views, he added:

The Shanghai Club diehards will die. Their representatives of forty and fifty years before drank 'To hell with Hart and d-n the Customs' . . . Hart never forgot the Lay experience.

(Lay, Hart's predecessor, had also tried to act independently of the government and was forced out of office.)

2. SOAS, Maze, PPMS2, Vol. VI, pp. 55–58, 14 June 1931. Maze responded with further argument to support his view that Aglen had presented other examples of ignoring the de facto government with dangerous results (SOAS, Maze, PPMS2, Vol. VI, pp. 51–54, 21 July 1931). Given the way Maze castigates Aglen with descriptions such as 'stupid' and 'senile', it is worth quoting Aglen's fulsome expression of faith in Maze when he appointed Maze Commissioner in Canton at the time of the Revolution in 1911:

I had complete confidence in both your loyalty and your judgement — [you] more than justified my selection. I always knew you would rise to the occasion but you have developed qualities of tact, diplomacy, and administrative ability of a high order which I didn't give you credit for, latent talents which it required unusual circumstances of heat and difficulty to bring out. (SOAS, Aglen, PPMS211355, 2 February 1913)

The strength of Maze's attack is another example of a successor tending to do down his predecessor.

3. B-T's brother-in-law Michie (with whom he continued to correspond) knew Maze well from their early days in the Service; he also continued to correspond with Maze intermittently, writing with familiarity to 'My old mess-mate Freddie Maze' (SOAS, Maze, PPMS2, Vol. VI, pp. 67–9, 5 January 1930).
4. Peg, February 1930.
5. Peg, 3 June 1933.
6. Peg, 3 August 1933.
7. PRO, FO678/1144, 1145. Lot 1 of FO678/1144 was not sold.
8. British Library Archives, OR 5896, p. 34.
9. BL OR 11127/2/3/4. The volumes contain the following *chüan* of the encyclopaedia: 8268–9, 8275, and 18244.
10. BL Archives, Donation Reports, 12 January 1931.
11. BL Archives, Official Letters, Private Correspondence, 4 January 1931.
12. Peg, 2 February 1930.
13. Peg, 29 March 1932.
14. B-T, Letter to Elizabeth, 23 January 1934.
15. Daisy's budge dated 2 March for February 1934. The family would certainly have possessed a telephone, so he could have phoned.
16. Peg, 1 December 1934.
17. Peg, 31 March 1935.
18. Peg, 31 December 1933.
19. B-T, letter to Joan. The letter is simply dated '30 Oct', with no year, but was probably written in the early to mid-1930s.
20. Evelyn, letter to Peg, 1 April 1937. Elizabeth and her daughters probably made their annual visit in the summer.

21. Peg, 31 March 1938.
22. Royal Astronomical Society, *Monthly Notices*, Vol. 99, p. 300. The obituary contains a couple of minor errors: B-T's first wife died in 1890 not 1891, and he was survived by two daughters-in-law not daughters, though he did have had strong affection for them.
23. The National Archives of Scotland, SC70/7/420, Probate, 1 June 1938.
24. Nevill, *London Clubs*, p. 273. B-T joined early in the life of the club, having been a member since 1899 according to the Royal Societies Club's booklet 'Foundation and Objects, Rules, and By-laws and List of Members, 1914'. The same publication lists his son Leonard as having joined the club in 1912, seemingly through being a member of the Siam Society.
25. *Survey of London*, p. 472:

    No description can give a true idea of the ingenuity and perverted taste displayed in this extraordinary front, which looks rather like a late Victorian music-hall . . . although the vulgarity is redeemed by the use of Portland stone throughout.

26. According to the 1901 Census, when the Taylors were already living in Carew Lodge, Herbert had five children: the two daughters, Dorothy and Marjorie, and three sons, Herbert Lionel, who later died of tuberculosis; Douglas, who was killed in the First World War; and Reginald, who was probably established in his career by the time B-T drew up his will. Herbert, who is known to have become a civil servant, is described as a 'gold and silver refiner'; this was initially thought to be an enumerator error, frequent at the time, but a recently discovered family tree clearly records him as a jeweller, so he must have changed career. In the same census, his mother could not be found (she would have been around seventy-four by then, so could well have already died), nor could two of B-T's sisters, the only one recorded in the census being Rebecca Barber, who B-T's first wife, Alice, stayed with in Southsea; Rebecca's son, Charles H., was an eighteen-year-old ironmonger's assistant. The parents of B-T's first wife, Alice, George and Emma Vale, were still alive and living in Lambeth. Ann refers to communicating with one of B-T's sisters living in Southsea (near Portsmouth) in 1916, alleging that the sister had commented that B-T did not know how to treat Ann and also that B-T paid regular trips to Portsmouth (see Appendix II).
27. FO917/3748. The value of the whole of B-T's property in China was sworn for probate at £2,511; of this amount, the Peitaiho property was valued at Ch.$5,390, which at the prevailing exchange of just over 8d.:Ch.$, was worth around £450, about the price of a modest suburban semi-detached house in Britain at the time.
28. Though adoption had become legal in 1926, there was no right to equal inheritance until 1949; J. P. Triselcotis, *Evaluation of Adoption Policy and Practice*, pp. 8ff.
29. See Appendix II.
30. Unlike the case for B-T, there was an announcement of her death in *The Times*, 1 May 1947.
31. Telephone conversation with John Linton, now a resident of Elie, adjacent to Earlsferry.
32. National Archives of Scotland, JC 20/56//69, ff1055; JC20/50/177, ff3115–118.
33. Letter from Dr. K. Bhanthumnaviv to Frances Brewitt-Taylor, 12 February 1995.

34. *SOAS Annual Report*, 1955–56, p. 123. Also see Helliwell, 'Holdings of *Yongle dadian* in United Kingdom Libraries'. The *chüan* is 10115–6.
35. *SOAS Bulletin*, 1958.
36. Bickers, 'Coolie Work', pp. 396–9.
37. SOAS, Evangeline Dora Edwards, pp. 38–40.

Chapter 18

1. The concepts of 'marginality' and the 'marginal man' have wide currency in the social sciences, where numerous studies have noted how marginality may confer the ability to bestride two cultures. See, for example, Gould and Kolb, *A Dictionary of the Social Sciences*, pp. 406–7.
2. CHC, Vol. 12, p. 183.
3. Wright, *Hart and the Chinese Customs*, p. 866.
4. SHAC, 27 September 1918.
5. See Appendix II.
6. See Appendix II.
7. Any interpretation of passivity would be false, for several examples of strongly expressed views can be found: his criticism of the naivety of the novice expatriate thinking he can change an ancient culture in 'A Handful of Cash'; concern over his status in Shanghai; his defence of Aglen against Maze's criticism; various expressions of bitterness relating to his wife's mental illness; and his general detachment being severely tested by suspicion of his wife's infidelity.
8. Much of his life was associated with the sea. He was born and brought up in the home of a coastguard on the south coast of Britain, and he retired and died in a seaside village in Scotland. His life was strongly marine-oriented: first through his early maritime-related education in the Royal Hospital School, then his teaching in a naval college in China, publishing a book on navigation and his main career in the Chinese Maritime Customs. In China he also owned a holiday home and other property at a popular seaside resort. Travel between postings and his regular journeys back to Britain on long leave were mainly by ship. So, B-T's work and domestic life were both strongly flavoured by maritime connections.
9. Bickers, *Britain in China*, p. 14.
10. Appendix III, Number 2.
11. Unusual perhaps but not absent, for friendships were by no means unknown; one description of a departure of an expatriate refers to it as a sad moment for 'there were many friends, both Chinese and foreign, whom I shall be sorry to leave' (Williams, *Chinese Tribute*, p. 181). There were sexual relationships, but marriage was rare and only much later would become socially more acceptable. However, relationships were often close between expatriate child and amah servant.
12. The term is derived from an as yet unpublished lecture given by Professor Peter Newmark, the translation theorist, who speaks of 'genteel anti-semitism'.
13. I am indebted to Chung Yuehtsen for noting this from a Customs circular.
14. SHAC, 8 August 1907.

15. Evidence of this is provided through his correspondence with Maze (see chapter Final Years).

16. One could speculate whether these and especially the sinologists among them would have formed a conscious 'brotherhood', another kind of freemasonry bound by their knowledge of China and their experience of the Customs. In particular, those who shared the experience of the Siege of the Legations must have felt a special kind of camaraderie, honed by knowledge of one another's behaviour under pressure.

17. See, for example, Hevia, *English Lessons*.

Appendices

1. Letter from Ann Brewitt-Taylor to G. E. Morrison, State Reference Library of New South Wales, MSS. 312, vol. 62, pp. 455–7, undated, but circa Dec. 1911. In her letter Ann notes that she had been in contact with an American grandchild of her errant grandfather, a Miss Fox, but had lost her address.

2. The obituary in the *East Fife Record,* 22/8/1902 refers to the Thins as half–brothers to Michie. The DNB for Michie (Supplement 1901–1911 and later) describes them as step-brothers. I first thought that without knowing the year of the second marriage we couldn't be sure about the degree of brotherhood, but the Old Parish Register for Kilconquhar clearly show that George and Robert were parented by George Thin and his wife Ann Laing, so they were Michie's half-brothers. The records also reveal that Michie was illegitimate, though he did take the name of his natural father; whether the parents later married (as Ann B-T suggests) couldn't be established, though it seems unlikely; the records use Michie's mother's maiden name, Laing, not Michie. Census data on the Thin births was also misleading, however the Parish records show George was born in November 1838 and Robert in December 1843; when Robert died in 1867 he was 23 (NCH, 22/4/1867, p. 26) not 17 as stated in the *East Fife Record*.

3. Alexander Michie, DNB, 1912; 1851 Census for Scotland, Earlsferry, Parish of Kilconquhar; and *East Fife Record,* 15/8/02, p. 4.

4. Lane-Poole, vol. I, pp. 417 and 422. There's a nice story related by Michie to Lane Poole about Sir Harry Parkes who visited a Taiping prince about stationing a gunboat to protect the river factories at Nanking. The prince had to refer the decision to his chief, the Heavenly King, who communicated directly with the Almighty. The Heavenly King received a vision saying no foreign ship could stay near Nanking. When this was relayed to Parkes, he displayed anger and replied, 'Tut, tut, tut! Won't do at all, he must have another vision.' The first vision was duly amended by another, more acceptable one.

5. Haan, p. 64.

6. Michie, A., 1864, pp. 357 and 369.

7. From Office of National Statistics records.

8. Baptismal records held in the Lambeth Palace Library.

9. SOAS, Addis, PPMS/14/144. An obituary of Michie in the *Peking and Tientsin Times* for 23/8/02, refers to 1868 as the year that his 'accomplished wife' died; the death was recorded by the local Shanghai newspaper (NCH, 14/3/1868, p.110). She, was believed to have had a drink problem, as was seen earlier her son had too (Addis, PPMS 14/10-21, Diary for 1898, 22 Aug.).

10. George Thin died in Nice on 27/12/1903. *The Lancet* records that it was in China that

> he gained an extensive experience in all forms of tropical disease, an experience which with ripened judgment in after years brought him considerable fame.

Both Thins were Registered Non-Residents in the *UK Medical Directories* during their years in China. Obituaries of George are in the *British Medical Journal*, 23/1/1904, p. 221 and *The Lancet*, 13/2/1904, p. 74.

11. SOAS, Addis, PPMS 14/67, 17 April 1892.

12. Fairbank, et al, 1975, 1215.

13. DNB, Listing for Michie, vol. II, 1912. There is a memorial to Robert Thin as well as to other members of the Thin family in the cemetery of the parish church, Kilconquhar, Fife.

14. Keppel, vol. iii, p. 238. British merchants were interested in opening up new treaty ports. Sir Rutherford Alcock had selected for the expedition Swinhoe, the late Consul to Taiwan and a scholar, linguist, and naturalist. Swinhoe and Michie were accompanied by a Mr. Francis, another Shanghai merchant. They were taken there by gunboat. Apparently no important developments followed. Blue, p. 118.

15. Noted in various reports of meetings recorded in the NCH over the period.

16. Office of National Statistics and DNB listing for MIchie.

17. PTT, Obit, 23/8/1902, p. 4. I have not been able to find any information about this Agency.

18. King, Frank H. H., 1987, Vol. I, p. 322.

19. *Chinese Times*, 6/11/1886.

20. CT, 20/7/1889. It should be said that a propensity to dissimulate could sometimes be a function of courteousness, telling people what they would like to hear rather than possibly causing offence by being frank. Making this finer distinction would not have been Michie's style.

21. CT, 28/3/1891.

22. Frank King and Prescott-Clarke, p. 98. The authors say that there was some uncertainty about who financed the paper, but also comments appreciatively:

> It appears to have had the facts, to have thought the matter out carefully before advising the foreign community, the Chinese and Japanese governments, and the world at large on the best course of action.

(This publication p.137 refers to Michie dying in 1891, in fact he died in 1902.) The leader in the *Peking and Tientsin Times* announcing Michie's death also states that 'Competent judges pronounced this paper [*Chinese Times*] to be the best ever produced in the East.' (P&TT, 23/8/1902, p. 2.)

23. King, P. pp. 83–4.

24. Chen and Han, 2680, letter from Campbell. Detring was also at the meeting which included M.P.s from both sides of the House. This was another momentous period in China's history when major reforms were attempted, but in the struggle between conservative and progressive forces, the would-be Chinese reformers lost out and were severely dealt with by the Empress Dowager, who proved more powerful than the reform-sympathetic Emperor. The M.P.s could well have been getting advice about policy over China.

25. SOAS, Addis, PPMS14/130-144, Box 18, 144 contains a copy of an obituary notice for Michie, but without noting the source.

26. Clearly Li Hung-chang and Michie got on well and the latter wrote a long article on Li Hung-chang when he died, aged 78, in November 1901. Michie, 'Li Hung-chang', Blackwoods Edinburgh Magazine, MXXXIV, Dec. 1901, vol. CLXX, pp. 838–51. When Michie was editing the *Chinese Times,* a leader lauded Li as one of the leading powers in China:

> The collective weight of [all the provincial governors and viceroys] falls short of Li Hung-chang alone ... Beyond the arena of palace intrigue, the malice of discontented placemen, the happy hunting grounds of eunuchs and concubines, there is really in China, a weather-beaten old pilot who, according to the light that is in him, has done his best to keep the ship off the breakers, and even to make it appear that she was really heading for some destination, without whom the most utter shipwreck would have been effected many times – and that is Li Hung-chang. The China which is known to the West is in fact the China of Li Hung-chang. (CT, 4/1/90, pp. 2–3.)

Michie had also attended the celebrations in Tientsin in February, 1892 for Li's 70th birthday, where the banquet provided by Li for foreign residents consisted of alternating English and Chinese dishes. Brewitt-Taylor, *Celebration of the Seventieth Birthday of Li Hung-chang.*

27. *The Times* 12/8/1902. A somewhat more critical comment on his biography of Alcock is to be found in Fairbank, Coolidge, Smith, 220:

> Using Alcock's career as a thread, Michie surveyed the events of Anglo-Chinese relations as a British success story meriting high praise. It is a distinctly Shanghai-minded narrative ... Michie offered few footnotes but a good deal of the conventional wisdom of the day.

Michie's death is noted in the Dictionary of National Biography (Second Supplement, vol. II, 1912), and in addition to *The Times* and the P&TT leader and obituary, other obituaries appeared in the local *East Fife Record* (15/8/1902, p. 4 and also 22/8/1902), and a very brief one in *The Graphic* (16/8/1902, p. 218), which includes the only known portrait of him. The source of this was a letter dated 4/11/1911 from Michie's daughter Ann to G.E. Morrison when the latter was China Correspondent for *The Times;* she also refers without giving details to other death notices, including German newspapers (State Reference Library of New South Wales, vol. 27–31, 1911). Some of Michie's writings will be found in the Bibliography.

28. P&TT, 23/8/1902, p. 2.

29. SOAS, Addis, PPMS 14/67, item163, 13/8/1902.

30. SOAS, Addis, PPMS 14/67, 21 March, 1893.

31. The grave number is 34786.

32. Ann may well have suffered mental disturbances when her first baby had died in Tientsin in 1896, but no details of this could be found.

33. Dr. George Matthew Robertson was well-regarded internationally. He combined the post of Physician-Superintendent at the Royal Edinburgh Hospital for Mental and Nervous

Disorders with the Chair of Psychiatry at the University of Edinburgh. He was active in the movement for treating mental disorders on similar lines to physical ones, and was a proponent of the hospitalization of asylum treatment. See Obituary, *British Medical Journal,* 9/4/1932, pp. 688–9.

Bibliography and Other Sources

Aitcheson, Jean. *The Chinese Maritime Service in the Transition from the Ch'ing to the Nationalist Era*. Ph.D. thesis, University of London, SOAS, 1983.

Allen, Rev. Roland. *The Siege of the Peking Legations, Beijing*. Smith, Elder, 1901.

Anderson, Perry. 'A Belated Encounter', parts 1 and 2, *London Review of Books*, 30 July 1998 and 20 August 1998. [Two articles on the career of the author's father in the Chinese Customs Service.]

Atkins, Martyn. *Informal Empire in Crisis: British Diplomacy and the Chinese Customs Succession, 1927–1929*. Cornell University Press, 1995.

Aylmer, Charles. 'The Memoirs of H. A. Giles'. *Journal of East Asian History* 13–14 (1997).

Benson, Stella, Diaries, 1902-1933, University of Cambridge Microfilm, published by Marlborough, 2005; also available at the BL shelf mark Mic.A 20024.

Bickers, Robert. 'Coolie Work: Sir Reginald Johnston at the School of Oriental Studies, 1931–1937'. *Journal of the Royal Asiatic Society* 5.3 (November 1995).

———. *Britain in China*. Manchester University Press, 1999.

———. *Empire Made Me: An Englishman Adrift in Shanghai*. Allen Lane, 2003.

———. 'Purloined Letters: History and the Chinese Maritime Customs Service'. *Modern Asian Studies* 40.3 (July 2006).

Biggerstaff, Knight. *The Earliest Modern Government Schools in China*. Cornell University Press, 1961.

Biggs, Roy W. *'Chinese' Wilson: A Life of Ernest H. Wilson*. HMSO, 1993.

Blue, A. D. 'European Navigation of the Yangtse'. *JHKBRAS* 3 (1963).

Blyth, Edmund Kell. *Life of William Ellis: Founder of the Birkbeck Schools*. Kegan Paul, Trench, 1889.

Boorman, H. L., and Richard, C. H. *Biographical Dictionary of Republican China*. Columbia University Press, 1967–71.

Brewitt-Taylor, Charles Henry. *Economic Policy (Li ts'ai chieh lüeh [Licai jielüe])*. BL microfiche 15259.c.39. [This is a summary in Chinese by B-T of articles for the use of Chinese Customs officers; the original, by Chen Yauyan, seemingly based on numerous writings, was summarized by B-T in 1899 and published 1900.]

– – – . Translation of *Celebrations of the Seventieth Birthday of Li Hung-chang at Tientsin, Feb. 1892*. Tientsin Press, 1892.

– – – . *Chats in Chinese: A Translation of the* T'an Lun Hsin Pien. Peking: Pei-Tang Press, 1901.

– – – , ed. *Textbook of Modern Documentary Chinese for the Special Use of the Chinese Customs Service*. By F. Hirth. Second edition rearranged, enlarged and edited. Shanghai: Statistical Department, Inspector General of Customs, Vol. 1 in 1909, Vol. 2 in 1910.

– – – . Translation, *San Kuo, or Romance of the Three Kingdoms*. An English version of *San Kuo Chih Yen-i*. 2 Vols. By Lo Kuan-chung. Kelly and Walsh, 1925.

– – – . *Problems and Theorums of Navigation and Nautical Astronomy*. N.p., n.d. [See also Chapter 5 and Appendix III for various other published writings of B-T.]

Brook, Timothy, and Wakabayashi, Bob Tadish, eds. *Opium Regimes: China, Britain, and Japan, 1839–1952*. University of California Press, 2000.

Brown, William, *Is Love a Disease?* The Strand magazine, January 1912.

Bruner, K., Fairbank, J. K., and Smith, *Entering China's Service*. Harvard University Press, 1986.

Brunero, Donna. *Britain's Imperial Cornerstone in China: The Chinese Maritime Customs Service, 1854–1949*. Routledge, 2006.

Burnett, John. *Plenty and Want*. Nelson, 1966.

– – – . *A History of the Cost of Living*. Penguin Books, 1969.

– – – . *A Social History of Housing, 1815–1970*. Methuen, 1978.

Caine, P. J., and Hopkins, A. G. *British Imperialism, 1868–2000,* 2nd ed. Longman, 2002.

Cannon, I. C. *The Social Situation of the Skilled Worker: A Study of the Compositor in London*. Ph.D. diss., University of London, 1961.

– – – . 'Charles Henry Brewitt-Taylor, 1857–1938: Translator and Chinese Customs Commissioner'. *JHKBRAS* 45 (2005).

Chen, Xiafei, and Han, Rongfang, eds. *Archives of China's Imperial Maritime Customs: Confidential Correspondence Between Robert Hart and James Duncan Campbell, 1874–1907,* compiled by the Second Historical Archives of China and the Institute of Modern History, Chinese Academy of the Social Sciences. Beijing: Foreign Languages Press, 1990.

Cheng, Ying-wan. *Postal Communication in China and Its Modernization, 1860–1896*. Harvard University Press, 1970.

Chinese Maritime Customs. *Documents Illustrative of the Origin, Development, and Activities of the Chinese Customs Service*. 7 Vols. Shanghai: Statistical Department of the Inspector General, 1939.

Chu, Samuel C., and Liu, Kwang-Ching, eds. *Li Hung-chang and China's Early Modernization*. M. E. Sharpe, 1994.

Chung, Hilary. Book review of *Psychoanalysis in China, Literary Transformations 1919–49* by Jingyuan Zhang *China Quarterly* (September 1994).

Coates, P. D. *The China Consuls: British Consular Officers, 1843–1943*. Oxford University Press Hong Kong, 1988.

Cohen, Paul A. *History in Three Keys: The Boxers as Event, Experience and Myth*. Columbia University Press, 1997.

Cole, G. D. H., and Postgate, Raymond. *The Common People, 1746–1946*, 3rd ed. Methuen, 1949.

Cordier, Henri. *Bibliotheca Sinica*. Paris: Libraire Orientale and Americaine, 1904.

Couling, Samuel. *Encyclopaedia Sinica*. Kelly and Walsh, 1917.

Cranmer-Byng, J. L. 'The Old British Legation at Peking, 1860–1959'. *JHKBRAS* 3 (1963).

———. 'The Establishment of the Tsungli Yamen: A Translation of the Memorial and Edict of 1861'. *JHKBRAS* 12 (1972).

Danielson, Eric N. 'Shanghai's Lost Libraries Rediscovered'. *JHKBRAS* 44 (2004).

Davidson, Martha. *List of Published Translations from the Chinese into English, French and German*. Edwards Brothers, 1952.

Dawson, Raymond. *The Chinese Experience*. Phoenix Press, 2000.

Dikother, Frank, Lamaan, L., and Zhou Xun. *Narcotic Culture: A History of Drugs in China*. London: Hurst, 2004.

Drage, Charles. *Servants of the Dragon Throne: Being the Lives of Edward and Cecil Bowra*. Peter Dawney, 1966.

Eastman, Lloyd E. *Throne and Mandarins: China's Search for a Policy During the Sino-French Controversy, 1880–1885*. Harvard University Press, 1967.

Edwards, Evangeline Dora. *The Dragon Book: An Anthology of Chinese Literature in Translation*. Wm. Hodge, 1938.

Elder, Chris. *China's Treaty Ports: An Anthology*. Oxford University Press, 1999.

Esherick, Joseph W. *Reform and Revolution in China: The 1911 Revolution in Hunan and Hubei*. University of California Press, 1976.

———. *The Origins of the Boxer Uprising*. University of California Press, 1987.

Fairbank, J. K. *Trade and Diplomacy on the China Coast: The Opening of the Treaty Ports, 1842–54*. Harvard University Press, 1953.

Fairbank, J. K., Bruner, K. F., and Matheson, E. M. *The I.G. in Peking*. Belknap Press, Harvard University Press, 1975.

Fairbank, J. K., Coolidge, M. H., and Smith, R. J. *H.B. Morse: Customs Commissioner and Historian of China*. University of Kentucky Press, 1995.

Fairbank, J. K., and Teng, S. Y. 'On the Types and Uses of Ch'ing Documents'. *Harvard Journal of Asiatic Studies* 5 (1940).

Ferro, Marc. *The Use and Abuse of History*. Routledge Classics, 2003.

Firth, A. E. *Goldsmiths' College: A Centenary Account*. Athlone Press, 1991.

Fleming, Peter. *The Siege at Peking*. Rupert Hart-Davis, 1959.

Forrester, John. '1919: Psychology and Psychoanalysis, Cambridge and London in Myers, Jones and MacCurdy'. *Psychoanalysis and History* 10.1 (2008).

Foster-Hall, B. *The Chinese Maritime Customs: An International Service, 1854–1950*. Maritime Monographs 26. Greenwich: National Maritime Museum, 1977.

Giles, H. A. *Two Romances* in The Chinese Student, a review published by the Central Union of Chinese Students in GB and Ireland. Inaugural Number, 1927.

Giles, Lancelot. *The Siege of the Peking Legations*. University of Western Australia Press, 1970.

Girardot, Norman J. *The Victorian Translation of China: James Legge's Oriental Pilgrimage*. University of California Press, 2002.

Giquel, Prosper. *The Foochow Arsenal and Its Results: From the Commencement in 1867, to the End of the Foreign Directorate on the 16 Feb 1874*. Translated from the French by H. Lang. Shanghai Evening Courier, 1874.

Goodrich, L. C., and Fang, C. *Dictionary of Ming Biography*. Columbia University Press, 1976.

Gould, Julius, and Kolb, William L. *A Dictionary of the Social Sciences*. Tavistock Publications, 1964.

Grant, Joy. *Stella Benson: A Biography*. Macmillan, 1987.

Haan, J. H. 'Origin and Development of the Political System in the Shanghai International Settlement'. *JHKBRAS* 22 (1982).

Hart, Robert, *These from the Land of Sinim*. Chapman & Hall, 1901.

– – –. See also correspondence and papers in various archives at Queen's University, Belfast, SOAS, and the University of Hong Kong, cited in the text.

Helliwell, David. 'Holdings of *Yongle dadian* in United Kingdom Libraries'. Paper presented at the International Symposium on the Six-hundredth Anniversary of the Compilation of the *Yongle dadian* at the National Library of China, Beijing, April 2002.

Hevia, James L. *English Lessons: The Pedagogy of Imperialism in Nineteenth Century China*. Hong Kong University Press, 2003.

Higham, Robin. *Britain's Imperial Air Routes*. G. T. Foulis, 1960.

Hobsbawm, Eric. *Uncommon People: Resistance, Rebellion and Jazz*. Weidenfeld & Nicolson, 1998.

Hoe, Susanna. *Women at the Siege: Peking, 1900*. Oxford: Holo Books, The Women's History Press, 2000.

Hong Kong Museum of Art. *Gateways to China: Trading Ports of the 18th and 19th Centuries*. Hong Kong Government Press, 1987.

Hooker, Mary. *Behind the Scenes in Peking*. John Murray, 1910.

Hopkins, A. G., ed. *Globalization in World History*. Pimlico, 2002.

Horowitz, Richard S. *Mandarins and Customs Inspectors: Western Imperialism in Nineteenth Century China Reconsidered*. Papers on Chinese History 7. The Fairbank Centre, East Asian Research, Harvard University, 1998.

———. 'Power, Politics and the Chinese Maritime Customs'. *Modern Asian Studies* 40.3 (July 2006).

Hsia, C. T. *The Classic Chinese Novel*. Columbia University Press, 1968; reprint, Cornell University Press, 1996.

Hsu, Immanuel C. Y. *The Rise of Modern China*. Oxford University Press, 2000.

Humnel, Arthur W. *Eminent Chinese of the Ch'ing Period*. Taipei, 1967.

Hung, Eva, and Pollard, David. 'Chinese Tradition'. In *Routledge Encyclopaedia of Translation Studies,* ed. Mona Baker and Kirsten Malmkjaer. Routledge, 1998.

Hutcheon, Robin. *Shanghai Customs*. Self-published, 2000.

Jay, Douglas. *Sterling: Its Use and Misuse*. Sidgwick & Jackson, 1985.

Johnston, Reginald F. *Twilight in the Forbidden City*. Oxford University Press, 1985.

Johnston, Tess, and Deke, Erh. *Near to Heaven: Western Architecture in China's Old Summer Resorts*. Old China Hand Press, 1994.

———. *Far from Home: Western Architecture in Northern Treaty Ports*. Old China Hand Press, 1996.

———. *The Last Colonies: Western Architecture in China's Southern Treaty Ports*. Old China Hand Press, 1997.

Kennerley, Alston. 'Early State Support of Vocational Education: The Department of Science and Art Navigation Schools, 1853–63'. *Journal of Vocational Education and Training* 52.2 (2000).

Keppel, Sir Henry. *A Sailor's Life under Four Sovereigns*. MacMillan, 1899.

King, Frank H. H. *The History of the Hongkong and Shanghai Banking Corporation*. Cambridge University Press, 1987.

———. 'The Boxer Indemnity — "Nothing But Bad."' *Modern Asian Studies* 40.3 (July 2006).

King, Frank H. H., and Clarke, Prescott, eds. *A Research Guide to China Coast Newspapers, 1822–1911*. East Asian Research Center, Harvard University, 1965.

King, Paul. *In the Chinese Customs Service*. T. Fisher Unwin, 1924.

Kwong, Luke. 'The Chinese Maritime Customs Remembered'. *JHKBRAS* 19 (1979).

Lam, Lok Ming. *Memoirs of 35-Year Service in the Chinese Maritime Customs*. Hong Kong: Lung Men Press, 1982.

Lan, Li, and Wildly, Deidre. 'Declaration Made by Robert Hart on His Domestic Life'. JHKBRAS 43 (2003).

Lane-Poole, Stanley. *Consul in China,* Vol. 1 of *The Life of Sir Harry Parkes*. MacMillan, 1894.

Leibo, Steven A., ed. *A Journal of the Chinese Civil War 1864 by Prosper Giquel*. University of Hawaii Press, 1985.

———. *Transferring Technology to China: Prosper Giquel and the Self-Strengthening Movement*. China Research Monograph. Institute of East Asian Studies, University of California, 1985.

Leslie, Donald, and Davidson, Jeremy. *Author Catalogue of Western Sinologists*. Australian National University, 1965.

Li, Xiaocong. *A Descriptive Catalogue of Pre-1900 Chinese Maps Seen in Europe*. British Library OIK 912.

Lin, Tai-Yi, trans. *Flowers in the Mirror*. By Li Ju-chen [Li Ruzhen]. Peter Marsh, 1965.

Lo, Hui-min, ed., *The Correspondence of G. E. Morrison*. Cambridge University Press, 1976.

Liu, Hong. *Startling Moon*. Hodder and Stoughton, 2001.

MacDonald, Sir Claude. *The Siege of the Peking Embassy: Report on the Boxer Rebellion*. The Stationery Office, 2000.

Macleod, Norman. 'History of the Royal Hospital School'. *Mariners' Mirror* 3513 July 1949.

MacNair, Harley Farnsworth. *Modern Chinese History: Selected Readings*. Shanghai: Commercial Press, 1923.

Mair, Victor, ed. *The Columbia Anthology of Traditional Chinese Literature*. Columbia University Press, 1994.

Marchant, L. R. *The Siege of the Peking Legations: Diary of Lancelot Giles*. University of Western Australia Press, 1970.

Mateer, A. H. *Siege Days: Personal Experiences of American Women and Children during the Peking Siege*. Fleming H. Revell, 1903; reprinted 1913, the Chinese Maternity Centre.

Maugham, W. Somerset. *On a Chinese Screen*. Heinemann, 1922.

McAleavy, Henry. *The Modern History of China*. Weidenfeld and Nicolson, 1967.

Meales, V. E., ed. *Highways of the Air*. Michael Mason, 1948.

Michie, Alexander. *The Siberian Route from Peking to Petersberg: Through the Deserts and Steppes of Mongolia, Tartary, etc*. John Murray, 1864.

———. *Missionaries in China*. London: E. Stanford, 1891.

———. *China and Christianity*. Boston: Knight and Millett, 1900.

———. *An Englishman in China during the Victorian Era as Illustrated in the Career of Sir Rutherford Alcock*. W. Blackwood, 1900.

———. 'China Revisited'. *Blackwood's Magazine* (October 1901).

———. 'Li Hung-chang'. *Blackwood's Magazine* 170 (December 1901).

Michie, Alexander, Jnr. 'Day's Sport Near Peking'. *Blackwood's Magazine* 1 (November 1900).

———. 'A Chinese Dinner Party'. *Blackwood's Magazine* 2 (December 1900).

———. 'Sir Robert Hart'. *Blackwood's Magazine* 212 (May 1923).

Morrison, G. E. *An Australian in China*. London: Horace Cox, 1902 edition.

Morse, H. B. *The International Relations of the Chinese Empire*. 3 Vols. Longmans, Green, 1918.

Moser, Michael J., and Moser, Yeone Wei-chih. *Foreigners within the Gates*. Hong Kong: Oxford University Press, 1993.

Murphey, Rhoads. *Shanghai: Key to Modern China*. Harvard University Press, 1953.

Needham, Joseph. *Paper and Printing,* Vol. 5, Part 1 of *Science and Civilization in China*. Cambridge University Press, 1954–.

Nevill, Ralph. *London Clubs: Their History and Treasures*. Chatto & Windus, 1911.

Newman, Oksana, and Foster, Allan. *The Value of the Pound: Prices and Incomes in Britain 1900–1993*. Manchester Business School and Information Service, 1995.

Nienhauser, William H., ed. *The Indiana Companion to Traditional Chinese Literature*. Indiana University Press, 1986.

Oliphant, Nigel. *A Diary of the Siege of the Legations in Peking*. Longman, Green, 1901.

Perkins, Dorothy. *Encyclopaedia of China*. Roundtable Press, 1999.

Plummer, Ken. *Documents of Life: An Introduction to the Problems and Literature of Humanities Method*. Unwin Hyman, 1990.

Pong, David P.T. 'Li Hung-chang and Shen Pao-chen: The Politics of Modernization'. In *Shen Pao-chen and China's Modernization in the Nineteenth Century,* ed. Samuel C. Chu and Kwang-Ching Liu. Cambridge University Press, 1994.

Poole, Francis Gordon, Capt. *A Diary in Peking*. Unpublished, Brit. Lib. OR.Micro 399.

Porter, Francis Knowles. *From Belfast to Peking*. Irish Academic Press, 1996.

Power, Brian. *The Ford of Heaven*. Peter Owen, 1984.

Preston, Diana. *Besieged in Peking: The Story of the 1900 Boxer Rising*. Constable, 1999.

Ransome, Jessie. *The Story of the Siege Hospital in Peking and Diary of Events from May to August 1900*. SPCK, 1901.

Rapp, Dean. 'The Early Discovery of Freud by the British General Educated Public, 1912–1919'. *Society for the Social History of Medicine* 3.2 (August 1990).

Roberts, Moss, trans. with an Afterword *Three Kingdoms: A Historical Novel*. University of California Press, full version 1991, abridged version 1999.

Roche, James F., and Cowen, L. L. *The French at Foochow*. Shanghai, 1884.

Royal Hospital School Prospectus. Undated, but circa 1999.

Schwarz, Benjamin. *In Search of Wealth and Power: Yen Fu and the West*. Harper Torchbooks, 1964.

Scully, Eileen P. 'The Low Road to Sino-American Relations'. *Journal of American History* 82.1 (June 1995).

Slack, Edward R. *Opium, State and Society: China's Narco-Economy and the Guomindang, 1924–37*. University of Hawaii Press, 2001.

Smith, Carl. 'Notes on Friends and Relatives of Taiping Leaders'. *JHKBRAS* 16 (1976).

Smith, D. Warren. *European Settlements in the Far East*. London: Sampson, Low, Marston, 1900.

Smith, R. J., Fairbank, J. K., and Bruner, K. *Robert Hart and China's Early Modernization*. Harvard University Press, 1991.

Snow, Edgar. *Journey South of the Clouds*. Ed. with commentary by Robert M. Farnsworth. University of Missouri Press, 1991.

SOAS. *Catalogue of the Papers of Sir Charles Addis*. SOAS, 1986.

Solly, Henry. *These Eighty Years: The Story of an Unfinished Life*. Simpkin and Marshall, 1893.

Solly, Henry Shaen. *Life of Henry Morley*. Edward Arnold, 1898.

Soothill, Lucy. *A Passport to China: Being the Tale of Her Long and Friendly Sojourning amongst a Strangely Interesting People*. Hodder & Stoughton, 1931.

Spence, Jonathan D. *To Change China: Western Advisers in China 1620–1960*. Little, Brown, 1969.

———. *God's Chinese Son*. Norton, 1996.

———. *The Chan's Great Continent: China in Western Minds*. Norton, 1998.

———. *The Search for Modern China*. Norton, 1999.

Stewart, W. A. C., and McCann, W. P. The Educational Innovators. Vol. 1. Macmillan, 1967.

Strachey, Lytton. *Eminent Victorians*. Harmondsworth: Penguin, 1975.

Survey of London, Vol. 30. Athlone Press, 1960.

Symonds, John, and Grant, Kenneth. *The Confessions of Aleister Crowley*. Routledge and Kegan Paul, 1979.

Teng, Ssu-yu, and Fairbank, J. K. *China's Response to the West*. Harvard University Press, 1954.

Ting, Joseph C. *British Contributions to Chinese Studies*. Typescript, SOAS, 1951.

Toyo Bunko. *Catalogue of the Asiatic Library of Dr. G. E. Morrison*. Tokyo: Oriental Library, 1924.

Trevor-Roper, Hugh. *The Hermit of Peking: The Hidden Life of Sir Edmund Backhouse*. Papermac, Macmillan, 1986.

Triselcotis, J. P. *Evaluation of Adoption Policy and Practice*. Department of Social Administration, University of Edinburgh, 1970.

Turner, H. D. *The Cradle of the Navy*. William Sessions, 1990.

Tyler, W. F. *Pulling Strings in China*. Constable, 1929.

Usher, H. J. K., Black-Hawkins, C. D., and Carrick, G. J. *An Angel without Wings: History of University College School, 1830–1980*. University College School, 1981.

Van de Ven, Hans. 'The Onrush of Modern Globalization in China'. In *Globalization in World History,* ed. A. G. Hopkins. Pimlico, 2002.

–––. 'Robert Hart and Gustav Detring during the Boxer Rebellion'. *Modern Asian Studies* 40.3 (July 2006).

Wang, Chi-chen, translated by, *The Dream of the Red Chamber*. Doubleday, Doran, 1929.

Wang, Y. C. *Chinese Intellectuals and the West, 1872–1949*. University of North Carolina Press, 1966.

Webb, William. *Coastguard! An Official History of HM Coastguard*. HMSO, 1976.

Werner, E. T. C. *Autumn Leaves: An Autobiography with a Sheaf of Papers, Sociological, Sinological, Philosophical and Metaphysical*. Kelly and Walsh, 1928.

Williams, C. A. S. *Chinese Tribute*. Literary Services and Production, 1969.

Wood, Frances. *No Dogs and Not Many Chinese: Treaty Port Life in China, 1843–1943*. John Murray, 1998.

Wright, Mary Clabaugh. *The Last Stand of Chinese Conservatism: The T'ung-chih Restoration, 1862–74*. Stanford University Press, 1957.

Wright, Richard N. J. *The Chinese Steam Navy, 1862–1945*. Chatham Publishing, 2000.

Wright, Stanley F. *Origin and Development of the Chinese Customs Service, 1843–1911: An Historical Outline*. Private Circulation, Shanghai, 1939.

–––. *Hart and the Chinese Customs*. Belfast University, Wm. Mullan, 1950.

Yule, Henry, and Burnell, A. C. *Hobson-Jobson: A Glossary of Colloquial Anglo-Indian Words and Phrases, and of Kindred Terms, Etymological, Historical, Geographical, and Discursive*, new 2nd ed. Routledge and Kegan Paul, 1985.

Journals, Newspapers and Encyclopedias

Australian Dictionary of Biography

Blackwood's Magazine

British Medical Journal

CBD: *Chambers Biographical Dictionary*

CHC: *Cambridge History of China*

China Directories

CJSA: *China Journal of Science and Arts*

CLEAR: *Chinese Literature, Essays, Articles, Reviews*

CR: *China Review, or Notes and Queries on the Far East* (Shanghai)

CRcdr.: *Chinese Recorder*

CSPSR: *Chinese Social and Political Science Review*

CT: *Chinese Times*

CY: *China Yearbook*

DNB: *Dictionary of National Biography*

EFR: *East Fife Record*

EB: *Encyclopaedia Britannica*

Folklore Review

The Gower (journal of the University College School, London)

ILN: *Illustrated London News*

JNCBRAS: *Journal of the North China Branch of the Royal Asiatic Society*

The Lancet

Modern Asian Studies

NCH: *North China Herald*

PTT: *Peking and Tientsin Times*

The Times

WSG: *West Sussex Gazette*

Libraries, Archives and Other Collections

Bethlem Royal Hospital Archives and Museum, Kent

British Library Archives

British Library, Morrison G. E. Diaries, Mic.A19829, and Stella Benson Diaries, Mic.A 20024

British Library Newspaper Library, Colindale

FRC: Family Record Centre for record of births, marriages and deaths in England & Wales; British Nationals Overseas lists; and Census records [moved to National Archives, Kew, Surrey in spring 2008]

Guildhall Library, London

Hongkong and Shanghai Bank Archives

London Metropolitan Archives

London School of Economics

Lothian Health Services Archive, Edinburgh University Library

National Archives of Scotland

National Library of Scotland

National Maritime Museum and Library, London

Probate Registry, London

PRO: Public Record Office, or National Archives (see also FRC)

Queens University, Belfast, Robert Hart Special Collections

Royal Astronomical Society, *Bulletins, Monthly Notices* and archives of correspondence

SHAC: Second Historical Archives of China (Nanjing) [When only a date is referenced it is to one of B-T's semi-official reports.]

SOAS Annual Reports and Bulletins

SOAS Archives: Addis Letters and Diaries

> Aglen Letters
>
> Bowra Papers
>
> Evangeline Dora Edwards, MS 14560
>
> Hart Letters
>
> Maze Papers

St. Andrew's Hospital Archives, Northampton

State Reference Library of New South Wales, G. E. Morrison Letters

University of Bristol, Maritime Customs Services Archive

University of Cambridge, Department of Manuscripts

University of Cambridge, Royal Observatory Archives

University College School, Roll of Honour

University of Hong Kong, Special Collection of Robert Hart material arranged by Elizabeth Sinn, assisted by Rev. Carl Smith, 1990.

Wellcome Medical Museum

West Sussex County Council Records

Private collections of family correspondence, including letters from Charles Henry Brewitt-Taylor and from his son Raymond; correspondence and conversations between the author and B-T's grandchildren E. G. (Teddy) Brewitt-Taylor and Joan Leaf; 'budges' and letters from Margaret (Peg) Ellis; and the correspondence and diaries of her daughters, Evelyn Brewitt-Taylor, 'Daisy' Suttill and Winnie Ellis.

Index